THE COLLECTOR'S GUIDE TO
20TH CENTURY MODERN
CLOCKS
DESK, SHELF AND DECORATIVE
WITH MARKET VALUES

MARK V. STEIN

RADIOMANIA® BOOKS
2109 Carterdale Road
Baltimore, Maryland 21209

NOTICE

The market values indicated in this reference are based on a number of different sources. Actual prices will vary dependent on many variables. Neither the author nor the publisher assumes responsibility for losses which might result from the use of this book.

© 2002 By Radiomania, Inc.

Published by
RADIOMANIA® BOOKS
2109 Carterdale Road
Baltimore, Maryland 21209
USA

E-MAIL: rpbook@bellatlantic.net

FAX: (800) 891-4484

WEBSITE: www.radiomania.com

ISBN: 0-9647953-5-3

Library of Congress Control Number: 2001118800

Printed in The United States of America

Cover designed by Jane Rubini
Book designed by Mark V. Stein and Jane Rubini

Production Assistance by Bruce B. Engle and Karen Peng

OTHER RADIOMANIA® BOOKS BY MARK V. STEIN

Machine Age to Jet Age: Radiomania's Guide to Tabletop Radios 1933-1959 Vol. I

Machine Age to Jet Age: Radiomania's Guide to Tabletop Radios 1930-1959 Vol. II

Machine Age to Jet Age: Radiomania's Guide to Tabletop Radios 1930-1962 Vol. III

The Complete Price Guide to Antique Radios: Pre-War Consoles

The Complete Price Guide to Antique Radios: The Sears Silvertone Catalogs 1930-1942

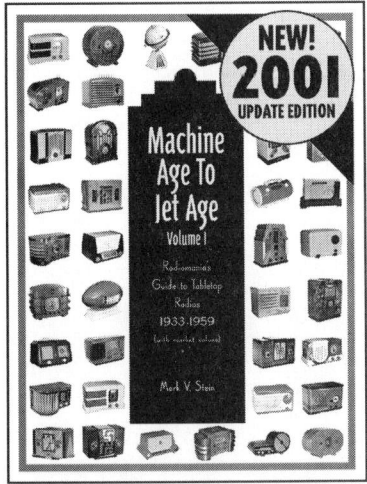

ISBN 0-9647953-02 $24.95*

ISBN 0-9647953-10 $28.95*

ISBN 0-9647953-29 $29.95*

ISBN 0-9647953-02 $29.95*

ISBN 0-9647953-02 $34.95*

ISBN 0-9647953-02 $29.95*

Additional copies of this and other Radiomania® Books may be purchased or ordered from your local bookseller.

Signed copies are available directly from the publisher. Please visit www.radiomania.com for further information about our books, vintage merchandise, and appraisal service. You may also mail, fax or e-mail your order or inquiry to:
Radiomania® Books   2109 Carterdale Road   Baltimore, MD   21209   USA
E-mail: rpbook@bellatlantic.net   Website: www.radiomania.com   Fax: (800) 891-4484

*Suggested Retail Price

ACKNOWLEDGEMENTS

This book was realized through the cooperative efforts of many collectors and enthusiasts. I'd like to express my sincere gratitude for their support and contributions.

Special thanks to the following individuals and businesses:

Jane and Paul Landersman
JanePaul Antiques
www.janepaul.com

Steven Sandler
SSCSI Consulting Services

Alan Voorhees
AntiqueRadios.com

Ed and Diane Hannah

Ellen Miller
Cordier Antiques & Fine Art

David Maloney
Maloney's Antiques & Collectibles
Resource Directory

Polly Exum

Steven Caiati
MachineAge.com

Luciano Clemente

Steven P. Berglund

Drake H. Damerau

There are many more who have contributed in one way or another. If I omitted your name, please accept my apologies for not thanking you individually.

TABLE OF CONTENTS

Preface 7

Introduction to Pricing 9

Fine Tuning Values .10

Valuing Plastic Clocks 12

Valuing Wood Clocks 13

Key to Listings 14

ILLUSTRATED LISTINGS:

Illustrated Listings: Clocks 15

Weather Guides, Switches and Timers 185

APPENDIX NO.1: MARKET VALUES: CLOCKS . . .207

APPENDIX NO.2: MARKET VALUES: Weather Guides, Switches and Timers 243

APPENDIX NO.3: Manufacturers and Brands . . .247

Bibliography 255

PREFACE

I am pleased to publish the first reference devoted exclusively to 20th Century Modern American Clocks. This book represents the culmination of more than fifteen years of research and development.

The design of 20th Century consumer goods including clocks, radios, lighting and other items, both functional and decorative, has been of interest to me personally for the past three decades. Although this realm, now called Industrial Design has only recently begun to receive serious attention, there has for some time existed a subculture of enthusiasts. These enthusiasts, whose interests lie less in the mechanism and more in its packaging, have both confused and amused the traditional antique collecting community.

As a collector, I began gathering information and developing resources for vintage radios due to the lack of any complete visual reference. I established Radiomania® Books in 1995. To date Radiomania has published five reference guides for radio collectors. These guides have become the standard for identification and valuation of vintage radios manufactured from 1930 into the 1960's, the 'Golden Age' of Industrial Design.

Having been a collector of clocks as well as radios, I find each a reflection of both the architecture and popular culture that has defined our recent American past. Unfortunately there continues to be a significant void in resources for the contemporary, non-horologically oriented, clock collector. As with radios, to date there has been no comprehensive attempt to catalog and value 20th Century Modern American clocks. This book is the by-product of both my frustration with available references and my interest as a collector. With the publication of this series, I hope provide such a resource.

In compiling this reference series, my primary purpose has been to identify, picture, describe and establish baseline values on a comprehensive basis. Other than identification of the movement type (i.e., AC Electric as opposed to 1 day wind, 8 day wind, alarm, etc.) the inner workings of clocks are not addressed here. I leave this to the horological community which continues to more than adequately cover the subject. I have included basic information about modern clock cabinetry, materials and finishes. Additionally, I have provided guidelines for fine tuning values based on several visual variables.

This first volume of "The Collector's Guide to 20th Century Modern Clocks" focuses on smaller clocks. That is, those which might have sat on a desk, night stand, bureau, shelf or other vertical surface. Both manual and electric clocks are included. Standard, alarm, chiming and striking clocks are represented as well. A chapter on related items such as weather meters (barometers, thermometers, hygrometers), and clocks with dual functions such as appliance switches, timers and gauges has also been included.

A forthcoming second volume will focus on mantle, tall (floor) and wall clocks and will include a chapter on related devices as well.

This series will be continually expanded and updated as with my other guides. I encourage others to share their resources with fellow collectors through the continuation of this series. Your thoughts, comments and contributions are welcomed.

Thank you and enjoy!

Mark V. Stein

INTRODUCTION TO PRICING

In compiling this book the question as to whether to include prices was one of major concern to both the author and contributors. As most collectors are aware, even the best price guide, if not initially flawed, is soon obsolete. The range of prices paid for most items is wide. One can pay anywhere from a few dollars to a few hundred for a given item, dependent on where it was purchased and from whom. Thus the task of establishing a "market value" is difficult. This problem given, it was still generally felt that the usefulness of including prices, at least as a general market gauge, would outweigh the disadvantages of omitting them completely.

As a point of reference, The **prices, as listed in Appendices Nos. 1 and 2, in this book represent retail prices for items in excellent cosmetic and working condition.**

The following pages of guidelines and information have been developed to assist the collector in developing a more precise value for a clock.

Notice: In establishing values a number of sources were utilized including auction results, classified ads, dealer pricing, collector valuations and the author's personal experience. Actual prices will vary dependent on many variables. Neither the author nor the publisher assumes responsibility for losses which might result from the use of this book.

FINE TUNING VALUES

To assist the collector in fine tuning the value of a given clock, some general rules of thumb are offered. Please remember that, as with all rules, there are exceptions. If you are uncertain about a specific item you will always do best to ask another collector whom you trust.

GENERAL CONSIDERATIONS

NON-WORKING WIND TYPE MOVEMENT: Most of the mass produced clocks with which this book is concerned utilized simple, and often interchangeable, movements. The most common problem causing movement failure is accumulation of dust and deteriorated oils, gumming and halting the gear train. In such cases the mainspring does not have enough power to keep the movement going and the wind key will not turn any further without breaking it. First, the mainspring should be released. Second the movement should be cleaned and oiled. I have found this to be all that is necessary to bring most wind clocks back to running order. If the wind key turns freely and does not tighten the spring, the mainspring is most likely broken and must be replaced. The movement should also be cleaned and oiled. Less common are stripped gears. These can be replaced, but at significant cost due to the labor involved.

Fortunately, since the same movements were used in multiple models, working replacement movements are often relatively easy to locate, particularly with the advent of the internet and internet auctions. Repairing your clock may be as simple as replacing the broken movement with a working one.

NON-WORKING ELECTRIC TYPE MOVEMENT: AC Electric movements are similar to the wind type with replacement of the main spring by an electric motor. **Extreme caution must be used in the handling of any vintage electric device due to electric shock and related hazards.** Unless you are experienced in the repair of electric powered devices and are familiar with the proper precautions necessary for your own safety, it is recommended that you either identify a resource for repair or steer clear of non-working electric clocks. Should you desire to pursue repair or replacement of the mechanism on your own, there are good resources available which explain the workings and repair of electric clocks in addition to appropriate precautions.

The state of the movement should be considered in valuing your potential purchase. The value of a non-working clock is typically reduced by 25-50% as compared with a working model in similar condition.

DESIGN PEDIGREE: In this book a designer is cited as documented ('des.') or attributed ('attr.'). Many designs have been attributed but not with 100% certainty. Few design patents were pursued and much collateral documentation has been lost with time. Some common knowledge attributions have been discovered to be incorrect upon further research. Many will never be verified or disproved. When buying a clock whose design is undocumented, try to make your decision as informed as possible. Discuss the assertion with the seller. He may have information which makes the pedigree a high probability.

A clock whose architect was a known and important industrial designer commands a higher price for this fact alone.

CASE CONDITION: Considerations are discussed in the pages that follow.

DAMAGED CRYSTAL: Covering the face on most clocks pictured in this book is a convex glass "crystal". A damaged or missing round crystal is generally easy to replace. A well-stocked clockmaker or supplier should have a suitable match.

Oval and odd shaped crystals are more difficult to replace. A piece of flat glass or acrylic may be cut to fit, but make certain a flat crystal will allow sufficient room for movement of the hands. If not, there are two remaining options: (1) find a junker with the same crystal intact, or; (2) have the glass crystal replaced with a made-to-order plastic crystal. Similar resources are available for radio dial lenses. Check the internet for resources.

The cost of a replacement crystal will vary from $5-10 for a standard stocked item to $20 for a custom made plastic piece.

DIAL FACE DAMAGE: It is often the dial which initially attracts one to a clock. A blemish or flaw in this face will undoubtedly be the first thing to draw the eye. Many times scoring from the hands and small scratches can be touched up with colored pencil or a well matched paint. Oftentimes the dial face is too far gone for repair due to excessive wear or staining. In such cases a junker clock can be a good alternative. Another option might be the use of a computer and scanner to produce a high resolution image, repair of that image using Photoshop® or similar software, and high quality output on appropriate stock. Although it sounds complicated, this process has become more accessible and less expensive in recent years.

A flawed dial face will reduced the value of a clock by 10-30%, dependent on the extent of damage.

VALUING PLASTIC CLOCKS

CHIPS AND CRACKS: Early plastics such as bakelite, plaskon, beetle and catalin are all susceptible to damage over time. Superficial stress lines are common in plaskon and beetle, as is darkening from UV exposure. Catalin shrinks with time and will often crack from the pressure created against the inner mechanism cylinder. Bakelite, the first and most common of the vintage plastics, is the best survivor. Bakelite will chip and crack but not due solely to age. It must be hit or dropped at some point in its lifetime.

So long as it remains displayable, a flaw in a plastic clock case, such as a significant visible chip, crack or stress line, will decrease value by 30-50%.

FRAGILITY: Dependent on the thickness of the casting, materials used in construction and the extremity of design, some clocks are inherently more delicate than others. The most fragile are rarely found in excellent condition. This 'universe' from which each clock is drawn must be considered in determining its value.

A fragile clock in what would appear to be marginal condition, might, in fact, be an excellent example of that model, given the condition of other surviving cases.

REPAIRS: Although there have been some relatively successful attempts at bakelite and catalin repair, no repair can go completely undetected.

A well repaired flaw can increase the value of a clock but will never raise its value to that of an unflawed one.

PAINT CHIPS: While many early plastic clocks were available in different colors (typically walnut, black and ivory), oftentimes the ivory colored cases were brown or black bakelite which had been painted at the factory. This factory painting process was similar to that used in the automobile industry and was also used with metal cased clocks. After several layers of paint were applied, the case was baked for several hours. As a result, the paint became 'hard' and much more susceptible to chipping over time. In addition to the problem of chipping, the baking process made the paint that much more difficult to remove. Stripping old baked paint is extremely time intensive.

The value of a factory painted clock with paint chips will be reduced by 20-40% dependent on the extent and placement of chipping.

VALUING WOOD CLOCKS

The following are some basics to keep in mind when considering the purchase of a wood case clock:

FINISH: Most wood clocks produced from the 1920s through the 1950s were finished with either clear or toned lacquer. Over the years many things can, and usually do, happen to a lacquer finish. The finish can dry, scratch, chip, peel or separate ('alligator'). Rarely does one come across an original lacquer finish without some evidence of the passage of time. Unless horrendous, it is probably worthwhile trying to salvage the original finish. There are various products available which allow you to easily clean the surface and replenish the moisture in the lacquer. Additionally, you may want to amalgamize the finish to cover bare spots. This involves dissolving the original finish with denatured alcohol or other substance and respreading it. Many antique restoration and refinishing books address this process.

As opposed to clear lacquer, toned lacquers present more of a problem. Many manufacturers, instead of decorative woods or veneers, used a solid, inexpensive wood finished with toned lacquers. Originally, the difference was difficult to discern. Today it is often evident. When toned lacquers age they reveal the original color of the wood underneath, usually in deep contrast. The darker the toner, the more significant the problem. Tiny blemishes may be hidden using markers, stains and other techniques. However, the purchaser of a clock with severe surface scratches may ultimately need to resign himself to live with the clock as is or refinish it completely.

The value of a Clock requiring finish restoration should be decreased by 10-30% dependent on the extent of damage. If in need of a total refinish, the value should be decreased by 30-50%.

VENEER: Most mass produced wood clock cases were made using wood veneer: a thin layer of hard or exotic wood glued to the surface of a case which had been constructed of inexpensive wood. Over time the glue which bonds the veneer can deteriorate, resulting in damage ranging from small veneer chips to loosening of large sections of veneer. The best scenario is veneer which has separated but is still present. This is easily remedied with proper gluing and clamping. If pieces of veneer are missing, they must be replaced. Often the remainder of the veneer on the damaged surface must be removed as well. You may be able to find a matching piece with original finish on a junker clock or other vintage item. Otherwise, you will need to procure, apply and finish a piece of new veneer. If the damage is small and in a relatively concealed area you may chose to fill the gap with a matching wood putty, shellac stick or toner pencil. Alternatively, some restoration experts are able to create a faux finish over a small damaged area.

Veneer work can be time consuming and difficult. It is usually expensive if performed by a professional.

REFINISHING: All but the absolute purist will agree that some clock cases need to be refinished in order to be displayable. Many collectors have not seen a well executed and historically correct refinished clock case and cannot appreciate the potential transformation. The process is long, involved and extremely labor intensive, but the result is astonishing. Of course there is refinishing and there is "refinishing". Many a novice hobbyist has used a caustic solvent to remove an original finish, followed by staining the case and then applying a coat of polyurethane or tung oil. Unfortunately, the result looks like it came from craft shop and is certainly not historically correct.

A clock with a poorly executed new finish should be valued as one needing a complete refinish.

Other types of refinishing are less objectionable and easier to remedy. Oftentimes one encounters a clock with the original finish intact, but under a coat of varnish or shellac which had been applied by a previous owner. Various solvents can be used to carefully remove the unwanted top coat and leave the original finish. There is a science to the process of both identifying the correct solvent and its application. Read up on refinishing and talk to other collectors about their experiences before attempting this on a valuable acquisition. If the top coat is polyurethane, all finishes must be removed.

If the original finish is salvageable, the value of the clock will be reduced by about 25%.

KEY TO LISTINGS

Listings are ordered: **1st** by Brand Name; **2nd** by Year of Manufacture; **3rd** by Model No. and **4th** By Model Name

1. Plate Number
Allows for exact identification for use in pricing Appendix Nos. 1 & 2 and otherwise.

2. Brand Name*
May not necessarily equate to specific manufacturer. Refer to Appendix No.3.

3. Model Year*
Approximate year first produced or marketed

4. Model Number*
Manufacturer or Brand Model Number (Source Manufactuer Provided in Parentheses Where Known)

5. Model Name*
Manufacturer or Brand Model Name (Source Manufactuer Provided in Parentheses Where Known)

6. Industrial Designer*
Documented Industrial Designer (Des.) or undocumented but Attributed (Attr.)

7. Movement Type(s), Options*
Mechanical (Wind) vs. Electric (AC or DC Electric), movement options (i.e., alarm, chime, strike).

8. Cabinet Material(s)*
Cabinet manufacture materials and alternates.

9. Variations*
Variations in color, trim, dial type, etc.

10. Dimensions*
Height (H), Width (W), Depth (D), Diameter (Diam), Square (Sq) in Inches

11. Image/Plate

*As ascertained utilizing period literature, clock markings and other references (refer to Bibliography)

PLATE 0111
GENERAL ELECTRIC
c.1935, 8B-04, New Executive (Teague des.)
AC Electric
Bakelite: Black w/Silver or Brow w/Gold
5H X 8.5W

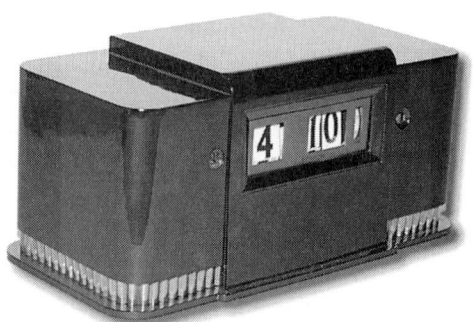

1. Plate 0111
2. General Electric
3. 1935
4. 8B-04
5. New Executive
6. (Teague des.)
7. AC Electric
8. Bakelite:
9. Black w/Silver or Brown w/Gold
10. 5H X 8.5W
11. Photo or rendering of clock

SECTION ONE

CLOCKS

ALDINE · BELMONT

PLATE 0001
ALDINE
c.1930, #9212
8-Day Wind, Chimes
Wood: Mahogany
15.5H X 10.5W X 6.5D

PLATE 0002
ARISTOCRAT
c.1951, #6828, Minuet
1-Day Wind, Alarm,
Metal: Red or Blue
3.25 Diameter

PLATE 0003
ARISTOCRAT
c.1951, #6844, Fleetwood (Ingraham)
1-Day Wind, Alarm
Metal: Ivory or Black
8.75H X 5W

PLATE 0004
ARTCRAFT
c.1931 (Ingraham)
1-Day Wind, Alarm
Metal: Green or Rose
5H X 5.5W

PLATE 0005
AUTODEX
c.1940, #700, Clock Index (New Haven)
40-Hour Wind
Wood: Walnut
5.75H X 9.75L X 5.25W

PLATE 0006
AUTODEX
c.1940, #701, Clock Index (New Haven)
40-Hour Wind
Wood: Mahogany
5H X 9.75L X 5.25W

PLATE 0007
AUTODEX
c.1940, #702, Clock Calindex (New Haven)
40-Hour Wind
Wood: Walnut
5H X 10L X 5.25W

PLATE 0008
BARR
c.1938, AC-46 (Pennwood)
AC Electric, Cyclometer
Plaskon: Ivory

PLATE 0009
BELMONT
c.1932, #2820, 21, 22, 23 Boudoir
AC Electric
Plaskon: Blue, Green, Lavender or Ivory
6.5H X 4.75W

BUGLE BOY

Plate 0010
BUGLE BOY
c.1934, #2460, Modernistic (Lux)
1-Day Wind, Alarm
Metal: Brown Lacquer w/Chrome Trim

Plate 0011
BUGLE BOY
c.1936, #6207 (Lux)
1-Day Wind, Alarm, Luminous Dial Optional
Metal: Black, Copper or Green
4.5H X 4.25W

Plate 0012
BUGLE BOY
c.1937, #1800, Octagon (Lux)
1-Day Wind, Alarm
Metal: Rose, Green or Ivory
4.5H

Plate 0013
BUGLE BOY
c.1939, #1652 (Lux)
8-Day Wind, Alarm, Luminous Dial
Metal: Black w/Chrome or Ivory w/Brass,
5.25H X 5.75W

Plate 0014
BUGLE BOY
c.1939, #1655 Ingraham)
8-Day Wind, Luminous Dial
Metal: Ivory or Green
5.5H X 6W

Plate 0015
BUGLE BOY
c.1939, #1656, Claridge (Lux)
1-Day Wind, Alarm
Metal: Pink, Ivory, or Green
4 Square

Plate 0016
BUGLE BOY
c.1939, #1657 (Lux)
1-Day Wind, Alarm
Metal: Ivory, Green, or Red
4.25 Square

Plate 0017
BUGLE BOY
c.1939, #1658 (Lux)
1-Day Wind, Alarm
Metal: Ivory, Green, or Red
6.5H X 5.25W

Plate 0018
BUGLE BOY
c.1939, #1659, Commander (Ingraham)
8-Day Wind, Alarm
Metal, Ivory w/Brass or Grey w/Chrome
5.75H X 7W

BUGLE BOY

Plate 0019
BUGLE BOY
c.1939 (Lux)
1-Day Wind, Alarm, Luminous Dial
Plastic: Ivory, Green, or Coral
4.5H X 5.5W

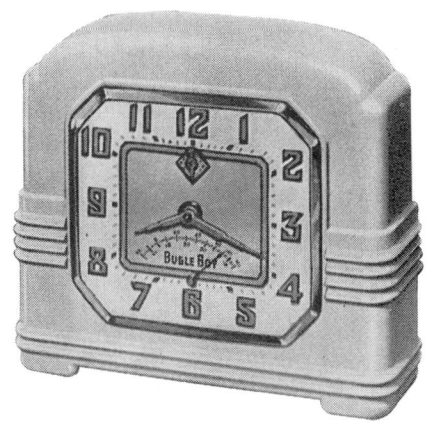

Plate 0020
BUGLE BOY
c.1939, #1650, 1651 (Lux)
1-Day Wind, Alarm, Luminous Dial
Metal: Ivory, Green, or Red
5H X 6.5W

Plate 0021
BUGLE BOY
c.1940, #5154, Defender (Lux)
30-Hour Wind, Alarm
Metal: Black or Green
4.5H X 4W

Plate 0022
BUGLE BOY
c.1940, #5155, Non-Tip (Lux)
30-Hour Wind, Alarm
Metal: Ivory, Green, or Coral
5H X 4.5W

Plate 0023
BUGLE BOY
c.1940, #5156, Landscape (Lux)
30-Hour Wind, Alarm
Metal: Ivory or Green
4.5H X 5W

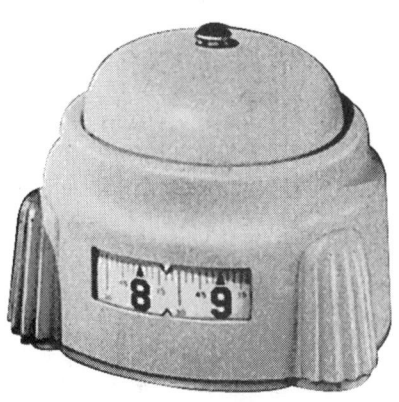

Plate 0024
BUGLE BOY
c.1940, #5157, Dome Style Rotary (Lux)
30-Hour Wind
Metal: Ivory or Antique Bronze
5H X 4W

Plate 0025
BUGLE BOY
c.1940, #5162, Round Thin (Lux)
30-Hour Wind, Alarm
Metal: Ivory or Black
5H X 4.5W

Plate 0026
BUGLE BOY
c.1940, #8916, Footed Octagon (Lux)
30-Hour Wind, Alarm
Metal: Ivory, Green or Mahogany
5.25H X 4.75W

Plate 0027
BUGLE BOY
c.1940, #8917, Chum (Lux)
30-Hour Wind, Alarm
Metal: Ivory or Black with Tan Base
3.25 Square

BUGLE BOY

Plate 0028
BUGLE BOY
c.1940, #8918, Gabled Top (Ingraham)
8-Day Wind, Alarm
Metal: Ivory or Black
5H X 4.5W

Plate 0029
BUGLE BOY
c.1940, #8920, Console (Lux)
30-Hour Wind, Alarm, Luminous Dial
Metal: Ivory or Black
4.5H X 7W

Plate 0030
BUGLE BOY
c.1940, #8922, Valley Brook (Lux)
30-Hour Wind, Alarm
Metal: Ivory, Green, or Blue
5.5H X 4.5W

Plate 0031
BUGLE BOY
c.1940, #8923, Fireside (Lux)
30-Hour Wind, Alarm, Animated
Metal: Ivory, Green, or Blue
5.5H X 4.5W

Plate 0032
BUGLE BOY
c.1940, #8925, Horseshoe (Ingraham)
30-Hour Wind, Alarm
Metal: Chrome
7.5H X 9W

Plate 0033
BUGLE BOY
c.1941, #7568, 4-In-1 Calendar (Lux)
30-Hour Wind, Alarm, Calendar
Metal: Chrome
7.5H X 5W

Plate 0034
BUGLE BOY
c.1941, #7574, The Flag Waves (Howard)
AC Electric
6.5H X 8.25W

Plate 0035
BUGLE BOY
c.1942, #5202, Stylized Square
30-Hour Wind, Alarm
Bakelite/Plaskon: Ivory, Black or Brown
4H X 5W

Plate 0036
BUGLE BOY
c.1942, #5204, Thin Streamline
30-Hour Wind, Alarm
Bakelite/Plaskon: Ivory or Brown
4.5H X 6.5W

BUGLE BOY · CHELSEA

PLATE 0037
BUGLE BOY
c.1942, #6581
8-Day Wind, Alarm, Luminous Dial Optional
Metal: Ivory or Black
5.75H X 5.25W

PLATE 0038
BUGLE BOY
c.1951, #3463, Swinging Girl (Mastercrafters)
AC Electric, Animated
Bakelite
10.75H X 7.5W X 3D

PLATE 0039
BUGLE BOY
c.1951, #3464, Swinging Playmates (Mastercrafters)
AC Electric, Animated
Bakelite
10.75H X 7.5W X 4D

PLATE 0040
BUGLE BOY
c.1951, #3535, Fireball
30-Hour Wind, Alarm, Luminous Dial
Metal: Ivory or Black
5.5 Square

PLATE 0041
BUGLE BOY
c.1951, #3576, Home Sweet Home (Haddon)
AC Electric, Animated
7.5H X 12W X 3.5D

PLATE 0042
BUGLE BOY
c.1951, #3581, Bank Clock
AC Electric
Metal: Ivory
6.5H X 6.5W

PLATE 0043
BULOVA
c.1935, #1209, Skyscraper (Ingraham)
AC Electric
Wood: Walnut and Maple
12H X 9W

PLATE 0044
CHEIFTAIN
c.1940, Executive (Pennwood)
AC Electric
Bakelite: Walnut

PLATE 0045
CHELSEA
c.1947, #7382, Manhattan (Ingraham)
8-Day Wind
Wood: Walnut
4.75 Diameter

CHELSEA · COMET

PLATE 0046
CHELSEA
c.1947, #7383, Clinton
AC Electric
Metal: Bronze
5H X 4W

PLATE 0047
CHELSEA
c.1947, #7384, Alden
AC Electric
Metal: Brass
4 Square

PLATE 0048
CLINTON
c.1955, #1
40-Hour Wind, Alarm
Metal: Gold
3.75H X 2.5W

PLATE 0049
CLINTON
c.1955, #2
8-Day Wind, Alarm, Luminous Dial
Black and Gold
3H X 4.5W

PLATE 0050
CLINTON
c.1955, #6
8-Day Wind, Alarm, Luminous Dial
Metal: Satin Silver and Gold
5H X 5W

PLATE 0051
CLINTON
c.1955, #7
8-Day Wind, Alarm
Metal with Leather: Green, Blue, Red or Tan
3.5H X 4.25W

PLATE 0052
CLINTON
c.1955, #14, Musical Cigarette Holder/Clock
8-Day Wind
Metal: Gold
6.25H X 5 Diameter

PLATE 0053
COMET
c.1930 (Ingraham)
8-Day Wind, Alarm, Luminous Dial Optional
Metal: Nickel
4.5H

PLATE 0054
COMET
c.1930, #1264, 1265 (Ingraham)
1-Day Wind, Alarm, Luminous Dial Optional
Metal: Nickel
6H

CONNECTICUT · DELUXE

PLATE 0055
CONNECTICUT
c.1932
AC Electric, Alarm
Bakelite: Walnut
4H X 4W

PLATE 0056
CONNECTICUT
c.1932
AC Electric, Alarm
Metal: Black
4.75S

PLATE 0057
CONNECTICUT
c.1932, #52, 53
AC Electric, Alarm
Bakelite: Black or Ivory
6.5H X 5.25W

PLATE 0058
CUTEY
c.1929, #L-15
1-Day Wind, Alarm
Metal: Green, Ivory or Pink

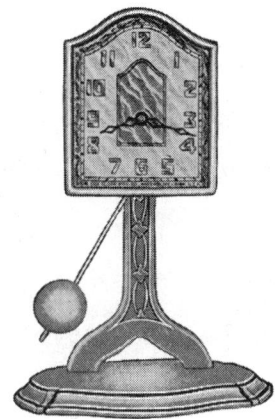

PLATE 0059
DELUXE
c.1931, #194, Pendulette (Lux)
1-Day Wind
Metal: Green, Blue, Pink or Lavender
6H X 4.25W

PLATE 0060
DELUXE
c.1932, Organ Grinder (Lux)
AC Electric, Alarm, Animated
Metal: Brass, Green, Blue or Pink
4H X 4W

PLATE 0061
DELUXE
c.1932, #151, Gothic (Lux)
AC Electric
Wood, Mahogany
7H X 6W

PLATE 0062
DELUXE
c.1932, #167, Junior (Lux)
1-Day Wind, Alarm
Metal: Green, Blue or Red
3H X 3W

PLATE 0063
DELUXE
c.1932, #337, 437 (Lux)
AC Electric
Bakelite: Black w/ Nickel Trim
3.25H X 3W

DELUXE

Plate 0064
DELUXE
c.1932, #582 (Lux)
AC Electric
Metal: Brass, Green, Blue or Pink
3.75H X 4W

Plate 0065
DELUXE
c.1932, #1781, Gothic (Lux)
AC Electric
Wood: Mahogany
7H X 6.5W

Plate 0066
DELUXE
c.1932, #1782, Elite (Lux)
AC Electric
Wood: Mahogany
7H X 6.5W

Plate 0067
DELUXE
c.1932, #1783, Doric (Lux)
AC Electric
Wood: Mahogany
7H X 5.75W

Plate 0068
DELUXE
c.1934, #432 (Pennwood)
AC Electric
Wood: Walnut
4.75H X 8.5W

Plate 0069
DELUXE
c.1938, #951 (Lux)
1-Day Wind, Alarm
Metal: Ivory, Green or Black
4.75H X 5.25W

Plate 0070
DELUXE
c.1938, #954 (Lux)
1-Day Wind, Alarm
Metal: Ivory
4.25H X 7.25W

Plate 0071
DELUXE
c.1938, #1054 (Lux)
1-Day Wind, Alarm
Metal: Ivory w/Gold or Black w/Nickel
4.25H

Plate 0072
DELUXE
c.1939, #1660, Skyline (Ingraham)
8-Day Wind, Alarm
Metal: Ivory w/Gold, Walnut or Black w/Gold
5.75H X 6.75W

DELUXE · DINSON

PLATE 0073
DELUXE
c.1939, #8591 (Lux)
1-Day Wind
Metal: Chrome
6H X 6W

PLATE 0074
DELUXE
c.1939, #8595 (Lux)
8-Day Wind
Crystal Glass
4.25H X 5W

PLATE 0075
DELUXE
c.1939, #8606 (Lux)
8-Day Wind
Metal: Chrome
4.25H X 4.75W

PLATE 0076
DELUXE
c.1940, #688,689 (Lux)
40-Hour Wind
Metal: Chrome w/Marble Base
4.5 X 7.5B

PLATE 0077
DELUXE
c.1940, #8568 (Lux)
40-Hour Wind
Wood: Walnut
5.5H X 4.75W

PLATE 0078
DELUXE
c.1940, #5806, Swinging (Lux)
1-Day Wind
Metal: Chrome
13H

PLATE 0079
DELUXE
c.1942, Esquire (Lux)
1-Day Wind, Alarm, Luminous Dial Optional
Metal: Ivory or Black

PLATE 0080
DELUXE
c.1942, #1052 (Lux)
1-Day Wind, Alarm
Metal: Ivory or Black
5H X 4.75W

PLATE 0081
DINSON
c.1951, #6852, Jeweled
1-Day Wind, Alarm, Luminous Dial
Metal: Gold
3.5H X 3.25W

DINSON · EMPRESS

PLATE 0082
DINSON
c.1952, #6834
1-Day Wind, Alarm, Luminous Dial
Metal: Ivory
3H X 3.75B

PLATE 0083
DUOKRON
c.1932, #535, 536 (Hammond)
AC Electric
Metal: Green, Blue, Ivory or Red

PLATE 0084
EDWARDS & CO.
c.1937, Tower
AC Electric
Wood: Walnut and Maple

PLATE 0085
ELEXA
c.1941
1-Day Wind
Plastic: Brass and Black

PLATE 0086
ELEXA
c.1941
1-Day Wind
Acrylic: Black and Clear
6H X 6.25W

PLATE 0087
ELTIME
c.1932, #2835
AC Electric
Metal: Nickel
4.5H X 3.5W

PLATE 0088
ELTIME
c.1934, #46107, 6605, Utility
AC Electric, Luminous Dial Optional
Wood: Walnut
9H X 8W

PLATE 0089
ELTIME
c.1934, #4628, 4828, Dresser
AC Electric, Alarm
Metal: Chrome plated, Black, White
5H X 4.25W

PLATE 0090
EMPRESS
c.1931, #3505
AC Electric
Metal: Crystal Green, Black, Ivory, Pink or Blue
5.5H

FASHION · GENERAL ELECTRIC

PLATE 0091
FASHION
c.1931, Easel
40-Hour Wind, Alarm
Metal: Green, Blue or Rose
5.5H X 6.75W

PLATE 0092
FORESTVILLE
c.1962, #3300, Tambourine (Sessions)
Wind, Chime
Wood
8H X 16.25W X 5.25D

PLATE 0093
GABLE
c.1933 (Lux)
8-Day Wind, Alarm,
Metal: Black
5.5H X 4.5W

PLATE 0094
GENERAL ELECTRIC
c.1930, #604, Brittany
AC Electric
Wood: Mahogany
11.5H X 8.5W

PLATE 0095
GENERAL ELECTRIC
c.1931, #3F-54, Super Hostess
AC Electric
Green, Chrome
5.5H

PLATE 0096
GENERAL ELECTRIC
c.1931, #3F-56, Vogue
AC Electric
Metal: Copper or Chrome w/Black
5H X 6.5W

PLATE 0097
GENERAL ELECTRIC
c.1931, 3F-60, Fleet
AC Electric
Bakelite/Plaskon: Green, Ivory or Black
5 Square

PLATE 0098
GENERAL ELECTRIC
c.1931, 7F-52, Morning Star
AC Electric
Bakelite/Plaskon: Black or Ivory
5H X 4.75W X 3D

PLATE 0099
GENERAL ELECTRIC
c.1931, 7F-56, Vedette
AC Electric, Alarm, Luminous Dial Optional
Bakelite/Plaskon: Black or Ivory
5H X 4.5W

GENERAL ELECTRIC

PLATE 0100
GENERAL ELECTRIC
c.1931, 7F-58, Lumalarm
AC Electric, Alarm, Luminous Dial
Bakelite/Plaskon: Ivory or Black
5H X 5.5W

PLATE 0101
GENERAL ELECTRIC
c.1932, #5, Auxiliary
Wood: Mahogany
6.25H X 5W

PLATE 0102
GENERAL ELECTRIC
c.1932, #28
AC Electric
Wood: Mahogany
7.5H X 5.5W

PLATE 0103
GENERAL ELECTRIC
c.1932, #52, Petite
AC Electric
Bakelite: Black
4.75H X 3.75W

PLATE 0104
GENERAL ELECTRIC
c.1932, #57
AC Electric
Bakelite: Black
7.5H X 4.75W

PLATE 0105
GENERAL ELECTRIC
c.1932, 7F-62, Englewood
AC Electric, Alarm
Wood: Mahogany
5H X 5W

PLATE 0106
GENERAL ELECTRIC
c.1933, 8B-02, Executive
AC Electric
Bakelite: Brown w/Brass or Black w/Silver Face
6.5H X 4W

PLATE 0107
GENERAL ELECTRIC
c.1934, 3F-58, Secretary
AC Electric
Wood: Mahogany with Marquerry Inlay
5.5H X 5.5W

PLATE 0108
GENERAL ELECTRIC
c.1935, 3F-64, Wellfleet
AC Electric
Bakelite: Green, Ivory or Black
5 Square

GENERAL ELECTRIC

Plate 0109
GENERAL ELECTRIC
c.1935, 4F-60, Rex
AC Electric
Mirror & Metal: Blue Mirror with Chrome Bezel
5 Diameter

Plate 0110
GENERAL ELECTRIC
c.1935, 7F-52, Morning Star
AC Electric, Alarm, Luminous Dial Optional
Bakelite/Plaskon: Black or Ivory
5H X 4.5W

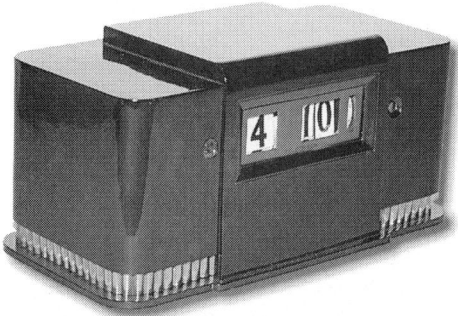

Plate 0111
GENERAL ELECTRIC
c.1935, 8B-04, New Executive (Teague des.)
AC Electric
Bakelite: Black w/Silver or Brow w/Gold
5H X 8.5W

Plate 0112
GENERAL ELECTRIC
c.1936, 3F-70, Park Avenue
AC Electric
Wood: Zebrawood with Black Trim

Plate 0113
GENERAL ELECTRIC
c.1936, 4F-52, Debutante
AC Electric
Metal: Chrome or Brass
5 H X 5 W

Plate 0114
GENERAL ELECTRIC
c.1936, 4F-58, Lotus
AC Electric
Chrome w/Black Bakelite Base, Lighted Mirror Dial
6H X 6.5W

Plate 0115
GENERAL ELECTRIC
c.1936, 4F-62, Blue Night
AC Electric
Blue Mirror
5.75 Diameter

Plate 0116
GENERAL ELECTRIC
c.1936, 4F-64, Blue Night
AC Electric
Blue Mirror
5.75 Square

Plate 0117
GENERAL ELECTRIC
c.1936, 4F-66, Blue Night
AC Electric
Blue Mirror
5.75 H X 5.75 W

GENERAL ELECTRIC

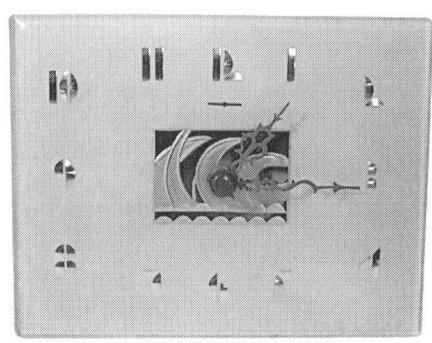

PLATE 0118
GENERAL ELECTRIC
c.1936, 5F-50, Mirage
AC Electric
Ivory or Black Glass w/Silver Detail
5.75H X 7.5W

PLATE 0119
GENERAL ELECTRIC
c.1936, 7F-60, Morning Glory
AC Electric, Alarm
Wood: Mahogany
6H X 5W

PLATE 0120
GENERAL ELECTRIC
c.1936, 7F-70, 'Overseer
AC Electric, Alarm
Wood: Mahogany
5H X 8W

PLATE 0121
GENERAL ELECTRIC
c.1936, 7F-72, Heralder
AC Electric, Alarm
Bakelite: Black or Brown
4.25H X 4W

PLATE 0122
GENERAL ELECTRIC
c.1936, 8B-06, Budgeteer
AC Electric
Wood: Mahogany w/Brass Trim
5H X 8.5W

PLATE 0123
GENERAL ELECTRIC
c.1937, 3F-72, Brever
AC Electric
Wood: Mahogany
6.5 Square

PLATE 0124
GENERAL ELECTRIC
c.1937, 3F-74, Duncan
AC Electric
Bakelite: Black or Blue
5H X 4.75W

PLATE 0125
GENERAL ELECTRIC
c.1937, 3H-78, Basque
AC Electric
Catalin: Butterscotch or Black
4.25H X 5W

PLATE 0126
GENERAL ELECTRIC
c.1937, 3H-80, Morgan
AC Electric
Wood: Mahogany
6H X 5W

GENERAL ELECTRIC

PLATE 0127
GENERAL ELECTRIC
c.1937, 4H-68, Tuileres
AC Electric
Mirror: Blue or Peach
6.25H X 5.5W

PLATE 0128
GENERAL ELECTRIC
c.1937, 5F-54, Salon
AC Electric
White Glass w/Silver Detail
5.75 Diameter

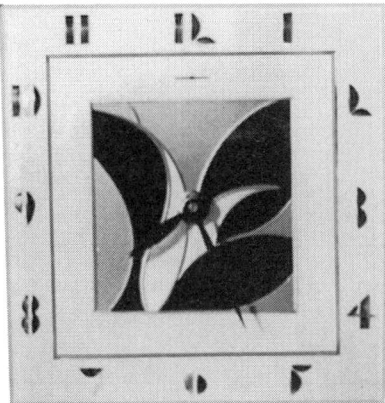

PLATE 0129
GENERAL ELECTRIC
c.1937, 5F-56, Soiree
AC Electric
White Glass w/Silver Detail
5.75 Square

PLATE 0130
GENERAL ELECTRIC
c.1937, 5F-58, Ecsracy
AC Electric
Mirror: Cobalt or Light Blue-Grey
5.75 Diameter

PLATE 0131
GENERAL ELECTRIC
c.1937, 7F-74, Heralder
AC Electric, Alarm
Bakelite: Black w/Brass Trim
4.5H X 4W

PLATE 0132
GENERAL ELECTRIC
c.1937, 7F-76, Geneva
AC Electric, Alarm
Mirror: Cobalt, Light Blue-Grey or Silver
5.75H X 5.5W

PLATE 0133
GENERAL ELECTRIC
c.1937, 7H-82, Sophist
AC Electric, Alarm
Wood: Mahogany
5.25H X 7.25W

PLATE 0134
GENERAL ELECTRIC
c.1938, 5F-60, Ecsracy
AC Electric
Mirror: Cobalt or Light Blue-Grey
5.75 Square

PLATE 0135
GENERAL ELECTRIC
c.1938, 5H-64, Lorraine
AC Electric
Mirror: Blue or Peach
5.75 Square

GENERAL ELECTRIC

PLATE 0136
GENERAL ELECTRIC
c.1938, 6H-02, Alencon
AC Electric
Mirror: Blue or Peach
7.5H X 16.5W

PLATE 0137
GENERAL ELECTRIC
c.1938, 7H-86, Warburton
AC Electric, Alarm
Catalin: Tortoise or Alabaster
5H X 4.75W

PLATE 0138
GENERAL ELECTRIC
c.1938, 7H-88, Dawning
AC Electric, Alarm
Mirror: Cobalt or Light Blue-Grey
5.75H Square

PLATE 0139
GENERAL ELECTRIC
c.1938, 7H-90, Eldorado
AC Electric, Alarm
Mirror: Blue or Peach w/Chrome Pedestal
7H X 5.5W

PLATE 0140
GENERAL ELECTRIC
c.1939, 3H-88, World's Fair
AC Electric
Bakelite: Walnut
5H X 4.5W

PLATE 0141
GENERAL ELECTRIC
c.1939, 3H-90, Norfolk
AC Electric
Wood: Striped Veneer w/Back Base
5H X 4.5W

PLATE 0142
GENERAL ELECTRIC
c.1939, 3H-92, New Lorraine
AC Electric
Walnut w/Inlay, Black base
4.75H X 5W

PLATE 0143
GENERAL ELECTRIC
c.1939, 4H-72, Breton
AC Electric, Alarm, Luminous Dial
White Glass on Chrome Base

PLATE 0144
GENERAL ELECTRIC
c.1939, 4H-78, Ballard
AC Electric
Brass
5H X 5.5W

GENERAL ELECTRIC

Plate 0145
GENERAL ELECTRIC
c.1939, 4H-80, Tuscan
AC Electric
Wood: Walnut and Zebrawood
6.5H X 8W

Plate 0146
GENERAL ELECTRIC
c.1939, 4H-84, Athens
AC Electric
Wood: Walnut
7.5H X 6.5W

Plate 0147
GENERAL ELECTRIC
c.1939, 7H-78, Acorn
AC Electric, Alarm
Black or Walnut Bakelite with Ivory Front Panel
4.75H

Plate 0148
GENERAL ELECTRIC
c.1939, 7H-80, Julep
AC Electric, Alarm
Catalin: Pink or Ivory
4.5H

Plate 0149
GENERAL ELECTRIC
c.1939, 7H-92, Circe
AC Electric, Alarm
White Glass w/Silver Detail and Chrome Base
7H X 8W

Plate 0150
GENERAL ELECTRIC
c.1939, 7H-94, Sergeant
AC Electric, Luminous Dial Optional
Black Bakelite or Ivory Plaskon
5.5H X 4.5W

Plate 0151
GENERAL ELECTRIC
c.1939, 7H-95, Colonade
AC Electric, Alarm
2-Tone Wood
5H X 4.5W

Plate 0152
GENERAL ELECTRIC
c.1939, 8H-76, Ithaca
AC Electric
Bakelite: Black or Walnut
5 H

Plate 0153
GENERAL ELECTRIC
c.1940, 3H-152, Sherwood
AC Electric
Wood: Mahogany
5.5 Square

GENERAL ELECTRIC

Plate 0154
GENERAL ELECTRIC
c.1940, 3H-158, Gay
AC Electric
Bakelite: Walnut
4H X 5W

Plate 155
GENERAL ELECTRIC
c.1940, 7H-98, Corporal
AC Electric, Alarm
Metal: Ivory or Brown
5.5 Square

Plate 156
GENERAL ELECTRIC
c.1940, 7H-102, Ashby
AC Electric, Alarm
Mirror: Blue or Peach
4.75H X 5W

Plate 0157
GENERAL ELECTRIC
c.1940, 7H-104, Hesperas
AC Electric, Alarm
Marble: White
5.5H X 5.5W

Plate 0158
GENERAL ELECTRIC
c.1940, 7H-110, Orpheus
AC Electric, Alarm
Brass
6.5H X 5.75W

Plate 0159
GENERAL ELECTRIC
c.1940, 7H-112, Gallant
AC Electric, Alarm
Brass
5.5H X 3.5W

Plate 0160
GENERAL ELECTRIC
c.1941, 3H98, Navigator
AC Electric
Wood: Ivory or Walnut
4.25H X 4.25W

Plate 0161
GENERAL ELECTRIC
c.1941, 3H-154, Saddle
AC Electric
Leather

Plate 0162
GENERAL ELECTRIC
c.1941, 3H-156, Narcissus
AC Electric
Marble: White
5.25 Square

GENERAL ELECTRIC

Plate 0163
GENERAL ELECTRIC
c.1941, 3H-162, Thrill
AC Electric
Wood: Walnut

Plate 0164
GENERAL ELECTRIC
c.1941, 3H-164, Bounty
AC Electric
Wood: Walnut

Plate 0165
GENERAL ELECTRIC
c.1941, 3H-166, Nimbus
AC Electric
Wood: Walnut and Maple

Plate 0166
GENERAL ELECTRIC
c.1941, 4H-76, Grafton
AC Electric
Bakelite: Walnut
7.25H X 7.75W

Plate 0167
GENERAL ELECTRIC
c.1941, 7H-106, Morning Glory
AC Electric, Alarm, Luminous Dial
Metal: Nickel Alloy w/Black Bakelite Base

Plate 0168
GENERAL ELECTRIC
c.1941, 7H-118, Troubadour
AC Electric, Alarm, Luminous Dial
Walnut Bakelite or Ivory Plaskon

Plate 0169
GENERAL ELECTRIC
c.1941, 7H-120, Modern
AC Electric
Pigskin Grain and Walnut
4.75 Square

Plate 0170
GENERAL ELECTRIC
c.1941, 8H-14, Almanac
AC Electric, Alarm
Wood: Mahogany
5.25H X 6W

Plate 0171
GENERAL ELECTRIC
c.1942, 6B-14, Winthrop
AC Electric, Chime
Wood: Mahogany
10.75H X 8W

GENERAL ELECTRIC

PLATE 0172
GENERAL ELECTRIC
c.1942, 8B-10, Framingham
AC Electric, Rotary Digital
Wood: Walnut
4H X 8.75W

PLATE 0173
GENERAL ELECTRIC
c.1946, 7H-132, Brisk
AC Electric, Alarm
Wood: Mahogany with Black Lacquer Trim

PLATE 0174
GENERAL ELECTRIC
c.1946, 7H-134, Helper
AC Electric, Alarm
Ivory Plaskon

PLATE 0175
GENERAL ELECTRIC
c.1947, 7H-136, Gay Hour
AC Electric, Alarm
Catalin: Butterscotch

PLATE 0176
GENERAL ELECTRIC
c.1947, 7H-138, Chipper
AC Electric, Alarm
Walnut Bakelite

PLATE 0177
GENERAL ELECTRIC
c.1947, 7H-142, Contact
AC Electric, Alarm
Wood with Faux Leather

PLATE 0178
GENERAL ELECTRIC
c.1947, 7H-160, Heralder
AC Electric, Alarm, Luminous Dial Optional
Plastic: Ivory
4.5H

PLATE 0179
GENERAL ELECTRIC
c.1947, 7H-164, Beau
AC Electric, Alarm
Mahogany Bakelite
4H

PLATE 0180
GENERAL ELECTRIC
c.1948, 7H-196, New Heralder
AC Electric, Alarm
Plastic: Ivory
5H X 5W

GENERAL ELECTRIC

Plate 0181
GENERAL ELECTRIC
c.1949, 3H-176, Geneva
AC Electric, Alarm
Wood: Mahogany or Birch
4.5H X 7.25W

Plate 0182
GENERAL ELECTRIC
c.1949, 3H-180, Voyager
AC Electric
Catalin: Brown Marbleized
5.5H X 6W

Plate 0183
GENERAL ELECTRIC
c.1949, 6B-20, Ridgefield
AC Electric, Strike
Wood: Mahogany
9.5H X 7.25W

Plate 0184
GENERAL ELECTRIC
c.1949, 7H-154, Chantilly
AC Electric, Alarm
Plastic: Ivory
4.5H

Plate 0185
GENERAL ELECTRIC
c.1949, 7H-166, Morning Glory
AC Electric, Alarm
Metal: Silver and Brass
4.75H X 6.5W

Plate 0186
GENERAL ELECTRIC
c.1949, 7H-170, Morning Star
AC Electric, Alarm, Luminous Dial
Plastic: Ivory
4.5H X 4.25W

Plate 0187
GENERAL ELECTRIC
c.1950, 3H-182, Designer
AC Electric
Wood: Mahogany
4H X 5.5W

Plate 0188
GENERAL ELECTRIC
c.1950, 7H-174, The Informer
AC Electric, Alarm, Luminous Dial
Plastic: Ivory
4.75H X 5W

Plate 0189
GENERAL ELECTRIC
c.1950, 7H-180, The Chipper
AC Electric, Alarm
Plastic: Ivory
4H X 4W

GENERAL ELECTRIC

PLATE 0190
GENERAL ELECTRIC
c.1950, 7H-190, Gay
AC Electric, Alarm
Ivory Plastic and Chrome
3.25H

PLATE 0191
GENERAL ELECTRIC
c.1951, Repeater
AC Electric
Metal: Ivory
5.5H X 4W

PLATE 0192
GENERAL ELECTRIC
c.1951, 7H-116, Orderly
AC Electric, Alarm, Luminous Dial
Plastic: Ivory or Walnut
4H

PLATE 0193
GENERAL ELECTRIC
c.1951, 7H-188, Candlewick
AC Electric, Alarm
Wood: Mahogany
5.5H X 8W

PLATE 0194
GENERAL ELECTRIC
c.1951, 7H-192, Wink
AC Electric, Alarm
Plastic: Ivory
4H X 3.75W

PLATE 0195
GENERAL ELECTRIC
c.1951, 7H-194, Nudger
AC Electric, Alarm, Luminous Dial
Plastic: Ivory
4H

PLATE 0196
GENERAL ELECTRIC
c.1951, 7H-198, Lumalarm
AC Electric, Alarm, Luminous Dial
Plastic: Ivory
5H X 4.5W

PLATE 0197
GENERAL ELECTRIC
c.1951, 7H-204, Tweed
AC Electric, Alarm
Brass
5H X 6W

PLATE 0198
GENERAL ELECTRIC
c.1951, 7H-208, Riser
AC Electric, Alarm
Plastic: Ivory
4 Square

GENERAL ELECTRIC

Plate 0199
GENERAL ELECTRIC
c.1951, Clansman
AC Electric
Plastic: White
6.25H

Plate 0200
GENERAL ELECTRIC
c.1953, 7H-213, Perspective
AC Electric, Alarm
Black Plastic with Gold Trim
6H X 7W

Plate 0201
GENERAL ELECTRIC
c.1953, 7H-220, Starter
AC Electric, Alarm, Luminous Dial Optional
Plastic: Ivory
3.75H

Plate 0202
GENERAL ELECTRIC
c.1953, Woodsman
AC Electric
Wood: Mahogany
5.5H

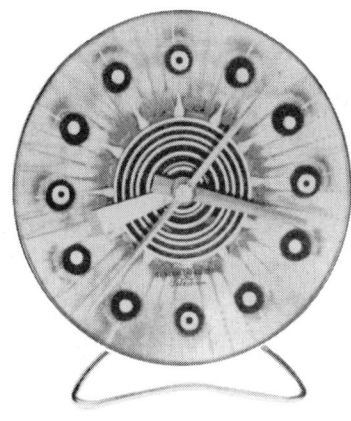

Plate 0203
GENERAL ELECTRIC
c.1954, 5H-70, Higgins Glass
AC Electric
Handblown Higgins Glass with Brass Trim
8.5H X 7.5W

Plate 0204
GENERAL ELECTRIC
c.1954, 7H-216, Brite-Dial
AC Electric, Alarm, Luminous Dial
Plastic: Blue, Pink, Green, Black or White
4.5H X 5.25W

Plate 0205
GENERAL ELECTRIC
c.1954, 7H-217, Telecrat
AC Electric, Alarm
Plastic: Ivory
4H X 4.5W

Plate 0206
GENERAL ELECTRIC
c.1954, 7H-224, Partner
AC Electric, Alarm, Luminous Dial
Metal Gilded
4.5H

Plate 0207
GENERAL ELECTRIC
c.1954, 7H-228, Architect
AC Electric, Alarm
Wood: Mahogany
4.25H

GENERAL ELECTRIC

Plate 0208
GENERAL ELECTRIC
c.1954, 7H-232, Caller
AC Electric, Alarm, Luminous Dial
Plastic: White
4H X 4.25W

Plate 0209
GENERAL ELECTRIC
c.1954, 7H-226, Urban
AC Electric, Alarm
Plastic: Black
5.5H

Plate 0210
GENERAL ELECTRIC
c.1955, 7H-215, Decor
AC Electric, Alarm, Luminous Dial
Wood: Birch
3.75H X 6W

Plate 0211
GENERAL ELECTRIC
c.1955, 7H-225, Luminary
AC Electric, Alarm, Luminous Dial
Plastic: Ivory
3.5H X 4.25W

Plate 0212
GENERAL ELECTRIC
c.1955, 7H-236, Revelation
AC Electric, Alarm
Plastic: Walnut
4.5H X 9.25W

Plate 0213
GENERAL ELECTRIC
c.1955, Versatile
AC Electric
Plastic: Red, White or Yellow w/Chrome
or Brown w/Gold

Plate 0214
GENERAL ELECTRIC
c.1956, 2H-103, Cupboard
AC Electric
Plastic: Red, Yellow, White or Walnut
5.25H X 6.25W

Plate 0215
GENERAL ELECTRIC
c.1956, 7H-204, Tweed
AC Electric, Alarm
Brass
5.25H X 6W

Plate 0216
GENERAL ELECTRIC
c.1956, 7H-223, Room-Mate
AC Electric, Alarm
Plastic: Ivory
3.75H X 3.5W

GENERAL ELECTRIC

Plate 0217
GENERAL ELECTRIC
c.1956, 7H-233, Circlewood
AC Electric, Alarm
Wood: Mahogany
4.5H X 5W

Plate 0218
GENERAL ELECTRIC
c.1957, Galaxy
AC Electric, Alarm
Plastic: Pink
4H X 5.75W

Plate 0219
GENERAL ELECTRIC
c.1957, Keynote
AC Electric
Plastic: Yellow, Red, or White
5.5H X 7.5W

Plate 0220
GENERAL ELECTRIC
c.1957, Radial
AC Electric, Alarm
Plastic: Tan
3.5H X 5.25W

Plate 0221
GENERAL ELECTRIC
c.1957, Snooz-Alarm
AC Electric, Alarm, Luminous Dial
Plastic: Grey
4.25 Square

Plate 0222
GENERAL ELECTRIC
c.1958, Concord
AC Electric
Wood: Mahogany
8H X 5W

Plate 0223
GENERAL ELECTRIC
c.1958, Chorus
AC Electric, Chime
Wood: Mahogany
9.75H X 8.25W

Plate 0224
GENERAL ELECTRIC
c.1958, Little Snooz
AC Electric, Alarm, Luminous Dial
Plastic: Grey
3.75 Square

Plate 0225
GENERAL ELECTRIC
c.1958, Scope
AC Electric, Alarm, Luminous Dial
Plastic: Grey
3.75H X 5.75W

GENERAL ELECTRIC

Plate 0226
GENERAL ELECTRIC
c.1958, Tempo
AC Electric, Alarm, Luminous Dial
Plastic: Ivory
3.75H X 4.25W

Plate 0227
GENERAL ELECTRIC
c.1958, Trend
AC Electric, Alarm, Luminous Dial
Plastic: Red or Black
3.75H X 6.25W

Plate 0228
GENERAL ELECTRIC
c.1958, Tune Alarm
AC Electric, Alarm
Plastic: Mahogany
4.25 Square

Plate 0229
GENERAL ELECTRIC
c.1958, Twinkle
AC Electric, Alarm
Wood: Mahogany
5.5 Square

Plate 0230
GENERAL ELECTRIC
c.1958, Twinkle
AC Electric, Alarm
Plastic: Mahogany
5.5H X 7.75W

Plate 0231
GENERAL ELECTRIC
c.1958, Warbler
AC Electric, Alarm
Wood: Mahogany
5H X 5.25W

Plate 0232
GENERAL ELECTRIC
c.1958, Lumalarm
AC Electric, Alarm
Plastic: Ivory
4.5H X 5W

Plate 0233
GENERAL ELECTRIC
c.1960, Royal Snooz
AC Electric, Alarm, Luminous Dial
Plastic: Tan
3.75H X 6.25W

Plate 0234
GENERAL ELECTRIC
c.1960, Snooze
AC Electric, Alarm, Luminous Dial
Plastic: White
3.5H X 4.25W

GENERAL ELECTRIC · GILBERT

Plate 0235
GENERAL ELECTRIC
c.1960, Snooze
AC Electric
Wood: Mahogany
3H X 4W

Plate 0236
GENERAL ELECTRIC
c.1960, Soft Tick
AC Electric, Alarm, Luminous Dial
Metal: Ivory
3.75 Diameter

Plate 00237
GENERAL ELECTRIC
c.1960, Wakewood
AC Electric, Alarm, Luminous Dial
Wood: Blond or Mahogany
4H X 5W

Plate 0238
GENERAL ELECTRIC
c.1960, #7381K, Atomic
AC Electric, Alarm
Plastic: Pink
4H X 6W

Plate 0239
GENERAL ELECTRIC
c.1960, Twin Bell
Alarm, Luminous Dial
Brass
6H X 5W

Plate 0240
GENERAL ELECTRIC
c.1960
Alarm, Luminous Dial
Metal: Ivory

Plate 0241
GENERAL ELECTRIC
c.1960
AC Electric, Alarm, Luminous Dial
Plastic: White

Plate 0242
GILBERT
c.1931
AC Electric, Alarm
Brass
4.75H

Plate 0243
GILBERT
c.1931
40-Hour Wind, Alarm, Luminous Dial
Metal: Green, Blue or Red
3.5H

GILBERT

PLATE 0244
GILBERT
c.1931
40-Hour Wind, Alarm
Metal: Green, Blue or Red
4.5H X 4.5W

PLATE 0245
GILBERT
c.1931
40-Hour Wind, Alarm, Luminous Dial Optional
Metal: Green, Blue, Red or Nickel
4.25H

PLATE 0246
GILBERT
c.1932, #605
Alarm
Metal: Black and Nickel
2" Dial

PLATE 0247
GILBERT
c.1932, #414
AC Electric, Alarm
Metal: Chrome and Black
4.5 Square

PLATE 0248
GILBERT
c.1932
AC Electric
Bakelite
5H

PLATE 0249
GILBERT
c.1932
40-Hour Wind, Alarm, Luminous Dial
Metal: Green, Blue or Rose
4.75H

PLATE 0250
GILBERT
c.1932
40-Hour Wind, Alarm
Metal: Green, Blue or Rose
4.5 Square

PLATE 0251
GILBERT
c.1933
8-Day Wind or AC Electric, Alarm, Luminous Dial Optional
Metal: Nickel, Green, Blue or Red
5H X 4.5W

PLATE 0252
GILBERT
c.1933
40-Hour Wind
Metal: Green, Blue or Red
3.75H X 4.25W

GILBERT

Plate 0253
GILBERT
c.1934, Salute
1-Day Wind, Alarm
Metal: Green, Blue or Pink

Plate 0254
GILBERT
c.1934
AC Electric
Wood: Mahogany
8.75H X 8.25W

Plate 0255
GILBERT
c.1934, #940, 941
40-Hour Wind, Alarm
Metal: Green or Pink
4.5H X 3.5W

Plate 0256
GILBERT
c.1934, Mogul
1-Day Wind, Alarm
Metal: Chrome and Black
6.25H X 5.5W

Plate 0257
GILBERT
c.1934
40-Hour Wind, Alarm
Metal: Green, Blue or Pink
4.25H X 3.75W

Plate 0258
GILBERT
c.1935
1-Day Wind, Alarm, Luminous Dial
Metal: Green, Blue or Pink
4.25H

Plate 0259
GILBERT
c.1936
40-Hour Wind, Alarm, Luminous Dial
Metal: Ivory or Nickel
5.75H

Plate 0260
GILBERT
c.1936
40-Hour Wind, Alarm
Metal: Green w/Ivory trim
5H

Plate 0261
GILBERT
c.1937, #947, 968
1-Day Wind, Alarm, Luminous Dial Optional
Metal: Black or Green
4H X 3.5W

GILBERT

PLATE 0262
GILBERT
c.1938, #956, Little Gilbert
1-Day Wind, Alarm
Metal: Ivory w/Gold or Black w/Nickel
3.75H

PLATE 0263
GILBERT
c.1938, #908, 909
1-Day or 8-Day Wind, Alarm
Metal: Green w/Nickel or Ivory w/Gold trim

PLATE 0264
GILBERT
c.1939, #1202, 1203
8-Day Wind, Alarm, Luminous Dial Optional
Metal: Ivory or Rust w/Gold, Green w/Nickel trim
5.5H X 5.75W

PLATE 0265
GILBERT
c.1939
40 Hr. Wind, Alarm
Metal: Rose, Green, Black or Ivory
4H

PLATE 0266
GILBERT
c.1939
1-Day Wind, Alarm
Metal: Rose, Green or Ivory
5.5H

PLATE 0267
GILBERT
c.1939
1-Day Wind, Alarm
Metal: Rose, Green or Ivory
6H

PLATE 0268
GILBERT
c.1940, Calender
40-Hour Wind
Bakelite: Black
6.5H X 5.5W

PLATE 0269
GILBERT
c.1940, Charlie McCarthy
40-Hour Wind, Alarm
Metal: Ivory
6H X 5.75W

PLATE 0270
GILBERT
c.1940
8-Day Wind or AC Electric
Wood: Mahogany
6.5H X 6W

GILBERT

PLATE 0271
GILBERT
c.1941, #982
1-Day Wind, Alarm
Metal: Ivory or Black
4.5H X 7W

PLATE 0272
GILBERT
c.1942, #333
1-Day Wind, Alarm
Metal: Ivory
4.5H X 4.25W

PLATE 0273
GILBERT
c.1942, Bell
1-Day Wind, Alarm, Luminous Dial Optional
Metal: Ivory or Black
4.5H X 5W

PLATE 0274
GILBERT
c.1942
Modern
1-Day Wind, Alarm
Metal: Ivory or Black

PLATE 0275
GILBERT
c.1942
1-Day Wind, Alarm
Black Bakelite or Ivory Plaskon

PLATE 0276
GILBERT
c.1947
1-Day Wind, Alarm
Metal: Ivory
4.5H

PLATE 0277
GILBERT
c.1948
40-Hour Wind, Alarm, Luminous Dial Optional
Plastic: Ivory
5.25H X 5.25W

PLATE 0278
GILBERT
c.1949, Trophy
40-Hour Wind, Alarm, Luminous Dial Optional
Plastic: Ivory w/gold trim
4.5H

PLATE 0279
GILBERT
c.1950
1-Day Wind, Alarm, Luminous Dial Optional
Metal: Chrome w/Black or Ivory
5.75H X 5.25W

GILBERT

PLATE 0280
GILBERT
c.1951, Sovereign
40-Hour Wind, Alarm, Luminous Dial Optional
Plastic: Ivory
5H

PLATE 0281
GILBERT
c.1952
40-Hour Wind, Alarm, Luminous Dial Optional
Plastic: Ivory
4.75H X 5.25W

PLATE 0282
GILBERT
c.1962, #1265, Sprite
AC Electric, Alarm, Luminous Dial
Metal: Ivory, Black, Green or Pink
3.5H X 3.25W

PLATE 0283
GILBERT
c.1962, #1266, Vanguard
AC Electric, Alarm, Luminous Dial Optional
Plastic: Ivory, Black, Green or Pink
5H X 4.5W

PLATE 0284
GILBERT
c.1962, Nite-Glo
40-Hour Wind, Alarm, Luminous Dial
Metal: Ivory
4.5H

PLATE 0285
GILBERT
c.1962, Square Model
40-Hour Wind, Alarm, Luminous Dial
Metal: Ivory
4 Square

PLATE 0286
GILBERT
c.1962, Startime
40-Hour Wind, Alarm, Luminos Dial Optional
Plastic: Ivory, Black, Green or Pink
5H X 4.5W

PLATE 0287
GILBERT
c.1962
40-Hour Wind, Alarm, Luminous Dial
Ivory, Green or Tan

PLATE 0288
GILBERT
c.1965, Coronet
1-Day Wind, Alarm, Luminous Dial
Metal

GOLD SHIELD · HAMMOND

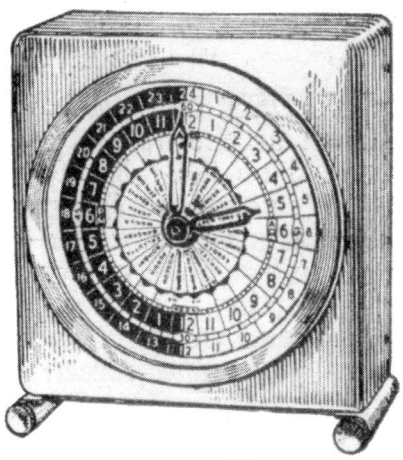

PLATE 0289
GOLD SHIELD
c.1942
World Time

PLATE 0290
GORDON
c.1938, #1076
AC Electric
Metal: Black
3.5D

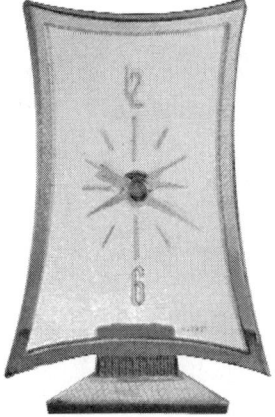

PLATE 0291
HADDON
c.1962, #156, Linear
AC Electric, Luminous Dial
Metal: Gold Plated
13H X 9W

PLATE 0292
HADDON
c.1962, #705, Vision
AC Electric, Luminous Dial
Metal: Gold Plated
8.75H X 7.75W

PLATE 0293
HAMILTON SANGAMO
c.1934, S-402
AC Electric Wind
Marble: Black, Green and Alabaster
8.5H X 7.5W

PLATE 0294
HAMILTON SANGAMO
c.1935, S-404
AC Electric Wind
Wood: Various Exotic Veneers

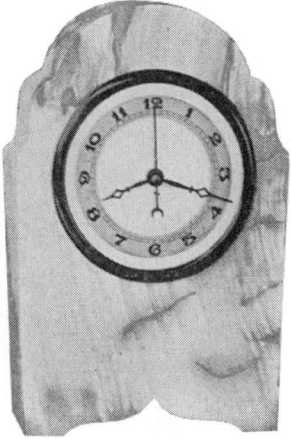

PLATE 0295
HAMMOND
c.1931, Old Durch
AC Electric
Marble: Predara Onyx
8H X 5.5W

PLATE 0296
HAMMOND
c.1931, Petite
AC Electric, Alarm
Marble: Predara Onyx
6H X 5.75W

PLATE 0297
HAMMOND
c.1931, Octagon
AC Electric
Marble: Onyx w/Black and Gold
6.75H X 7W

HAMMOND

PLATE 0298
HAMMOND
c.1931, Boudoir
AC Electric
Marble: Predara Onyx w/Black and Gold

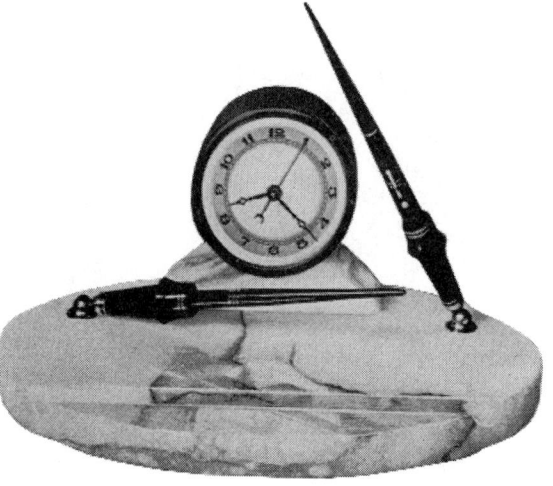

PLATE 0299
HAMMOND
c.1931, Double Director
AC Electric
Marble: Predara Onyx
5.5H, 8 X 13 Base

PLATE 0300
HAMMOND
c.1931, Arcadia
AC Electric
Wood: Mahogany
7.25H X 5W

PLATE 0301
HAMMOND
c.1931, Knickerbocker
AC Electric
Marble: Predara Onyx
8.5H X 6W

PLATE 0302
HAMMOND
c.1931, Melody
AC Electric, Alarm
Marble: Predara Onyx w/Black & Gold Spheres
5.75H X 7B

PLATE 0303
HAMMOND
c.1931, Columbia
AC Electric, Alarm
Wood: Mahogany w/Black and Gold Trim
8H X 6W

PLATE 0304
HAMMOND
c.1931, Duchess
AC Electric
Marble: Predara Onyx and Dark Green

PLATE 0305
HAMMOND
c.1931, Avondale
AC Electric, Calendar
Bakelite: Walnut
8H X 4.75W

PLATE 0306
HAMMOND
c.1931, Skyline
AC Electric, Alarm
Marble: Predara Onyx and Black Belgian
9.5H X 5.5B

HAMMOND

PLATE 0307
HAMMOND
c.1931, Parisian
AC Electric, Alarm
Marble: Green Argentine
7H X 6B

PLATE 0308
HAMMOND
c.1931, Valencia
AC Electric
Marble: Rance with Belgian Black

PLATE 0309
HAMMOND
c.1931, Double Executive
AC Electric
Marble: Green Argentine
5.5H, 8 X 12 Base

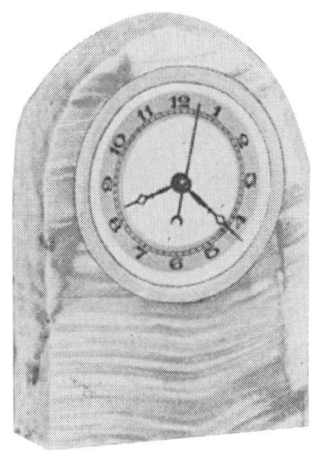

PLATE 0310
HAMMOND
c.1931, Ruff
AC Electric, Alarm
Marble: Pedrara Onyx
7H

PLATE 0311
HAMMOND
c.1931, Seneca
AC Electric
Marble: Green w/Black and Gold
7H X 6B

PLATE 0312
HAMMOND
c.1931, Junior (aka Beacon)
AC Electric, Alarm Optional
Bakelite: Walnut or Black
4.25H X 3.5W

PLATE 0313
HAMMOND
c.1931, Glenmora
AC Electric, Alarm
Wood: Walnut
9.5H X 7.75W

PLATE 0314
HAMMOND
c.1931, Gregory (aka Skyscraper)
AC Electric, Calendar
Bakelite: Walnut or Black
6.5H X 5.75W

PLATE 0315
HAMMOND
c.1931, Logan
AC Electric
Bakelite: Walnut
4.75H X 4W

HAMMOND

PLATE 0316
HAMMOND
c.1931, Oakwood
AC Electric, Alarm
Bakelite: Walnut
6.75H X 5W

PLATE 0317
HAMMOND
c.1931, Sherwood
AC Electric
Wood: Mahogany
10H X 8W

PLATE 0318
HAMMOND
c.1931
AC Electric
Wood: Mahogany
5H X 3.25W

PLATE 0319
HAMMOND
c.1931
AC Electric
Wood: Mahogany
9.25H X 7.25W

PLATE 0320
HAMMOND
c.1931
AC Electric
Wood: Mahogany
7H X 8.5W

PLATE 0321
HAMMOND
c.1932, Firefly
AC Electric, Alarm, Luminous Dial
Bakelite: Walnut, Ivory, Green or Black
5.25H X 4.5W

PLATE 0322
HAMMOND
c.1932
AC Electric, Alarm
Bakelite: Walnut
4.75H X 4W

PLATE 0323
HAMMOND
c.1933, Modern
AC Electric
Bakelite: Walnut
4.25H X 3.5W

PLATE 0324
HAMMOND
c.1933, Gloria
AC Electric, Alarm
Metal: Chrome w/Green or Pink Dial
5H X 4.5W

HAMMOND

Plate 0325
HAMMOND
c.1934, Tower-Modernistic
AC Electric
Metal: Silver, Black

Plate 0326
HAMMOND
c.1934, Grenadier
AC Electric, Alarm
Metal: Chrome with Black Trim
5.5H X 4.75W

Plate 0327
HAMMOND
c.1934, Paris
AC Electric, Alarm
Bakelite/Plaskon: Brown, Black or Ivory
4.5H X 3.75W

Plate 0328
HAMMOND
c.1934, Polo
AC Electric, Alarm
Metal: Chrome with Black Trim
5.5H X 4.75W

Plate 0329
HAMMOND
c.1936, Falcon
AC Electric
Bakelite: Brown or Black

Plate 0330
HAMMOND
c.1936, Modern Firefly
AC Electric, Luminous Dial
Bakelite/Plaskon: Ivory or Black
5.25H X 4.5W

Plate 0331
HAMMOND
c.1937, Empress
AC Electric, Alarm
Black Bakelite, Chrome, Cobalt Mirror
4.75H X 5.5W

Plate 0332
HAMMOND
c.1937, Firefly
AC Electric
Plaskon: Ivory

Plate 0333
HAMMOND
c.1938, Tripoli
AC Electric, Alarm, Day/Date
Wood: Mahogany
5.25H X 6.5W

HAMMOND

Plate 0334
HAMMOND
c.1938, Aurora
AC Electric, Alarm, Luminous Dial
Wood: Burl Maple or Orientalwood
5.75H X 4.5W

Plate 0335
HAMMOND
c.1938, Chancellor
AC Electric, Alarm
Wood: Walnut
7.75H X 3.25W

Plate 0336
HAMMOND
c.1938, Courtier
AC Electric, Alarm
Wood: Walnut
5.75H X 5W

Plate 0337
HAMMOND
c.1938, Diplomat
AC Electric, Alarm
Wood: Redwood or Maple
5.75H X 5W

Plate 0338
HAMMOND
c.1939, Regent
AC Electric, Alarm
Onyx: White w/Gold Trim
5H X 5W

Plate 0339
HAMMOND
c.1939, Edgemont
AC Electric, Alarm
Metal: Chrome
4.5H X 5.25W

Plate 0340
HAMMOND
c.1939
AC Electric, Alarm
Blue Mirror
6.5H X 5.25W

Plate 0341
HAMMOND
c.1939, Asbury
AC Electric, Alarm
Bakelite/Plaskon: Ivory w/Gold or Black w/Chrome
5H X 5W

Plate 0342
HAMMOND
c.1939, Cathay
AC Electric, Alarm
Plaskon: Ivory
4.75H X 4W

HAMMOND

PLATE 0343
HAMMOND
c.1940
AC Electric
Onyx: Green
6.25H X 6.5W

PLATE 0344
HAMMOND
c.1940
AC Electric
Blue-Grey Mirror
6H X 8.5W

PLATE 0345
HAMMOND
c.1940
AC Electric
Blue Mirror
7.5L X 2.5W

PLATE 0346
HAMMOND
c.1941
AC Electric
Marble: White

PLATE 0347
HAMMOND
c.1941
AC Electric
Marble: White
5.5H X 7W

PLATE 0348
HAMMOND
c.1941, Arc of Time
AC Electric
Marble: White
6H X 5W

PLATE 0349
HAMMOND
c.1941, Dayton
AC Electric, Calendar
Wood: Mahogany
5.75H X 7.75W

PLATE 0350
HAMMOND
c.1941, Fantasy
AC Electric, Alarm
Plaskon: Ivory
4.5H X 4.25W

PLATE 0351
HAMMOND
c.1941, Mentor
AC Electric
Wood: Mahogany
4.75H X 6.5W

HAMMOND · HARMONY HOUSE

PLATE 0352
HAMMOND
c.1941, Luna
AC Electric, Luminous Dial
Wood: Mahogany
5.5H X 5.25W

PLATE 0353
HAMMOND
c.1941, Pilot
AC Electric
Wood: Walnut
7.25 Square

PLATE 0354
HAMMOND
c.1941, Riviera
AC Electric, Alarm
Metal: Gold plated, satin finish
4.5H X 6.75W

PLATE 0355
HARMONY HOUSE
c.1946, #7076
AC Electric, Alarm
Bakelite/Plaskon: Walnut or Ivory
4.5H X 4.5W

PLATE 0356
HARMONY HOUSE
c.1951, #7086
40-Hour Wind, Alarm
Wood: Mahogany
6.5H

PLATE 0357
HARMONY HOUSE
c.1951, #7029, 7032, Modern
40-Hour Wind, Alarm, Luminous Dial Optional
Wood: Mahogany
4.5

PLATE 0358
HARMONY HOUSE
c.1951, #7048, 7056, Precision
8-Day Wind, Alarm, Luminous Dial Optional
Metal: Mahogany, Black or Ivory
5H

PLATE 0359
HARMONY HOUSE
c.1951, #7063, 7064, Junior
40-Hour Wind, Alarm, Luminous Dial Optional
Metal: Pink, Ivory or Sky Blue
3.25H

PLATE 0360
HARMONY HOUSE
c.1952, #7011, 7012, Extra-Thin
1-Day Wind, Alarm, Luminous Dial Optional
Metal: Ivory
3.25H

HARMONY HOUSE

PLATE 0361
HARMONY HOUSE
c.1953, #7110
AC Electric, Alarm, Luminous Dial
Plastic: Ivory
4H X 4.25W

PLATE 0362
HARMONY HOUSE
c.1953, #7013, 7014, Square Design
1-Day Wind, Alarm, Luminous Dial Optional
Metal: Ivory
4.25H

PLATE 0363
HARMONY HOUSE
c.1954, #7040, Decorator
1-Day Wind, Alarm, Luminous Dial
Metal: Ivory, Pink or Blue
3.75H X 3.5W

PLATE 0364
HARMONY HOUSE
c.1954, #7035, 7036, Designer
8-Day Wind, Alarm, Luminous Dial Optional
Metal: Ivory
5.25H

PLATE 0365
HARMONY HOUSE
c.1959, #7068, Daisy Boutique
1-Day Wind, Alarm, Luminous Dial
Metal: Ivory
3H

PLATE 0366
HARMONY HOUSE
c.1959, #7069
8-Day Wind, Alarm, Luminous Dial
Metal: Ivory
4.5H X 4W

PLATE 0367
HARMONY HOUSE
c.1959, #7070
8-Day Wind, Alarm, Luminous Dial
Metal: Gold
5H

PLATE 0368
HARMONY HOUSE
c.1959, #7082
AC Electric, Alarm, Luminous Dial
Plastic: Ivory or Beige
4H X 5W

PLATE 0369
HARMONY HOUSE
c.1959, #7151, Add-a-Nap
AC Electric, Alarm, Luminous Dial
Plastic: White
3.5H X 4.5W

HARMONY HOUSE · HERMAN MILLER

Plate 0370
HARMONY HOUSE
c.1959, #7155, Add-a-Nap
AC Electric, Alarm, Luminous Dial
Wood: Mahogany
4H X 4.5W

Plate 0371
HARMONY HOUSE
c.1959, #7107, 7108
AC Electric, Alarm, Luminous Dial Optional
Plastic: Ivory
3.5H X 3.5W

Plate 0372
HARMONY HOUSE
c.1959, #7140, 7141, Shadow Box
AC Electric, Alarm, Luminous Dial Optional
Plastic: Ivory, White or Pink
6W

Plate 0373
HAVLIN
c.1930, Kennerly
AC Electric, Alarm
Wood: Walnut
10H X 7.5W

Plate 0374
HAVLIN
c.1930, Mary Lou
AC Electric
Bakelite: Walnut
5H X 4W

Plate 0375
HAVLIN
c.1931, #1033
AC Electric
Bakelite: Walnut
7.25H X 3.25W

Plate 0376
HAVLIN
c.1931, #1038
AC Electric
Bakelite: Walnut
5H X 5W

Plate 0377
HAVLIN
c.1932, Havalarm Delux
AC Electric, Alarm
Bakelite: Walnut
7H X 4.5W

Plate 0378
HERMAN MILLER
c.1931, #4018
AC Electric
Wood: Mahogany
10H X 7.25W

HERMAN MILLER

Plate 0379
HERMAN MILLER
c.1931, #4c.197
AC Electric
Wood: Mahogany
10.75H X 9W

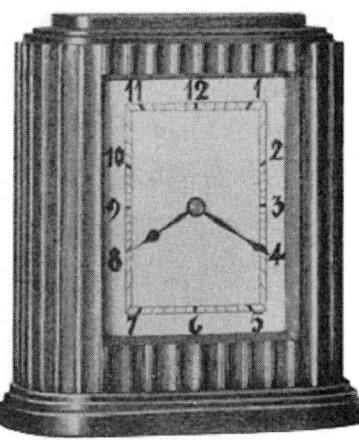

Plate 0380
HERMAN MILLER
c.1931, TR410 (Rohde Des.)
AC Electric
Wood: Mahogany
7.5H X 7W

Plate 0381
HERMAN MILLER
c.1931, TR410/Alternate Luminous Dial (Rohde Des.)
AC Electric
Wood: Mahogany
7.5H X 7W

Plate 0382
HERMAN MILLER
c.1931, #4776 (Rohde Des.)
AC Electric, Chime
Wood, Walnut
5.25H X 8.5W

Plate 0383
HERMAN MILLER
c.1931, #4784 (Rohde Des.)
AC Electric, Chime
Wood, Walnut
5.25H X 11.5W

Plate 0384
HERMAN MILLER
c.1931, #5187
AC Electric, Chime
Wood: Mahogany
11.5H X 9.75W

Plate 0385
HERMAN MILLER
c.1933, Moderne (Rohde Des.)
AC Electric
Metal: Chrome

Plate 0386
HERMAN MILLER
c.1934, (Rohde Des.)
AC Electric
Wood: Walnut w/Chrome
8.25H X 7.5W

HERMAN MILLER · HERSCHEDE

Plate 0388
HERMAN MILLER
c.1934 (Rohde Des.)
AC Electric, Alarm
Metal: Chrome w/White, Black
6.25H

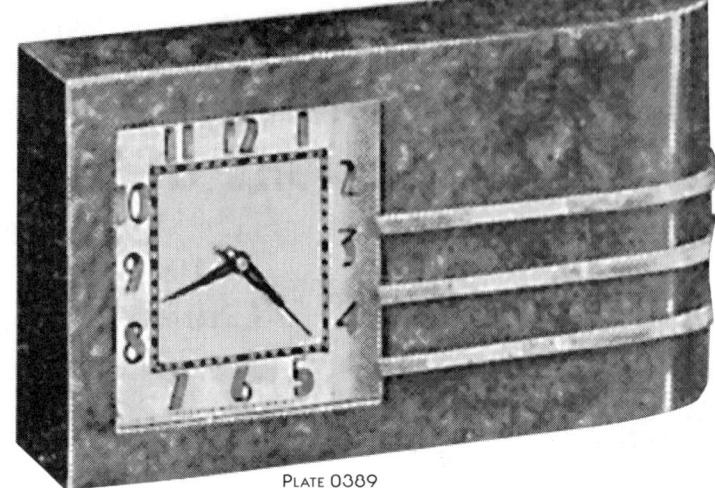

Plate 0389
HERMAN MILLER
c.1934 (Rohde Des.)
AC Electric
Wood, Walnut
7H X 13L

Plate 0390
HERSCHEDE
c.1932, #2053, French Gothic Style
AC Electric, Chime
Wood: Mahogany
14.5H X 10.25W X 7.25D

Plate 0391
HERSCHEDE
c.1932, #6046, Sheraton
AC Electric, Chime, Alarm
Wood: Mahogany, Maple Overlay
11.75H X 5.5D

Plate 0392
HERSCHEDE
c.1932, #6078, Sheraton-Colonial
AC Electric, Chime
Wood: Mahogany
11.5H X 8.25W X 5.5D

Plate 0393
HERSCHEDE
c.1933 #2005, Colonial
AC Electric, Chime
Wood
13.25H X 14W X 7D

Plate 0394
HERSCHEDE
c.1933, #2011, Gothic
AC Electric, Chime
Wood
18H X 10.5W X 7D

Plate 0395
HERSCHEDE
c.1933, #2013, Sheraton-Colonial
AC Electric, Chime
Wood w/Brass trimmings
14.75H X 11.5W X 7D

HERSCHEDE

Plate 0396
HERSCHEDE
c.1933, #2023, Gothic
AC Electric, Chime
Wood
14.5H X 11W X 7D

Plate 0397
HERSCHEDE
c.1933, #2035, Colonial
AC Electric, Chime
Wood: Redwood Burl Panels
13.25H X 11W X 7D

Plate 0398
HERSCHEDE
c.1933, #2041, Moderne
AC Electric, Chime
Wood: Rosewood, Amboyna/Madrone Inlay,
Green Catalin Feet
14.75H X 10.25W X 6.75D

Plate 0399
HERSCHEDE
c.1933, #2047, Sheraton-Colonial
AC Electric, Chime, Alarm
Wood: Maple
13.75H X 11W X 7.5D

Plate 0400
HERSCHEDE
c.1933, #2051, Louis XVI
AC Electric, Chime
Wood: Walnut, Satinwood inlay
15.75H X 10.5W X 7.5D

Plate 0401
HERSCHEDE
c.1933, #3002, Gothic
AC Electric, Chime
Wood: Mahogany
11.5H X 8W

Plate 0402
HERSCHEDE
c.1933, #3004, Colonial
AC Electric, Chime
Wood: Mahogany
11.25H X 8W

Plate 0403
HERSCHEDE
c.1933, #6002, Sheraton
AC Electric, Chime
Wood w/Brass finials
15H X 8W X 6.25D

Plate 0404
HERSCHEDE
c.1933, #6012, Gothic
AC Electric, Chime, Alarm
Wood: Mahogany
12.25H X 8.25W X 6D

HERSCHEDE · HOWARD

Plate 0405
HERSCHEDE
c.1933, #6016, Gothic
AC Electric, Chime
Wood: Mahogany
12.25H X 8.75W X 6D

Plate 0406
HERSCHEDE
c.1933, #6018, Georgian
AC Electric, Chime
Wood: Mahogany, Maple
12.75H X 8.5W X 6.25D

Plate 0407
HERSCHEDE
c.1933, #6020, Louis XIV
AC Electric, Chime, Alarm
Wood: Walnut
12H X 12.25W X 6.25D

Plate 0408
HERSCHEDE
c.1933, #6028, Chippendale
AC Electric, Chime, Alarm
Wood: Mahogany
13H X 8.25W X 6D

Plate 0409
HERSCHEDE
c.1933, #6040, Gothic
AC Electric, Chime
Wood: Mahogany
13H X 8.5W X 6.75D

Plate 0410
HERSCHEDE
c.1933, #6062, Moderne
AC Electric, Chime
Wood: Amboyna w/Ivory trim columns
12.5H X 8.25W X 6.75D

Plate 0411
HERSCHEDE
c.1963, #2177, Warren
AC Electric, Chime Optional
Wood: Cherry
8H X 6.75W X 4.5D

Plate 0412
HOWARD
c.1939, Mariner
AC Electric
Metal: Chrome
9.5H X 8.5W

Plate 0413
HOWARD
c.1939, Horseshoe-Good Luck
AC Electric
Metal: Chrome
9.5H X 9W

HOWELL · INGERSOL

Plate 0414
HOWELL LAMP
c.1957, #797, Future
AC Electric
Ceramic: Black or Blue
7H X 8W (Clock)

Plate 0415
HOWELL LAMP
c.1957, #800, Embassy
AC Electric
Ceramic: Blue or White
6H X 9W (Clock)

Plate 0416
HOWELL LAMP
c.1957, #1617, Musicale
AC Electric
Ceramic: White or Black
9H X 11W (Clock)

Plate 0417
HOWELL LAMP
c.1957, #801, Moderne
AC Electric
Ceramic: Pink or Blue
9H X 10W (Clock)

Plate 0418
IMPERIAL
c.1947, Zephyr
AC Electric, Rotary Digital
Bakelite/Plaskon/Tenite:
Black w/Ivory or Ivory w/Red

Plate 0419
INGERSOL
c.1931, #10
AC Electric, Alarm
Wood: Mahogany
7H X 5.75W

INGERSOL

PLATE 0420
INGERSOL
c.1931, #15
AC Electric
Wood: Mahogany
7H X 5.75W

PLATE 0421
INGERSOL
c.1931, #20
AC Electric
Wood: Mahogany
7H X 6W

PLATE 0422
INGERSOL
c.1931, #30
AC Electric
Wood: Mahogany
8.25H X 7W

PLATE 0423
INGERSOL
c.1931, #35
AC Electric
Wood: Mahogany
8.25H X 7W

PLATE 0424
INGERSOL
c.1931, #40
AC Electric
Wood: Mahogany
9H X 8W

PLATE 0425
INGERSOL
c.1931, #150
AC Electric
Wood: Mahogany
6H X 5W

PLATE 0426
INGERSOL
c.1931, #151
AC Electric
Wood: Mahogany
6H X 5W

PLATE 0427
INGERSOL
c.1931, #250
AC Electric
Wood: Mahogany
6H X 5W

PLATE 0428
INGERSOL
c.1931, #251
AC Electric
Wood: Mahogany
6H X 5W

INGERSOL

PLATE 0429
INGERSOL
c.1931, Photo Traveler
1 Day Wind, Luminous Dial Optional
Metal: Chrome w/Blue, Red, Pink, Tan or Green
3.5H

PLATE 0430
INGERSOL
c.1931, Traveler
1 Day Wind, Alarm, Luminous Dial Optional
Metal: Chrome w/Blue, Red, Pink, Tan or Green
3H

PLATE 0431
INGERSOL
c.1933, Pilot
1-Day Wind, Alarm
Metal: Black

PLATE 0432
INGERSOL
c.1934, #420, Mickey Mouse
1 day Wind, Alarm
Metal: Red or Green
4.25H

PLATE 0433
INGERSOL
c.1934
1-Day Wind, Alarm
Metal: Black
4H X 3.75W

PLATE 0434
INGERSOL
c.1934, #426, Dollar
1 Day Wind, Alarm
Metal: Chrome

PLATE 0435
INGERSOL
c.1934, Big Bad Wolf
1-Day Wind, Alarm
Metal: Red
4.25H

PLATE 0436
INGERSOL
c.1934
1-Day Wind, Alarm
Metal: Metallic Teal with Brass Trim

PLATE 0437
INGERSOL
c.1936, #2122
1 Day Wind, Alarm
Metal: Green or Black w/Chrome Trim

INGERSOL

Plate 0438
INGERSOL
c.1936, #2123, Gale
1 day Wind, Alarm
Metal: Green, Black

Plate 0439
INGERSOL
c.1936, #2147
1-Day Wind, Alarm
Metal: Green

Plate 0440
INGERSOL
c.1936, #2148, Daintie
1-Day Wind, Alarm
Metal: Green or Brass

Plate 0441
INGERSOL
c.1936, #2149, Daybreak
1-Day Wind, Alarm
Chrome w/Black or Ivory w/Gold

Plate 0442
INGERSOL
c.1936, #2150, Petire
1-Day Wind, Alarm
Metal: Chrome w/Brass or Black w/Chrome

Plate 0443
INGERSOL
c.1936, #2482, Measuring Tape
8-Day Wind, Rotary
Metal: Black or Copper w/Chrome

Plate 0444
INGERSOL
c.1936, #2482R, Gable
8-Day Wind, Alarm
Metal: Black w/Chrome

Plate 0445
INGERSOL
c.1947, #6828, 6830
40-Hour Wind, Alarm, Luminous Dial Optional
Metal: Red, Green, Blue or Grey w/Chrome
5.5H

Plate 0446
INGERSOL
c.1947
1-Day Wind, Alarm
Plastic: Ivory, Green, Navy, Yellow or Mahogany

INGERSOL - INGRAHAM

Plate 0447
INGERSOL
c.1949, #414, AMI
40-Hour Wind, Alarm, Luminous Dial Optional
Plastic: Ivory, Emerald Green, Navy or Mahogany
5H

Plate 0448
INGERSOL
c.1951, Sunrise
1-Day Wind, Alarm, Luminous Dial
Plastic, White
4.5H X 4.25W

Plate 0449
INGRAHAM
c.1930, Cathedral
8-Day Wind, Chimes
Wood: Mahogany

Plate 0450
INGRAHAM
c.1931, Colonial
8-Day Wind, Chimes
Wood: Mahogany
15H X 10.75W

Plate 0451
INGRAHAM
c.1931, Elton
8-Day Wind, Chimes
Wood: Mahogany
10H X 8.25W

Plate 0452
INGRAHAM
c.1932, Classic
1-Day Wind, Alarm
Metal: Blue, Green or Ivory
4.75H X 6.25W

Plate 0453
INGRAHAM
c.1932
1-Day Wind, Alarm
Metal: Pink, Green, or Blue
4.5H

Plate 0454
INGRAHAM
c.1932
AC Electric
Wood: Mahogany
8.5H X 7.75W

Plate 0455
INGRAHAM
c.1932
AC Electric
Wood: Mahogany
6.75H X 7.25W

INGRAHAM

PLATE 0456
INGRAHAM
c.1932, Automatic
8-Day Wind, Alarm, Luminous Dial Optional
Metal: Black, Green or Nickel Plated
5.5H X 5W

PLATE 0457
INGRAHAM
c.1933, Ace
1-Day Wind, Alarm
Metal: Black, Chrome or Green
4.25H

PLATE 0458
INGRAHAM
c.1933, Ace Luminous
1-Day Wind, Alarm, Luminous Dial
Metal: Black, Chrome or Green
4.25H

PLATE 0459
INGRAHAM
c.1933, Ace
1-Day Wind, Alarm
Metal: Black, Ivory, Chrome or Green

PLATE 0460
INGRAHAM
c.1933, Commander
8-Day Wind, Chimes
Wood: Mahogany
10H X 9W

PLATE 0461
INGRAHAM
c.1933, Magic
AC Electric, Alarm
Metal: Black, Ivory or Chrome
6.25H X 5.25W

PLATE 0462
INGRAHAM
c.1933, Modern
8-Day Wind, Alarm, Luminous Dial Optional
Metal: Black w/Nickel or Walnut w/Copper
3.25H X 2.75W

PLATE 0463
INGRAHAM
c.1933
8-Day Wind, Alarm, Luminous Dial Optional
Metal: Black or Green w/Nickel or Ivory w/Gold
5H X 4.5W

PLATE 0464
INGRAHAM
c.1933
AC Electric, Alarm
Wood: Mahogany
9.25H X 7.5W

INGRAHAM

Plate 0465
INGRAHAM
c.1933
AC Electric
Wood: Walnut
9.5H X 7W

Plate 0466
INGRAHAM
c.1933
AC Electric
Metal: Chrome plated
5.5H X 9W

Plate 0467
INGRAHAM
c.1933
8-Day Wind, Strike
Wood: Mahogany
10.5H X 9W

Plate 0468
INGRAHAM
c.1934, Mounted Buller
1-Day Wind
Metal: Blue or Green w/Nickel Trim
5H X 5W

Plate 0469
INGRAHAM
c.1934, Commander
8-Day Wind, Alarm
Metal: Chrome or Black w/Chrome
5.25H X 6.75W

Plate 0470
INGRAHAM
c.1934
8-Day Wind
Wood: Walnut w/Maple Inlay
7H X 6.25W

Plate 0471
INGRAHAM
c.1935, Calais
8-Day Wind, Chimes
Wood: Mahogany
11H X 9.5W

Plate 0472
INGRAHAM
c.1935, Timemaster
8-Day Wind, Alarm, Luminous Dial Optional
Metal: Chrome and Black
5.5 Square

Plate 0473
INGRAHAM
c.1935, Stylewood
1-Day Wind
Wood: Walnut with Marquetry Inlay
6H X 9.5W

INGRAHAM

PLATE 0474
INGRAHAM
c.1935
AC Electric, Alarm
Plastic: Black or Ivory w/Gold trim
5.25H

PLATE 0475
INGRAHAM
c.1935, SC-323
AC Electric
Wood: Walnut
7.25H

PLATE 0476
INGRAHAM
c.1935, SD-321
AC Electric
Wood: Walnut
6.5H X 5.5W

PLATE 0477
INGRAHAM
c.1936, Bullet
1-Day Wind, Alarm
Metal: Black, Ivory, Green or Lavender
4.25H X 3.5W

PLATE 0478
INGRAHAM
c.1936, Claridge
1-Day Wind, Alarm
Metal: Ivory or Black w/Chrome
6.5H X 4.75W

PLATE 0479
INGRAHAM
c.1936, Dover
8-Day Wind
Wood: Walnut
10.75H X 9W

PLATE 0480
INGRAHAM
c.1936, SSC-2, Gothic
AC Electric, Strike
Wood: Walnut
9.25H X 6W

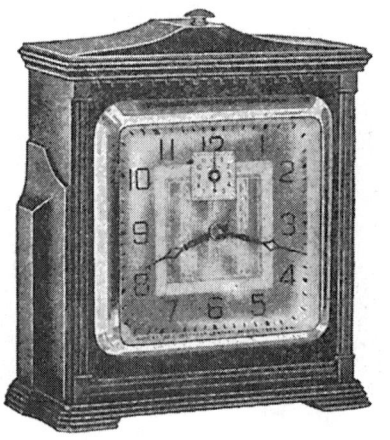

PLATE 0481
INGRAHAM
c.1936, Meteor
1-Day Wind, Alarm
Metal: Black, Ivory, Green or Rose
6.25H X 5.75W

PLATE 0482
INGRAHAM
c.1936, Penguin
1-Day Wind, Alarm
Metal: Black or Green w/Nickel or Ivory w/Gold
5.25H

INGRAHAM

Plate 0483
INGRAHAM
c.1936, SSC3, Self-Starting Upright
AC Electric, Strike
Wood: Walnut
9.5H X 6.25W

Plate 0484
INGRAHAM
c.1936, Victory
8-Day Wind, Alarm, Luminous Dial Optional
Metal: Nickel or Black
5.25H X 5W

Plate 0485
INGRAHAM
c.1936, X-Ray /Round
1-Day Wind, Alarm, Luminous Dial Optional
Metal: Green or Nickel
4.25H X 4.5W

Plate 0486
INGRAHAM
c.1936, X-Ray/Square
1-Day Wind, Alarm
Metal: Black, Green, or Pink w/Nickel; Ivory w/Gold
4.75H X 4.5W

Plate 0487
INGRAHAM
c.1936, X-Ray/Square Luminous
1-Day Wind, Alarm, Luminous Dial
Metal: Black, Green, or Pink w/Nickel; Ivory w/Gold
4.75H X 4.5W

Plate 0488
INGRAHAM
c.1936
1-Day Wind, Alarm
Metal: Black, Green, or Pink w/Nickel; Ivory w/Gold
4.5H

Plate 0489
INGRAHAM
c.1936
1-Day Wind, Alarm
Metal: Black, Green or Pink
4.25H

Plate 0490
INGRAHAM
c.1936
AC Electric
Wood: Mahogany
5.75H X 5.75W

Plate 0491
INGRAHAM
c.1936, SSD-1
AC Electric, Strike
Wood: Walnut w/Maple Inlay
6H X 8W

INGRAHAM

PLATE 0492
INGRAHAM
c.1936
1-Day Wind, Alarm
Metal: Ivory, Green or Black w/Nickel
4.75H

PLATE 0493
INGRAHAM
c.1937, Fireball
1-Day Wind, Alarm, Luminous Dial Optional
Metal: Black or Ivory
5 Square

PLATE 0494
INGRAHAM
c.1937, Gable
8-Day Wind, Alarm
Metal: Black and Chrome

PLATE 0495
INGRAHAM
c.1937, Modern
8-Day Wind, Alarm, Luminous Dial Optional
Metal: Ivory
5.25H X 5W

PLATE 0496
INGRAHAM
c.1937, Penglow
1-Day Wind, Alarm
Metal: Black or Green w/Nickel trim
5.5H

PLATE 0497
INGRAHAM
c.1937, #2-3W, Radio
AC Electric, Striking
Wood: Walnut & Maple w/Green or Red Inlay
7H X 11W

PLATE 0498
INGRAHAM
c.1937, D-157, Skyscraper
AC Electric
Wood: Walnut with Maple and Mahogany

PLATE 0499
INGRAHAM
c.1937, C-154
AC Electric, Striking
Wood: Walnut
11H X 9W X 4

PLATE 0500
INGRAHAM
c.1937
1-Day Wind, Alarm
Metal: Blue, Pink, or Green
6H X 6W

INGRAHAM

PLATE 0501
INGRAHAM
c.1937
AC Electric, Chime, Alarm
Bakelite/Plaskon: Black or Ivory
5.5H

PLATE 0502
INGRAHAM
c.1937
1-Day Wind, Alarm
Metal: Green or Black w/Nickel or Ivory w/Gold
4.5H X 4.75W

PLATE 0503
INGRAHAM
c.1938, Arcade
1-Day Wind, Alarm
Metal: Black, Rose, Ivory, or Green
4.75H X 6.5W

PLATE 0504
INGRAHAM
c.1938, Eagle
1-Day Wind, Alarm, Luminous Dial Optional
Metal: Ivory w/Yellow or Walnut
4.75H X 4.75W

PLATE 0505
INGRAHAM
c.1938, Fleetwood
1-Day Wind, Alarm
Metal: Black, Ivory, Green or Chrome

PLATE 0506
INGRAHAM
c.1938, Master
AC Electric, Alarm
Metal: Chrome
5.25 Square

PLATE 0507
INGRAHAM
c.1938, Radium
8-Day Wind, Alarm, Luminous Dial
Metal: Nickel

PLATE 0508
INGRAHAM
c.1938, Victorian
8-Day Wind, Alarm, Luminous Dial Optional
Metal: Black or Ivory
6H

PLATE 0509
INGRAHAM
c.1938, SSD-3, World's Fair
AC Electric, Chime
Wood: Mahogany
5.75H X 5.75W

INGRAHAM

PLATE 0510
INGRAHAM
c.1938, A-210
AC Electric, Striking
Wood: Walnut

PLATE 0511
INGRAHAM
c.1938, SSD-2
AC Electric, Striking
Wood: Walnut with Black Trim
6.5H X 8.25W

PLATE 0512
INGRAHAM
c.1938, X-Ray
1-Day Wind, Alarm
Metal: Black, Green or Ivory
4.5H X 4W

PLATE 0513
INGRAHAM
c.1938, X-Ray Luminous
1-Day Wind, Alarm, Luminous Dial
Metal: Black, Green or Ivory
4.5H X 4W

PLATE 0514
INGRAHAM
c.1938
8-Day Wind, Alarm
Metal: Ivory w/Gold trim
5.5H X 7W

PLATE 0515
INGRAHAM
c.1938
8-Day Wind, Strike, Alarm
Wood: Walnut
10.5H X 8.5W

PLATE 0516
INGRAHAM
c.1938
8-Day Wind, Alarm, Luminous Dial Optional
Metal: Black or Green w/Nickel or Ivory w/Gold
5H

PLATE 0517
INGRAHAM
c.1939, Cadet
8-Day Wind, Alarm, Luminous Dial
Metal: Ivory, Black, Walnut, Nickel or Coral
5.75H X 6.5W

PLATE 0518
INGRAHAM
c.1939, Cascade
1-Day Wind, Alarm
Metal: Ivory, Black, Nickel or Green
5.75H X 7W

INGRAHAM

Plate 05c.19
INGRAHAM
c.1939, Classic
1-Day Wind, Alarm
Metal: Blue, Green, Nickel or Ivory
4.75H X 6.25W

Plate 0520
INGRAHAM
c.1939, Guard
1-Day Wind, Alarm
Bakelite/Plaskon: Brown, Black or Ivory
4.75H X 5W

Plate 0521
INGRAHAM
c.1939, Mayfair
1-Day Wind
Wood: 2-Tone Finish
7.5W X 6.5H

Plate 0522
INGRAHAM
c.1939, Overland
1-Day Wind, Alarm
Metal: Black, Ivory, Green or Rose
5.5H X 5.25W

Plate 0523
INGRAHAM
c.1939, Salute
1-Day Wind, Alarm
Metal: Rose, Green or Blue
4.5H

Plate 0524
INGRAHAM
c.1939, Sentry
1-Day Wind, Alarm
Metal: Brown, Black, Nickel or Ivory
5H X 5.5W

Plate 0525
INGRAHAM
c.1939, Skyline
1-Day Wind, Alarm
Metal: Ivory, Black, Gold or Chrome
5.75H X 6.5W

Plate 0526
INGRAHAM
c.1939, York
8-Day Wind, Alarm
Wood: Walnut with Marquetry Inlay
5H X 8.75W

Plate 0527
INGRAHAM
c.1939, SA-12
AC Electric, Alarm
Catalin: Green or Yellow
4H X 3.75W

INGRAHAM

PLATE 0528
INGRAHAM
c.1939
1-Day Wind, Alarm
Metal: Black w/Chrome or Ivory w/Gold
5.25H

PLATE 0529
INGRAHAM
c.1939
8-Day Wind, Alarm
Wood: Walnut
6.5H X 6W

PLATE 0530
INGRAHAM
c.1939, Upright
8-Day Wind, Chimes
Wood: Mahogany
10.75H X 9W X 5D

PLATE 0531
INGRAHAM
1939
AC Electric, Chime, Alarm
Metal: Green w/Nickel or Ivory w/Gold
6H

PLATE 0532
INGRAHAM
c.1939
AC Electric, Alarm
Wood: Walnut w/Brass Inlay
6H X 5L

PLATE 0533
INGRAHAM
c.1939
AC Electric, Alarm
Wood: Walnut w/Maple Inlay
6H X 5.5W

PLATE 0534
INGRAHAM
c.1939
AC Electric
Wood: Walnut
8.75H X 7W

PLATE 0535
INGRAHAM
c.1939
1 Day Wind, Alarm, Luminous Dial Optional
Metal: Ivory or Black

PLATE 0536
INGRAHAM
c.1939
AC Electric, Alarm
Bakelite/Plaskon: Black or Ivory

INGRAHAM

Plate 0537
INGRAHAM
c.1940, Chilton
1-Day Wind, Alarm, Luminous Dial Optional
Metal: Black or Ivory
5H X 4.5W

Plate 0538
INGRAHAM
c.1940, Miracle-Tone
AC Electric, Chime
Wood: Walnut w/Red or Green Inlay
5.5H X 8W

Plate 0539
INGRAHAM
c.1940, Two-In-One
8-Day Wind or AC Electric, Alarm
Metal: Nickel
5.25H X 7.5W

Plate 0540
INGRAHAM
c.1940, SD-180
AC Electric
Wood: Walnut

Plate 0541
INGRAHAM
c.1940
8-Day Wind, Alarm
Wood: 2-Tone Finish

Plate 0542
INGRAHAM
c.1940
AC Electric, Strike
Wood: Walnut
9.25H X 6W

Plate 0543
INGRAHAM
c.1940, SSD4
AC Electric, Strike
Wood: Walnut w/Red or Green Inlay
6.25H X 8.25W

Plate 0544
INGRAHAM
c.1940
AC Electric, Strike, Alarm
Wood: Walnut
10.5H X 7.5W

Plate 0545
INGRAHAM
c.1940, Broadcast
8-Day Wind, Alarm, Luminous Dial
Metal: Nickel Plated or Ivory
5.5H X 5.25W

INGRAHAM

PLATE 0546
INGRAHAM
c.1940
1-Day Wind, Alarm
Metal: Black or Ivory
4.75H X 4W

PLATE 0547
INGRAHAM
c.1940
AC Electric, Alarm
Wood: Walnut or Maple
6.5H X 7W

PLATE 0548
INGRAHAM
c.1941, Ace Skyscraper
8-Day Wind, Alarm
Wood: Walnut w/Marquetry Inlay
5.25H X 5.25W

PLATE 0549
INGRAHAM
c.1941, Beacon
1-Day Wind, Alarm
Metal: Ivory, Black or Nickel

PLATE 0550
INGRAHAM
c.1941, Commander
8-Day Wind, Alarm, Luminous Dial Optional
Metal: Ivory w/Gold
5.75H X 7W

PLATE 0551
INGRAHAM
c.1941, Federal
8-Day Wind, Alarm
Metal: Black or Ivory
4.75H X 5W

PLATE 0552
INGRAHAM
c.1941, Rite-Vu
1-Day Wind, Alarm
Metal: Ivory, Walnut, Nickel or Gold
5.5H X 7W

PLATE 0553
INGRAHAM
c.1941, New Time Ball Clock
1-Day Wind
Chrome or Gold w/Black Bakelite Base

PLATE 0554
INGRAHAM
c.1941, Wakemaster
1-Day Wind, Alarm, Luminous Dial Optional
Metal: Ivory or Black
5H X 5W

INGRAHAM

Plate 0555
INGRAHAM
c.1941
1-Day Wind, Alarm
Metal: Ivory or Black
4.5H

Plate 0556
INGRAHAM
c.1941
8-Day Wind, Alarm
Wood: Walnut
5.25H X 7.25W

Plate 0557
INGRAHAM
c.1941
8-Day Wind, Alarm
Wood: Walnut w/Black Base
6.75H X 8W

Plate 0558
INGRAHAM
c.1941
1-Day Wind, Alarm, Luminous Dial Optional
Metal: Black, Green or Ivory
4.5H X 4W

Plate 0559
INGRAHAM
c.1941
8-Day Wind, Alarm
Wood: Walnut
5H X 8.75

Plate 0560
INGRAHAM
c.1941
AC Electric
Wood: Walnut
5.5H X 8.25W

Plate 0561
INGRAHAM
c.1941
8-Day Wind or AC Electric
Wood: Walnut
2.5H X 4.75W

Plate 0562
INGRAHAM
c.1941
AC Electric, Alarm
Metal: Gold or Silver

Plate 0563
INGRAHAM
c.1941
AC Electric
Catalin: Butterscotch, Brown or Green
3.75 Square

INGRAHAM

PLATE 0564
INGRAHAM
c.1942, Antique Replica,
AC Electric
Wood: Walnut
7.5H X 8W

PLATE 0565
INGRAHAM
c.1942, Broadcast
8-Day Wind, Alarm, Luminous Dial
Metal: Ivory
6.5H

PLATE 0566
INGRAHAM
c.1942, Midger
1-Day Wind, Alarm
Metal: Nickel, Ivory or Black
3.5H

PLATE 0567
INGRAHAM
c.1942, Modern
AC Electric
Wood: Walnut w/Maple Inlay
4.5H X 5.25W

PLATE 0568
INGRAHAM
c.1942, Utility Alarm
1-Day Wind, Alarm
Metal: Ivory
5.5H

PLATE 0569
INGRAHAM
c.1942
1-Day Wind, Alarm, Luminous Dial
Metal: Ivory or Black
5.75H X 5.25W

PLATE 0570
INGRAHAM
c.1942
1-Day Wind, Alarm
Metal: Ivory or Black
5.25H X 4.75W

PLATE 0571
INGRAHAM
c.1942
8-Day Wind, Alarm
Wood: Walnut
5.5H X 5.75W

PLATE 0572
INGRAHAM
c.1942
8-Day Wind, Alarm
Wood: Walnut

INGRAHAM

PLATE 0573
INGRAHAM
c.1946, Sentinel
8-Day Wind, Alarm
Metal: Ivory
5.25 Square

PLATE 0574
INGRAHAM
c.1947
8-Day Wind, Alarm, Luminous Dial
Metal: Ivory
5.5H X 5.25D

PLATE 0575
INGRAHAM
c.1948, Belle-alarm
1-Day Wind, Alarm, Luminous Dial Optional
Metal: Ivory w/gold trim
4.5H

PLATE 0576
INGRAHAM
c.1948, Night 'n' Day
1-Day Wind, Alarm, Luminous Dial Optional
Metal: Ivory w/Gold trim
4.5H

PLATE 0577
INGRAHAM
c.1948, Yearling
1-Day Wind, Alarm
Metal: Ivory or Brown
5H

PLATE 0578
INGRAHAM
c.1949, Ace
1-Day Wind, Alarm
Metal: Ivory, Gold
4.25H X 4W

PLATE 0579
INGRAHAM
c.1949, Guard
1-Day Wind, Alarm
Bakelite/Plaskon: Brown, Black or Ivory
4.75H X 5W

PLATE 0580
INGRAHAM
c.1949
8-Day Wind, Alarm, Luminous Dial Optional
Metal: Ivory w/gold trim
5H

PLATE 0581
INGRAHAM
c.1950, Sentinel
1-Day Wind, Alarm
Metal: Ivory
3.25H X 3.25W

INGRAHAM · JEFFERSON

PLATE 0582
INGRAHAM
c.1950, Sentinel
Alarm, Luminous Dial
Metal: Ivory
3.25H X 3W

PLATE 0583
INGRAHAM
c.1950, Princess
1-Day Wind, Alarm
Metal: Ivory
3.25H X 3.25W

PLATE 0584
INGRAHAM
c.1950
8-Day Wind
Wood: Walnut
5.75H X 8W

PLATE 0585
INGRAHAM
c.1951, Roy Rogers
40-Hour Wind, Alarm
Metal: Green, Sky Blue, Walnut, Tan
4.75H

PLATE 0586
INGRAHAM
c.1957, Eagle
1-Day Wind, Alarm
Metal: Ivory or Brown
4.5H

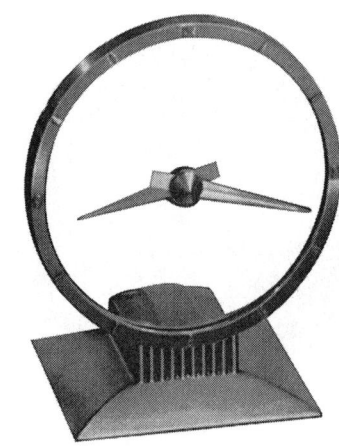

PLATE 0587
JEFFERSON
c.1956, Golden Hour
AC Electric, Mystery Movement, Luminous Dial
Metal: Gold Plated, Satin finish trim
9H X 6W

PLATE 0588
JEFFERSON
c.1955, Golden Helm
AC Electric, Mystery Movement, Alarm
Metal: 24k Gold-plated or Chrome

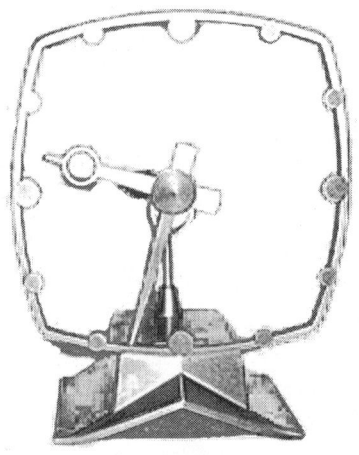

PLATE 0589
JEFFERSON
c.1956, Golden Secret
AC Electric, Mystery Movement
Metal: 24k Gold-plated

PLATE 0590
JEFFERSON
c.1963 (Eames attr.)
AC Electric
Metal: Chrome

JEFFERSON · LACKNER

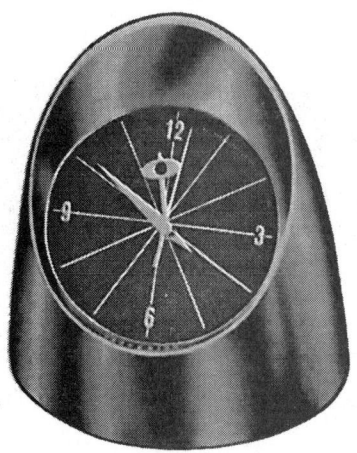

Plate 0591
JEFFERSON
c.1963 (Eames attr.)
AC Electric
Metal: Black

Plate 0592
JEWELITE
c.1963, #534
1-Day Wind, Alarm, Luminous Dial
Metal: Gold
3.5H X 7.75W

Plate 0593
KLOK·TENNA
c.1930, Klok Tenna
AC Electric
Bakelite: Walnut

Plate 0594
LACKNER
c.1935, Neon Glo
AC Electric, Neon Dial Illumination
Catalin: Butterscotch, Brown, Red or Green
7H X 6.5W

Plate 0595
LACKNER
c.1935, Neon Glo
AC Electric, Illuminared Dial (Non-Neon)
Wood: Maple

Plate 0596
LACKNER
c.1938, Pedestal
AC-Electric, Neon Dial Illumination
Bakelite: Brown or Black

Plate 0597
LACKNER
c.1939, Nassau
AC-Electric, Neon Dial Illumination
Bakelite: Walnut case with Etched Glass Panels

Plate 0598
LACKNER
c.1941
AC-Electric, Neon Dial Illumination
Walnut w/Acrylic
8H X 10W

LAWSON

Plate 0600
LAWSON
c.1932, Zephyr (Kem Weber Des.)
AC-Electric, Cyclometer Digital
Metal: Brass or Brass & Nickel

Plate 0601
LAWSON
c.1933, #215 (Kem Weber Attr.)
AC-Electric, Cyclometer Digital
Wood: Mahogany with Brass Trim
3.5H X 7.5

Plate 0602
LAWSON
c.1934, Moderne Desk (Kem Weber Attr.)
AC-Electric, Cyclometer Digital
Metal: Copper w/Brass Trim

Plate 0603
LAWSON
c.1934, Pyramid
AC-Electric, Cyclometer Digital
Metal: Copper

Plate 0604
LAWSON
c.1934, #303, Streamline (Kem Weber Attr.)
AC-Electric, Cyclometer Digital
Metal: Bronze

Plate 0605
LAWSON
c.1934, #480, Futurist (Kem Weber Attr.)
AC-Electric, Cyclometer Digital
Metal

LECTROLARM · LUX

PLATE 0606
LECTROLARM
c.1932
AC Electric, Alarm
Bakelite: Walnut
5.5H X 3.75W

PLATE 0607
LINCOLN
c.1932, No. 1, Gothic Synchromatic
AC Electric
Bakelite: Mahogany
7H X 5.5W

PLATE 0608
LINCOLN
c.1932, No. 80, Synchromatic
AC Electric
Bakelite: Walnut
7.75H X 6.5W

PLATE 0609
LINCOLN
c.1932, #B
AC Electric, Alarm
Bakelite: Walnut
5.75H X 4.5W

PLATE 0610
LINCOLN
c.1932, No.490
AC Electric, Alarm
Bakelite: Mahogany
5.25H X 4W

PLATE 0611
LINCOLN
c.1932, No.191
AC Electric
Bakelite: Walnut
6.5H X 5.5W

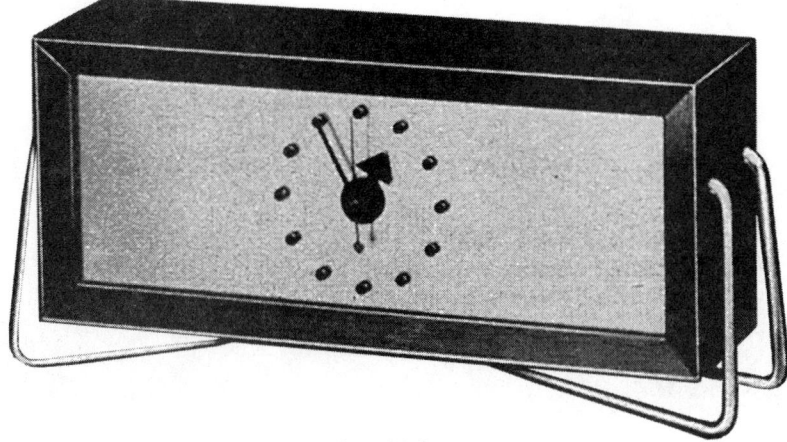

PLATE 0612
LOUIS
c.1956, La Moderne (Eames Attr.)
AC Electric
Metal: Black
5H X 8W

PLATE 0613
LUX
c.1930
1-Day Wind, Alarm, Luminous Dial
Metal: Green, Blue, Nickel
5.25H

LUX

PLATE 0614
LUX
c.1930
1-Day Wind, Alarm, Luminous Dial Optional
Metal: Nickel
6 Square

PLATE 0615
LUX
c.1930
1-Day Wind, Alarm
Metal: Green or Rose
4.75H X 6W

PLATE 0616
LUX
c.1930
1-Day Wind
Metal: Ivory or Rose
3.5H

PLATE 0617
LUX
c.1930
1-Day Wind
Metal: Orchid, Green or Rose
3.5 X 4W

PLATE 0618
LUX
c.1931, Chilton
1-Day Wind, Alarm
Metal: Ivory or Brown w/Brass Trim

PLATE 0619
LUX CLOCK
c.1932
AC Electric, Alarm
Metal
4.5H

PLATE 0620
LUX
c.1933, #70
AC Electric
Metal: Black and Nickel
3.75H

PLATE 0621
LUX
c.1933, #71, Gothic
AC Electric
Metal: Black and Nickel
3.75H X 3W

PLATE 0622
LUX
c.1933, #72
AC Electric, Alarm
Wood, Mahogany
7H X 6W

LUX

PLATE 0623
LUX
c.1933, #74
AC Electric
Metal: Black and Nickel

PLATE 0624
LUX
c.1933, DeLuxe
AC Electric, Alarm
Wood: Walnut

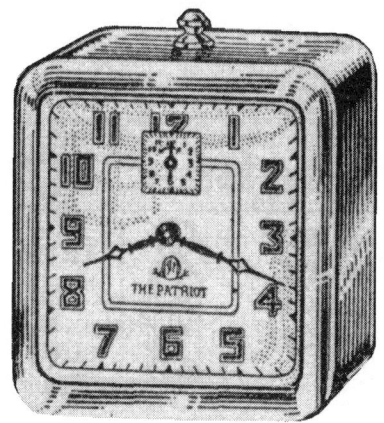

PLATE 0625
LUX
c.1933, Patriot
1-Day Wind, Alarm
Metal: White

PLATE 0626
LUX
c.1935, Tape Measure
1-Day Wind, Rotary
Metal: Brass

PLATE 0627
LUX
c.1936, Gong
1-Day Wind, Alarm
Metal: Black w/Nickel
4.75H

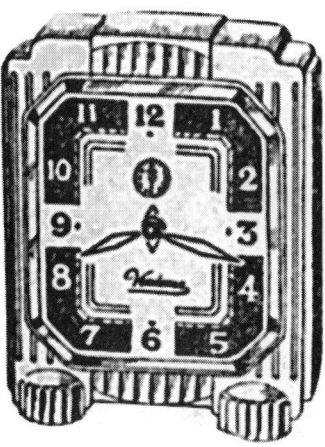

PLATE 0628
LUX
c.1938, Vendome
AC Electric, Alarm
Metal: Ivory, Blue, Green or Maroon
6.5H X 5.25W

PLATE 0629
LUX
c.1938, Spinning Wheel
AC Electric, Animated, Alarm
Metal: Ivory, Green, Black or Maroon
4.5H X 5.5W

PLATE 0630
LUX
c.1939, Streamline or Madison
AC Electric or 1-Day Wind, Alarm
Metal: Black, Ivory, Black, Green, Maroon or Rose
4H X 7.25W

PLATE 0631
LUX
c.1939, Apollo
1-Day Wind, Alarm
Metal: Ivory, Green or Black

LUX

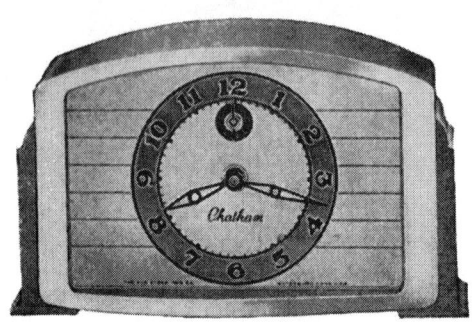

PLATE 0632
LUX
c.1939, Chatham
AC Electric, Alarm
Metal: Ivory w/Brass trim
4H X 7.75W

PLATE 0633
LUX
c.1939, Chatham
AC Electric, Alarm, Luminous Dial
Bakelite: Mahogany
4H X 7.75W

PLATE 0634
LUX
c.1939, Modern Eight
8-Day Wind, Alarm
Metal: Green or Black with Chrome
5.5H

PLATE 0635
LUX
c.1941, #948, Esquire/Round
1-Day Wind, Alarm
Metal: Ivory, Black or Green
5H

PLATE 0636
LUX
c.1941, #907, Esquire/Square
1-Day Wind, Alarm
Metal: Ivory, Black, Pink or Beige
4.75H X 5W

PLATE 0637
LUX
c.1940, #949, Utopia
1-Day Wind, Alarm, Luminous Dial
Metal: Ivory, Black or Green
5H X 4.75W

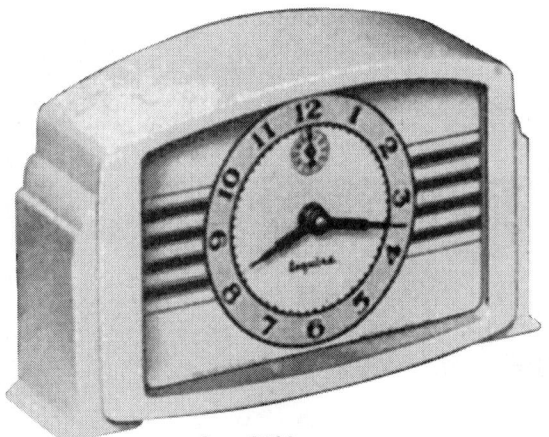

PLATE 0638
LUX
c.1941, #978, Esquire
1-Day Wind, Alarm
Metal: Ivory, Black or Tan
4H X 7W

PLATE 0639
LUX
c.1942, #336, Symphony
30-Hour Wind, Alarm
Bakelite: Walnut or Mahogany
4.5H X 6.25W

LUX

Plate 0640
LUX
c.1942, Pyramid
30-Hour Wind, Alarm
Metal: Ivory or Black
5.75H X 5.5W

Plate 0641
LUX
c.1947
1-Day Wind, Alarm
Metal: Ivory or Black
5H

Plate 0642
LUX
c.1951, #323
Alarm, 1-Day Wind
Metal: Green or Tan

Plate 0643
LUX
c.1962, #243
Alarm, Luminous Dial
Metal: Ivory and Gold

Plate 0644
LUX
c.1962, #240, Wren
Luminous Dial
Metal: Ivory

Plate 0645
LUX
c.1962, #385
Alarm, Luminous Dial
Plastic; Ivory

Plate 0646
LUX
c.1962, #995, Occasional Calender
AC Electric, Calender
Plastic: Black
6.25H X 7W

Plate 0647
LUX
c.1962, Gabriel
1-Day Wind, Alarm
Metal: Brass

Plate 0648
LUX
c.1965, Conqueror
1-Day Wind, Alarm
Metal: Ivory

LYCEUM · MASTERCRAFTERS

Plate 0649
LYCEUM
c.1940
8-Day Wind
Leather: Green or Blue
3H

Plate 0650
LYCEUM
c.1940
8-Day Wind, Alarm
Pink, Green or Blue
4H

Plate 0651
LYCEUM
c.1940
8-Day Wind, Alarm
Blue, Black or Green
3.75H

Plate 0652
MANNING·BOWMAN
c.1930, #907
AC Electric
Metal: Green w/Chrome & Black
6 Diameter

Plate 0653
MANNING·BOWMAN
c.1932, #911
AC Electric
Bakelite: Walnut
6.75H X 5W

Plate 0654
MARLBORO
c.1932
1-Day Wind, Alarm
Metal: Green or Rose
5.5H X 6.75W

Plate 0655
MASTERCRAFTERS
c.1955, #9, La Moderne
AC Electric
Wood: Mahogany
16H X 6.25W

Plate 0656
MASTERCRAFTERS
c.1955, #47, Flying Cloud
AC Electric, Alarm
Wood: Walnut
14.75H X 17.75W

Plate 0657
MASTERCRAFTERS
c.1960, #49, Starlight
AC Electric, Mystery Movement
Metal & Glass: Gold
9H X 8.5W

MASTERCRAFTERS

PLATE 0658
MASTERCRAFTERS
c.1955, #4740, Waterfall
AC Electric, Animated
Metal: Gold
12H X 8W

PLATE 0659
MASTERCRAFTERS
c.1955, #244, Dorell
AC Electric, Alarm
Metal: Gold
9.25H X 8.25W

PLATE 0660
MASTERCRAFTERS
c.1955, #591, Estate
AC Electric, Alarm
Metal: Gold
8.25H X 9W

PLATE 0661
MASTERCRAFTERS
c.1955, #425, Frell
AC Electric
Plastic: Walnut
8H X 8W

PLATE 0662
MASTERCRAFTERS
c.1955, #506, Benler
AC Electric
Plastic: Walnut
8H X 8W

PLATE 0663
MASTERCRAFTERS
c.1955, #830, Dean
AC Electric
Metal: Gold
9.5H X 8W

PLATE 0664
MASTERCRAFTERS
c.1955, #272, Fireplace
AC Electric, Animated
Plastic: Walnut
10.5H X 7.5W

PLATE 0665
MASTERCRAFTERS
c.1955, #551, Swinging Playmates
AC Electric, Animated
Plastic: Walnut or Onyx
10.5H X 7.5W

PLATE 0666
MASTERCRAFTERS
c.1955, #589, Merry-Go-Round
AC Electric, Animated
Plastic: Walnut or Onyx
10.5H X 7.5W

MASTERCRAFTERS · NATIONAL CALL

PLATE 0667
MASTERCRAFTERS
c.1960, Country Church
AC Electric, Animated, Alarm Optional
Plastic: White or Gold
12.5H X 7.5W

PLATE 0668
MASTERCRAFTERS
c.1963, Pot Belly
AC Electric
Black
11.75H X 6.75W

PLATE 0669
MASTERCRAFTERS
c.1963, Desktop
DC (Battery) Electric
Plastic: Black
3H X 6.75W

PLATE 0670
MATCH KING
c.1936, Imperial
1-Day Wind with Cigarette Lighter
Metal: Chrome

PLATE 0671
MCCRACKEN
c.1933
1-Day Wind, Alarm
Metal: Chrome

PLATE 0672
NATIONAL CALL
c.1930, #8501
8-Day Wind, Alarm
Metal: Chrome, Blue, Green or Rose
6H X 6W

PLATE 0673
NATIONAL CALL
c.1930, #8517 (Royal Kenmore)
1-Day Wind
Wood: Mahogany, Blue or Green
4.5H X 5.75W

PLATE 0674
NATIONAL CALL
c.1932, #8513, Monterey (Lux)
1-Day Wind
Metal: Green or Rose
5H X 5.25W

PLATE 0675
NATIONAL CALL
c.1932, #8542, Patriot (Lux)
1-Day Wind, Alarm
Metal: Green, Blue, Rose or Black
4.25H X 4W

NATIONAL CALL

PLATE 0676
NATIONAL CALL
c.1932, #8601, Thin
8-Day Wind, Alarm
Metal: Green, Blue, Rose or Nickel
5H X 4.5W

PLATE 0677
NATIONAL CALL
c.1932, #8645
AC Electric
Bakelite: Walnut or Black
4.25H X 3.5W

PLATE 0678
NATIONAL CALL
c.1932, #8650
AC Electric
Bakelite: Walnut
4.25H X 4W

PLATE 0679
NATIONAL CALL
c.1934, #8533, Thin Model New Style
1-Day Wind, Alarm
Metal: Black w/Nickel trim
4.75H X 6.5W

PLATE 0680
NATIONAL CALL
c.1936, #8501, Jubilee Special (Ingraham)
8-Day Wind, Alarm, Luminous Dial Optional
Metal: Green, Blue, Rose or Black
6H X 5.25W

PLATE 0681
NATIONAL CALL
c.1936, #8550 (Ingraham)
1-Day Wind, Alarm
Metal: Ivory
5.5H X 4.5W

PLATE 0682
NATIONAL CALL
c.1936, #8508, Modern Square (Ingraham)
8-Day Wind, Alarm, Luminous Dial Optional
Metal: Ivory
5.25H X 5.25W

PLATE 0683
NATIONAL CALL
c.1938, #8501 (Ingraham)
8-Day Wind, Alarm
Metal: Black, Red, Green or Blue w/Nickel or Ivory w/Yellow
6H X 5.25W

PLATE 0684
NATIONAL CALL
c.1938, #8577 (Ingraham)
AC Electric, Alarm
Wood: Walnut
6H X 3W

NATIONAL CALL

PLATE 0685
NATIONAL CALL
c.1940, #8580 (Hammond)
AC Electric, Alarm, Luminous Dial
Bakelite/Plaskon: Ivory or Black
5.5H

PLATE 0686
NATIONAL CALL
c.1940 (Westclox)
AC Electric, Alarm
Metal: Ivory
5H X 5W

PLATE 0687
NATIONAL CALL
c.1941
1-Day Wind,
Metal: Black or Coral
4H X 4W

PLATE 0688
NATIONAL CALL
c.1951, #7066, Belle-Alarm (Ingraham)
40-Hour Wind, Alarm, Luminous Dial Optional
Metal: Ivory
4.5

PLATE 0689
NATIONAL CALL
c.1951, 7317, Home Sweet Home
AC Electric, Animated (Haddon)
Plastic: Ivory, Walnut
7.5H X 12.5W X 3.5D

PLATE 0690
NATIONAL CALL
c.1952, #7322, Skipper
30-Hour Wind
Metal: Brass
9.25H

PLATE 0691
NATIONAL CALL
c.1951, #7361, Rancho (Haddon)
AC Electric, Animated
Plastic: Walnut
7H X 12W

NATIONAL CALL

PLATE 0692
NATIONAL CALL
c.1953, #7066 (Ingraham)
40-Hour Wind, Alarm, Luminous Dial Optional
Metal: Ivory
5.5H

PLATE 0693
NATIONAL CALL
c.1953, #7004, Utility (Ingraham)
40-Hour Wind, Alarm
Metal: Ivory
4.5H

PLATE 0694
NATIONAL CALL
c.1953, #7344
Wood: Mahogany
7.5H X 13.5W

PLATE 0695
NATIONAL CALL
c.1953, #7172 (Seth Thomas)
1-Day Wind, Chime
Wood: Mahogany
5.75H X 9.75

PLATE 0696
NATIONAL CALL
c.1954, #7044 (Ingraham)
8-Day Wind, Alarm
Metal: Ivory
5.5H

PLATE 0697
NATIONAL CALL
c.1954, #7134
8-Day Wind, Strike
Wood: Mahogany
7H X 10W

PLATE 0698
NATIONAL CALL
c.1954, #7300, Waterfall (Haddon)
AC Electric, Animated
Plastic: Walnut
11.25H

PLATE 0699
NATIONAL CALL
c.1954, #7377, Ballerina (Haddon)
AC Electric, Animated
Wood: Mahogany
10H X 12.5W

PLATE 0700
NATIONAL CALL
c.1954, #7095 (Ingraham)
40-Hour Wind, Alarm
Metal: Ivory
5H

NATIONAL CALL · NEW HAVEN

Plate 0701
NATIONAL CALL
c.1957, #7033, 7034
1-Day Wind, Alarm, Luminous Dial Optional
Metal: Ivory
4H

Plate 0702
NATIONAL CALL
c.1959, #7040
1-Day Wind, Alarm
Metal: Brass
4.5H

Plate 0703
NATIONAL CALL
c.1959, #7028, 7049, Pedestal Base
1-Day Wind, Alarm, Luminous Dial Optional
Metal: Ivory
4.5H

Plate 0704
NEW HAVEN
c.1928, Specialty
1-Day Wind
Metal: Brass

Plate 0705
NEW HAVEN
c.1929, Nouveau Budoir
1-Day Wind
Metal: Brass w/Marble Inserts

Plate 0706
NEW HAVEN
c.1930, Art Alarm
1-Day Wind, Alarm
Bakelite: Walnut
Two Sizes: 2.75H or 4.25H

Plate 0707
NEW HAVEN
c.1930, Tat-Too Junior
40-Hour Wind, Alarm, Luminous Dial Optional
Metal: Green or Blue
3H

Plate 0708
NEW HAVEN
c.1930, Abbey Artlarm
40-Hour Wind, Alarm, Luminous Dial Optional
Bakelite: Mahogany
5.75H X 4W

Plate 0709
NEW HAVEN
c.1930, Library
AC Electric, Alarm
Green Catalin w/Black Wood Base
3H X 4W

NEW HAVEN

PLATE 0710
NEW HAVEN
c.1930, Gothic Easel
AC Electric, Alarm
Wood: Mahogany
7.75H X 7.25W

PLATE 0711
NEW HAVEN
c.1930, Eldon
AC Electric
Wood: Mahogany and Birdseye Maple
5.5 X 5.25

PLATE 0712
NEW HAVEN
c.1930, Electric Taroo
AC Electric, Alarm
Metal: Nickel and Black
4.5H X 5W

PLATE 0713
NEW HAVEN
c.1930, Eureka
AC Electric, Alarm
Metal: Nickel w/Black
4.25H X 3.75W

PLATE 0714
NEW HAVEN
c.1930, Good Cheer
AC Electric, Alarm Optional
Bakelite: Mahogany
4.75H X 4.5W

PLATE 0715
NEW HAVEN
c.1930, Lantern
AC Electric
Metal: Copper w/Amber Glass Side Panels
6.75H X 3.5W

PLATE 0716
NEW HAVEN
c.1930, Pownal
AC Electric
Green Catalin w/Black Wood base
5H X 5W

PLATE 0717
NEW HAVEN
c.1931, #7015, Pandora
AC Electric
Wood: Mahogany
7.5H X 6.25W

PLATE 0718
NEW HAVEN
c.1931, Ideal
1-Day Wind
Metal: Nickel, Brass or Ivory
3.5H X 6.5W

NEW HAVEN

PLATE 0719
NEW HAVEN
c.1931, #8629
1-Day Wind
Green
4.5H X 7.75W

PLATE 0720
NEW HAVEN
c.1931, Artlarm Octagon
40-Hour Wind, Alarm, Luminous Dial Optional
Metal: Green or Red
4.5H

PLATE 0721
NEW HAVEN
c.1931, Artlarm Square
40-Hour Wind, Alarm, Luminous Dial Optional
Metal: Green or Blue
3.75H X 3.75W

PLATE 0722
NEW HAVEN
c.1931
40-Hour Wind, Alarm, Luminous Dial Optional
Metal: Nickel
6.5H

PLATE 0723
NEW HAVEN
c.1931, Cloister
AC Electric, Chime
Wood: Mahogany
14.5H X 10W

PLATE 0724
NEW HAVEN
c.1931, Don Garcia
AC Electric
Marble: Cream Onyx
7H X 5W

PLATE 0725
NEW HAVEN
c.1931, Don Pio Pico
AC Electric
Marble: Cream Onyx
6.25H X 5.25W

PLATE 0726
NEW HAVEN
c.1931, Don Santee
AC Electric
Marble: Cream Onyx
7.25H X 5.5W

PLATE 0727
NEW HAVEN
c.1931, Elwood
AC Electric, Strike
Wood: Mahogany
11.25H X 7.5W

NEW HAVEN

Plate 0728
NEW HAVEN
c.1931, Grenadier
AC Electric
Wood: Mahogany
6.5H X 5.25W

Plate 0729
NEW HAVEN
c.1931, Inca
AC Electric
Wood: Mahogany
7.75H X 5.25W

Plate 0730
NEW HAVEN
c.1931, Mentor (Montcalm w/Chime)
AC Electric, Strike
Wood: Mahogany
11.75H X 8.5W

Plate 0731
NEW HAVEN
c.1931, Palas
AC Electric
Marble: Black and Green
6H X 6.25W

Plate 0732
NEW HAVEN
c.1931, Penrose
AC Electric
Wood: Mahogany
6.25H X 5.25W

Plate 0733
NEW HAVEN
c.1931, Preston
AC Electric
Marble: Black and Green
6.75H X 6W

Plate 0734
NEW HAVEN
c.1931
40-Hour Wind
Bakelite: Mahogany
4.5 Square

Plate 0735
NEW HAVEN
c.1931
1-Day Wind, Alarm
Metal: Orchid, Green or Rose
3H X 3W

Plate 0736
NEW HAVEN
c.1931
1-Day Wind, Alarm
Bakelite: Walnut
Two Sizes: 5.25H X 4W or 3.5H X 2.75W

NEW HAVEN

Plate 0737
NEW HAVEN
c.1931
1-Day Wind
Metal: Nickel
4.75H X 3.25W

Plate 0738
NEW HAVEN
c.1932, Don Louis
AC Electric
Marble: Onyx
6H X 5.75W

Plate 0739
NEW HAVEN
c.1932, Don Pedro
AC Electric, Alarm
Marble: Onyx
6H X 5.5W

Plate 0740
NEW HAVEN
c.1932, Tattoo
AC Electric
Metal: Nickel and Black
4.5H

Plate 0741
NEW HAVEN
c.1932, Burton
AC Electric
Wood: Walnut w/Chrome Trim
5.75H X 5.5W

Plate 0742
NEW HAVEN
c.1932, Footed Octagon
AC Electric, Alarm, Luminous Dial
Metal: Nickel-plated
5.5H

Plate 0743
NEW HAVEN
c.1932, Colored Glass
AC Electric
Glass
3.75H

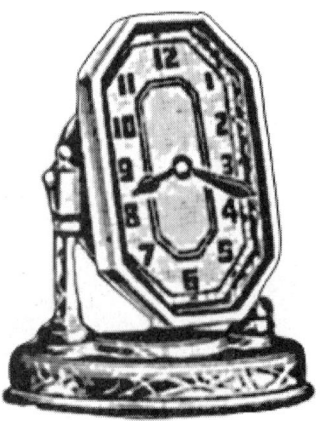

Plate 0744
NEW HAVEN
c.1932
1-Day Wind
Metal: Green w/Brass Trim
4.25H X 3.25W

Plate 0745
NEW HAVEN
c.1932
1-Day Wind
Metal: Black w/Nickel Trim
3H X 2.75W

NEW HAVEN

Plate 0746
NEW HAVEN
c.1932, Den
AC Electric, Alarm
Green Catalin w/Black & Chrome
3H X 3.25W

Plate 0747
NEW HAVEN
c.1933, #25
1-Day Wind, Chime
Metal: Black w/Gold Trim
6H X 4W

Plate 0748
NEW HAVEN
c.1933, #56
AC Electric, Alarm
Catalin and Onyx
3.75H X 5.75W

Plate 0749
NEW HAVEN
c.1933, #124
1-Day Wind, Luminous Dial
Walnut or Black

Plate 0750
NEW HAVEN
c.1933, #4604
AC Electric
Metal: Black
5.5H X 6W

Plate 0751
NEW HAVEN
c.1933, #4606
AC Electric, Alarm
Metal: Chrome Plated
3 Square

Plate 0752
NEW HAVEN
c.1933, #4608
Wood: Mahogany, Black, White
AC Electric
5H X 4.5W

Plate 0753
NEW HAVEN
c.1933, Stylis
AC Electric
Wood: Mahogany
3.75H X 7.75W

Plate 0754
NEW HAVEN
c.1933, Adare
AC Electric, Luminous Dial
Metal: Gold and Chrome Plated
6H X 5.75W

NEW HAVEN

PLATE 0755
NEW HAVEN
c.1933
8-Day Wind, Alarm, Luminous Dial Optional
Metal: Black, Green or Rose w/Nickel trim
6.25H X 4.5W

PLATE 0756
NEW HAVEN
c.1933, Geometric Series: Triple Tier
1-Day Wind
Wood: Mahogany and Maple

PLATE 0757
NEW HAVEN
c.1933, Geometric Series: Disc
1-Day Wind
Wood: Mahogany and Maple

PLATE 0758
NEW HAVEN
c.1933, Geometric Series: Skyscraper
1-Day Wind
Wood: Walnut and Maple

PLATE 0759
NEW HAVEN
c.1935, Hand Bag Watch
1-Day Wind
Metal: Black

PLATE 0760
NEW HAVEN
c.1936, #900, Boudoir
1-Day Wind, Alarm
Suede: Walnut
4.75H

PLATE 0761
NEW HAVEN
c.1936, #904, Keyless Alarm
1-Day Wind, Alarm
Metal: Silver
4.5 Square

PLATE 0762
NEW HAVEN
c.1936, #906
1-Day Wind, Alarm
Metal: Grey
4.5H

PLATE 0763
NEW HAVEN
c.1936, #927, Popeye
1-Day Wind, Alarm
Metal: Ivory w/Black trim
4.5H

NEW HAVEN

PLATE 0764
NEW HAVEN
c.1936, #928, New Style
1-Day Wind, Alarm
Metal: Black w/Nickel Trim
4.75H

PLATE 0765
NEW HAVEN
c.1936, #933, Midget Alarm
1-Day Wind, Alarm
Metal: Chrome plated
2.75H

PLATE 0766
NEW HAVEN
c.1936, #2781
1-Day Wind
Catalin: Transparent Jade or Amber
3H

PLATE 0767
NEW HAVEN
c.1936, Little Octagon
1-Day Wind, Alarm, Luminous Dial Optional
Metal: Ivory
3.25H

PLATE 0768
NEW HAVEN
c.1936, Slumber Stopper
1-Day Wind, Alarm
Metal: Chrome

PLATE 0769
NEW HAVEN
c.1938, Spinning Wheel
1-Day Wind, Animated, Alarm
Metal: Green or Ivory
5H X 5.25W

PLATE 0770
NEW HAVEN
c.1938, Mars
AC Electric, Alarm
Bakelite/Plaskon: Walnut or Ivory
5.25H X 4.5W

PLATE 0771
NEW HAVEN
c.1938, Rhonda
AC Electric
Metal: Gold Plated
5H X 4.75W

PLATE 0772
NEW HAVEN
c.1939, #571, Ideal Wind-Up Alarm
1-Day Wind, Alarm
Metal: Ivory, Gold or Chrome
4.25H X 6W

NEW HAVEN

PLATE 0773
NEW HAVEN
c.1939, #572, Seaman
AC Electric
Wood: Mahogany
7.5H X 7.5W X 3D

PLATE 0774
NEW HAVEN
c.1939
8-Day Wind or AC Electric, Chime
Wood: Walnut
11H X 7.75

PLATE 0775
NEW HAVEN
c.1939, #8587
1-Day Wind
Wood: Walnut
9.5H X 7.75W

PLATE 0776
NEW HAVEN
c.1939, #8588
AC Electric
Wood: Walnut
7.75H X 10.75W

PLATE 0777
NEW HAVEN
c.1939, #8597
1-Day Wind
Blue Mirror
4.25 Square

PLATE 0778
NEW HAVEN
c.1939
1-Day Wind
Blue Mirror
4 Square

PLATE 0779
NEW HAVEN
c.1939
1-Day Wind
Metal: Ivory or Brown
5.5H X 5W

PLATE 0780
NEW HAVEN
c.1939, #378, 384, Ideal Junior
1-Day Wind, Alarm
Metal: Ivory, Chrome or Gold
3H X 4W

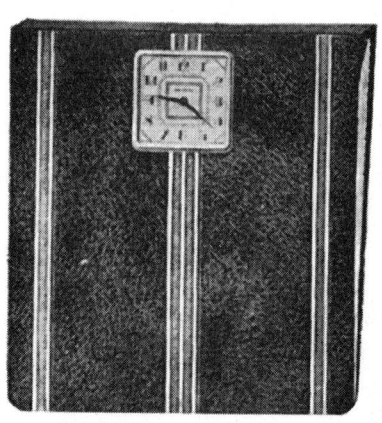

PLATE 0781
NEW HAVEN
c.1939, Silent Secretary
1-Day Wind
Leather: Walnut and Gold
9.25H X 8.5W X 1.25D

NEW HAVEN

Plate 0782
NEW HAVEN
c.1939, Colonial Highboy
8-Day Wind, Chimes
Wood: Mahogany
15.5H X 11.5W

Plate 0783
NEW HAVEN
c.1939, Streamliner
8-Day Wind or AC Electric, Chimes
Wood: Mahogany
8.25H X 16.5W

Plate 0784
NEW HAVEN
c.1940, #383, Bantry
AC Electric, Alarm
Metal: Black w/Chrome or Ivory w/Brass
4.25H X 3.75W

Plate 0785
NEW HAVEN
c.1940, #494, Lone Ranger
1-Day Wind
Metal: Black

Plate 0786
NEW HAVEN
c.1940, #640
AC Electric
Wood: Walnut
4.5H X 4.5W

Plate 0787
NEW HAVEN
c.1940, #647
AC Electric, Alarm
Wood: Walnut
4.25H X 6.75W

Plate 0788
NEW HAVEN
c.1940, #676, Tele-List and Clock
1-Day Wind
Wood: Walnut
6H X 10L X 5W

Plate 0789
NEW HAVEN
c.1940, #1031, Tele-List and Clock
1-Day Wind
Wood: Walnut w/Brass trim
6H X 14 X 5B

NEW HAVEN

Plate 0790
NEW HAVEN
c.1940, #1043, Gondolier
1-Day Wind
Metal: Blue and Chrome
9H X 9W

Plate 0791
NEW HAVEN
c.1940, #1051, Four Hundred
1-Day Wind
Wood
6H X 8.5W

Plate 0792
NEW HAVEN
c.1940, #1060, Nugget
1-Day Wind, Alarm
Bakelite/Plaskon: Ivory or Black
2.75H X 3W

Plate 0793
NEW HAVEN
c.1940, #1062, Nautical
AC Electric
Wood: Walnut
6.25H X 5.25D

Plate 0794
NEW HAVEN
c.1940, #1063, Ship's Wheel
AC Electric
Wood: Walnut
13.5H X 11W

Plate 0795
NEW HAVEN
c.1940, #1064, Arc
AC Electric
Wood: Walnut
10H X 13W

Plate 0796
NEW HAVEN
c.1940, #2069, Cigarette Server
Leather: Walnut or Blue cowhide

Plate 0797
NEW HAVEN
c.1940, Mem-O-Clock
1-Day Wind
Wood: Walnut
8.75H X 5.75

NEW HAVEN

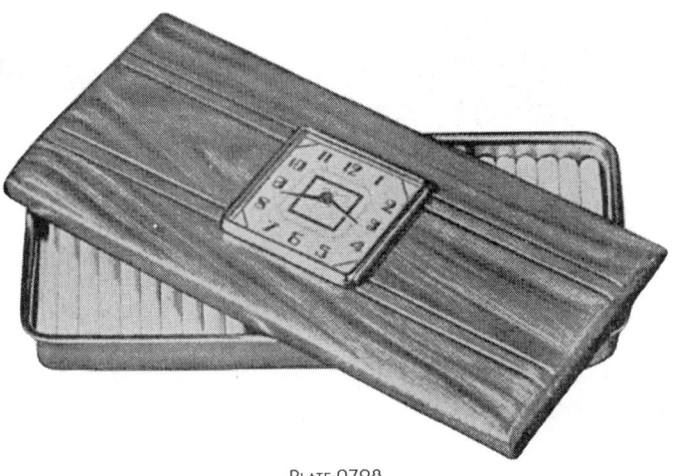

Plate 0798
NEW HAVEN
c.1940, #6916, Swing Top Cig Case/Clock
1-Day Wind
Wood: Walnut
2.75H X 9.5L X 4.5D

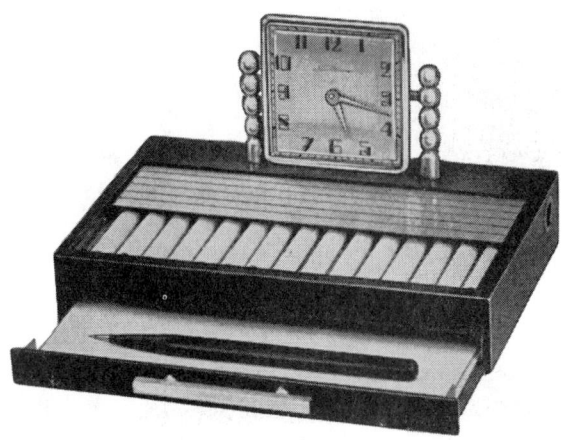

Plate 0799
NEW HAVEN
c.1940, #6910
1-Day Wind, Alarm
Wood: Walnut
1.75H X 7L X 4.5D

Plate 0800
NEW HAVEN
c.1940, #6906
40-Hour Wind
Wood: Walnut
4.5H X 7W X 8L

Plate 0801
NEW HAVEN
c.1940, #8577
1-Day Wind
Wood: Mahogany
4D X 3.25W

Plate 0802
NEW HAVEN
c.1940, #6914
1-Day Wind
Metal: Ivory
3.25H X 4W

Plate 0803
NEW HAVEN
c.1940, #8583
1-Day Wind
Blue Mirror
4.5H X 5W

Plate 0804
NEW HAVEN
c.1940, #8584
AC Electric
Blue Mirror
5H X 5.5W

Plate 0805
NEW HAVEN
c.1940, #8585
AC Electric
Blue Glass and Mirror
5.5H X 8W

NEW HAVEN

PLATE 0806
NEW HAVEN
c.1940, #686, Archon Mirror
8-Day Wind or AC Electric, Alarm
Blue or Peach Mirror
6.5H X 11.5W

PLATE 0807
NEW HAVEN
c.1940, Scottie
1-Day Wind, Alarm
Wood: Walnut with Chrome Dog
5H X 5W

PLATE 0808
NEW HAVEN
c.1940, #632
AC Electric or 1-Day Wind
Gold Plated w/Pink
4.5H X 5W

PLATE 0809
NEW HAVEN
c.1940, #642, 643
AC Electric or 1-Day Wind, Alarm
Gold Plated w/Pink or Blue
4.5D

PLATE 0810
NEW HAVEN
c.1940, #1855, 1856
1-Day Wind
Leather: Pigskin or Black
4.5H

PLATE 0811
NEW HAVEN
c.1940, Tele-List
1-Day or 8-Day Wind
Wood: Walnut
5H X 10L X 6W

PLATE 0812
NEW HAVEN
c.1940, Cloister
AC Electric or 8-Day Wind, Chime
Wood: Mahogany
13H X 8.5W

PLATE 0813
NEW HAVEN
c.1940, Durham
AC Electric or 8-Day Wind, Chime
Wood: Mahogany
11.75H X 8.75W

NEW HAVEN

Plate 0814
NEW HAVEN
c.1942, Strato
1-Day Wind
Wood: Mahogany
4.5H X 5.5W

Plate 0815
NEW HAVEN
c.1942, Culver
AC Electric
Wood: Walnut
5.75H X 5.5W

Plate 0816
NEW HAVEN
c.1942, Irma
1-Day Wind
Wood: Walnut
6.75H X 8W

Plate 0817
NEW HAVEN
c.1942, #140
1-Day Wind, Luminous Dial
Metal: Maroon or Ivory
1.5H X 1.25W

Plate 0818
NEW HAVEN
c.1942, #828, Mariner
1-Day Wind
Wood: Walnut
14W

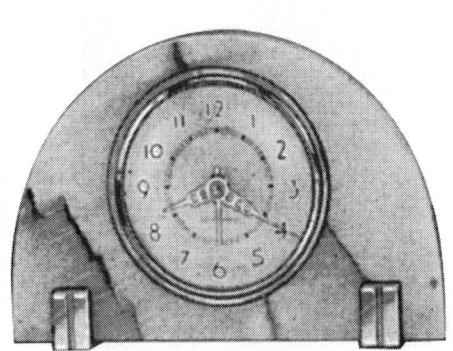

Plate 0819
NEW HAVEN
c.1942, Vista
AC Electric
Onyx
4.75H X 7W

Plate 0820
NEW HAVEN
c.1942, #345, Spica Jr Alarm
AC Electric, Alarm
Plaskon: Ivory
5.25H X 4.5W

Plate 0821
NEW HAVEN
c.1942, Regency Design
AC Electric
Wood: Mahogany
8.5H X 10W

NEW HAVEN

Plate 0822
NEW HAVEN
c.1942, Clock and Calender
1-Day Wind, Calendar
Metal: Brass w/Gold Trim
5H

Plate 0823
NEW HAVEN
c.1942, Echo
AC Electric, Alarm
Wood: Walnut
5.5 Square

Plate 0824
NEW HAVEN
c.1942, Library
1-Day Wind, Alarm
Caralin: Green or Ivory (Butterscotch)
4.25H X 5.25W

Plate 0825
NEW HAVEN
c.1942, Overnite
1-Day Wind, Alarm
Metal: Black w/Chrome or Ivory w/Brass
3.25H X 4.25W

Plate 0826
NEW HAVEN
c.1942, Peerless
AC Electric or 8-Day Wind, Strike
Wood: Walnut
11H X 7.75W

Plate 0827
NEW HAVEN
c.1942, Seaman
AC Electric
Wood: Walnut w/Brass
7.75H X 7.5W

Plate 0828
NEW HAVEN
c.1948, Ideal
1-Day Wind, Alarm, Luminous Dial
Metal: Chrome or Gold
3.25H

Plate 0829
NEW HAVEN
c.1957, #424, Ideal
8-Day Wind, Alarm, Luminous Dial
Metal: Black w/Nickel
3 Diameter

NEW HAVEN · OLD RELIABLE

PLATE 0830
NEW HAVEN
c.1957, #617, Whirl
AC Electric, Alarm, Luminous Dial
Plastic: Ivory
4.5 Square

PLATE 0831
NEW HAVEN
c.1957, #633, Viking
AC Electric, Alarm
Plastic: Maroon
4.5 Square

PLATE 0832
NEW HAVEN
c.1957, #671, Marlow
AC Electric, Alarm, Luminous Dial
Wood: Mahogany
5 Square

PLATE 0833
NEW HAVEN
c.1957, #685, Oxford
AC Electric, Alarm
Plastic: Green
5.25H X 5.5H

PLATE 0834
NEW HAVEN
c.1957, Halo
1-Day Wind, Alarm, Luminous Dial
Metal: Ivory
3.5H X 3W

PLATE 0835
NEW HAVEN
c.1957, Pocket Travel Watch
AC Electric, Alarm, Luminous Dial
Metal

PLATE 0836
NEW LUX
c.1951, Harvester (Lux)
2-Day Wind, Alarm, Luminous Dial Optional
Metal: Ivory or Grey
5H

PLATE 0837
OLD RELIABLE
c.1930, #1119,20,21,22, Pedestal Base (Ingraham)
1-Day Wind, Alarm, Luminous Dial Optional
Metal: Green, Blue or Red w/Gold, Nickel
5H

PLATE 0838
OLD RELIABLE
c.1930, #1198, 1199 (Ingraham)
8-Day Wind, Alarm, Luminous Dial Optional
Metal: Nickel
4.5H

OLD RELIABLE

PLATE 0839
OLD RELIABLE
c.1931, #1256 (Royal Kenmore)
AC Electric, Alarm, Calendar or Radio Control Optional
Bakelite: Walnut
6.75H X 4.5W

PLATE 0840
OLD RELIABLE
c.1931, #1151,52,57, DeLuxe Pedestal (Ingraham)
8-Day Wind, Alarm, Luminous Dial Optional
Metal: Nickel, Green, Blue or Red
6.25H X 6W

PLATE 0841
OLD RELIABLE
c.1931, #1262,63, Regular (Ingraham)
8-Day Wind, Alarm, Luminous Dial Optional
Metal: Nickel, Green, Black, White or Blue
5H X 5W

PLATE 0842
OLD RELIABLE
c.1932, #1196 (Royal Kenmore)
AC Electric, Alarm
Bakelite: Walnut
5.5H X 4W

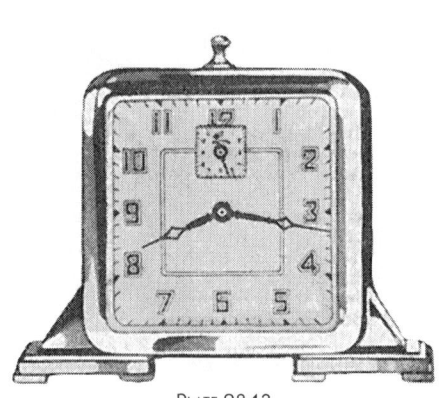

PLATE 0843
OLD RELIABLE
c.1933, #952 (Ingraham)
1-Day Wind, Alarm
Metal: Black and Chrome
3.5H X 3.5W

PLATE 0844
OLD RELIABLE
c.1933, #953 (Ingraham)
1-Day Wind, Alarm
Metal: Black and Chrome
6.25H X 5W

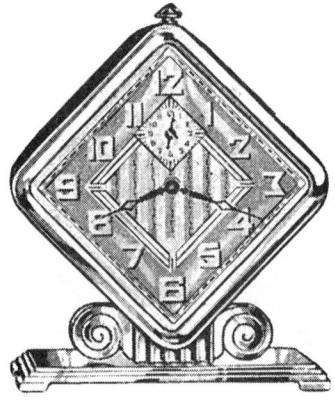

PLATE 0845
OLD RELIABLE
c.1933, #1174, 1175 (Ingraham)
8-Day Wind, Alarm, Luminous Dial Optional
Metal: Nickel
6.25H X 4.5W

PLATE 0846
OLD RELIABLE
c.1933, #1262, 1263 (Ingraham)
8-Day Wind, Alarm, Luminous Dial Optional
Metal: Nickel plated
7H X 5.75W

PLATE 0847
OLD RELIABLE
c.1933, #1264, 1265, Bell Top
1-Day Wind, Alarm, Luminous Dial Optional
Metal: Nickel
6H X 5.25W

OLD RELIABLE · PENNWOOD

PLATE 0848
OLD RELIABLE
c.1936, #1365, Twin Face
AC Electric, Alarm
Metal: Black and Chrome
4.75H X 5.5W

PLATE 0849
OTHELLO
c.1950, #90A
1-Day Wind, Alarm
Metal: Ivory
4.5H X 4W

PLATE 0850
PEERLESS
c.1933, Skyscraper (Sessions)
AC Electric
Wood: Black with Chrome Inlay

PLATE 0851
PENNWOOD
c.1934, #528
AC Electric, Cyclometer Digital
Wood: Walnut
5H X 8W X 4.5D

PLATE 0852
PENNWOOD
c.1934, #529
AC Electric, Cyclometer Digital, Alarm
Bakelite: Black with Aluminum Trim
5H X 7.25W X 3.5D

PLATE 0853
PENNWOOD
c.1936, #1362
AC Electric, Rotary Cyclometer Digital, Alarm
Wood: Walnut
4.5H X 8.5W X 4D

PLATE 0854
PENNWOOD
c.1936, #1364
AC Electric, Cyclometer Digital
Wood: Walnut
5.75H X 9.25W

PENNWOOD

PLATE 0855
PENNWOOD
c.1938, #100, Chieftain
AC Electric, Cyclometer Digital, Alarm
Bakelite/Plaskon: Brown, Black or Ivory
7.5"W X 3.75"H X 4"D

PLATE 0856
PENNWOOD
c.1938, Century
AC Electric, Cyclometer Digital, Alarm
Bakelite/Plaskon: Rosewood w/Ivory louvers
4.5H X 7.75W X 4D

PLATE 0857
PENNWOOD
c.1937, Bronze
AC Electric, Cyclometer Digital
Metal: Bronze

PLATE 0858
PENNWOOD
c.1940, AC-48, Federal Moderne
AC Electric, Cyclometer Digital
Tenite: Walnut and Ivory or Maroon and Silver
3.75H X 5.75W X 3.25D

PLATE 0859
PENNWOOD
c.1940, Chatham
AC Electric, Cyclometer Digital, Alarm
Wood: Walnut
4H X 7.75W X 3.5D

PLATE 0860
PENNWOOD
c.1940, Zephyr
AC Electric, Cyclometer Digital
Wood: Walnut
4H X 10.5W

PENNWOOD

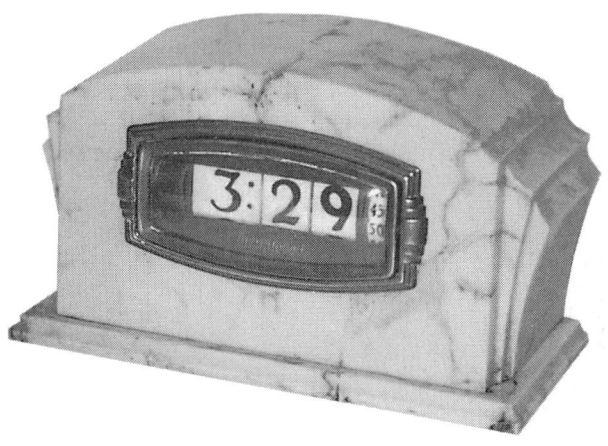

PLATE 0861
PENNWOOD
c.1940, #12A
AC Electric, Cyclometer Digital
Bakelite, Plaskon or Beetle: Brown, Ivory or Marbled Ivory
4.25H X 7.25W X 3.5D

PLATE 0862
PENNWOOD
c.1940, Century Executive
AC Electric, Cyclometer Digital
Bakelite/Plaskon: Black w/Ivory Louvers
4.25H X 14.75W X 4.5D

PLATE 0863
PENNWOOD
c.1948, #300, Numechron, Topper
AC Electric, Cyclometer Digital
Plastic: Walnut or Ivory
3.75H X 5.25L X 3.75D

PLATE 0864
PENNWOOD
c.1963, Numechron, Belvedere
AC Electric, Cyclometer Digital
Wood: Mahogany or Blond
4.5H X 7.5W X 3.5D

PLATE 0865
PENNWOOD
c.1954, N, Timeter
AC Electric, Cyclometer Digital
Plastic: Brown or Black w/Ivory Face

PLATE 0866
PENNWOOD
c.1963, Numechron, Satellite
AC Electric, Cyclometer Digital
Plastic: Black or Walnut
4H X 7.75W X 4.5D

PENNWOOD · PHINNEY·WALKER

Plate 0867
PENNWOOD
c.1963, Numechron, TV-Lamp
AC Electric, Cyclometer Digital, Alarm, Luminous Dial
Plastic: Walnut
5.75H X 6W

Plate 0868
PENNWOOD
c.1948, Starlet
AC Electric
Plastic: Walnut or Ivory
4H X 5.5L X 3.5D

Plate 0869
PENNWOOD
c.1963, Numechron, Explorer
AC Electric, Cyclometer Digital, Luminous Dial
Wood: Walnut
3.75H X 7.75W X 3.75D

Plate 0870
PHINNEY·WALKER
c.1940, Desk Set
1-Day Wind
Wood: Walnut
4.75H X 8.5W

Plate 0871
PHINNEY·WALKER
c.1952, #20, Clock/Cigarette Combo
1-Day Wind
Leather and Walnut
1.75H X 6L X 4.5W

Plate 0872
PHINNEY·WALKER
c.1952, #32
1-Day Wind
Metal: Gold
4H X 4W

Plate 0873
PHINNEY·WALKER
c.1952, #39
1-Day Wind
Metal: Gold
3H X 2.25W X 4.25D

Plate 0874
PHINNEY·WALKER
c.1955, #42
1-Day Wind, Alarm, Luminous Dial
Metal: Gold
3.25H X 5.25W X 1.75D

PHINNEY·WALKER

Plate 0875
PHINNEY·WALKER
c.1957, #30, Time For Royalty
1-Day Wind, Alarm, Luminous Dial
Acrylic: Pink, Clear, White, Amber or Blue
3.25H X 3.25W

Plate 0876
PHINNEY·WALKER
c.1957, #33, Calender Alarm
1-Day Wind, Alarm, Luminous Dial
Metal: Gold
4.5W X 4.75D

Plate 0877
PHINNEY·WALKER
c.1957, #34
1-Day Wind, Alarm, Luminous Dial
Metal: Gold w/Blue, Crystal or Pink
2.5H X 2.75W

Plate 0878
PHINNEY·WALKER
c.1957, #36, Desk Mates
1-Day Wind, Alarm, Luminous Dial
Metal: Gold
3.25H X 4.75L X 1.5D

Plate 0879
PHINNEY·WALKER
c.1957, #50
1-Day Wind, Alarm, Luminous Dial
Metal: Walnut, Blue, Ivory or Pink
3H X 4W

Plate 0880
PHINNEY·WALKER
c.1957, Tuck-Away
1-Day Wind, Alarm, Luminous Dial
Metal: Gold w/Tan, Green, Walnut or Maroon
2.75H X 2.5W

Plate 0881
PHINNEY·WALKER
c.1963, Crown Jewel
1-Day Wind, Alarm, Luminous Dial
Acrylic: Red, Blue, White or Amber
3.25H X 3.25H

Plate 0882
PHINNEY·WALKER
c.1963, Premier
AC Electric
Metal: Brass
3.5H X 2.5W

PHINNEY·WALKER · RELIDE

PLATE 0883
PHINNEY·WALKER
c.1963, Cirolet
1-Day Wind, Alarm, Luminous Dial
Plastic: White or Black
3.5D

PLATE 0884
PHINNEY·WALKER
c.1963, Heritage
AC Electric
Metal: Brass
5.5H X 6.5W

PLATE 0885
PLYMOUTH
c.1940, #654
8-Day Wind
Plastic: Black or Ivory
3.5H X 4W

PLATE 0886
PYRAMID
c.1942, #329, Pyramid (Lux)
1-Day Wind, Alarm
Metal: Ivory or Black
5.75H

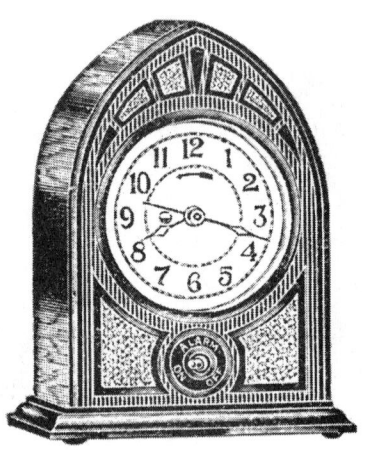

PLATE 0887
RAVENSWOOD
c.1931
AC Electric, Alarm
Bakelite: Walnut
7H

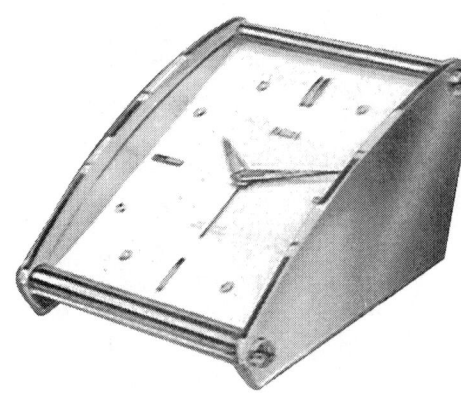

PLATE 0888
RELIDE
c.1962, Bell Companion
8-Day Wind, Alarm, Luminous Dial
Metal: Gold
5.75H X 4.25D

PLATE 0890
RELIDE
c.1962, Beside Manner
8-Day Wind
Metal: Gold
5H X 5W

PLATE 0891
RELIDE
c.1962, Boudoir Quadrille
1-Day Wind
Metal: Gold or Silver w/Gold
6H X 4W

PLATE 0892
RELIDE
c.1962, Calender
8-Day Wind, Alarm, Luminous Dial
Metal: Brass
1.75H X 1.75W

RELIDE

PLATE 0892
RELIDE
c.1962, Celestial
8-Day Wind
Metal: Gold
8.5H X 7.75D

PLATE 0893
RELIDE
c.1962, Chairman
8-Day Wind
Metal: Gold
4H X 5.25W

PLATE 0894
RELIDE
c.1962, Chalet Suisse
8-Day Wind, Alarm, Luminous Dial
Metal: Brass
3.H X 3.5W

PLATE 0895
RELIDE
c.1962, Classique
AC-Battery
Metal: Gold
4.75H X 4.25W

PLATE 0896
RELIDE
c.1962, Deluxe Mantle
8-Day Wind
Metal: Gold
5.5H X 9.25W

PLATE 0897
RELIDE
c.1962, Elite
8-Day Wind
Metal: Brass
2.25H

PLATE 0898
RELIDE
c.1962, Executive Director
8-Day Wind
Metal: Gold or Silver
4H X 4.75W

PLATE 0899
RELIDE
c.1962, Globe Clock
8-Day Wind
Metal: Gold
6H X 7W

PLATE 0900
RELIDE
c.1962, Globemaster
8-Day Wind
Metal: Gold
5.75H X 4.75W

RELIDE

PLATE 0901
RELIDE
c.1962, Globemaster Deluxe
8-Day Wind
Metal: Gold
6.5H X 5D

PLATE 0902
RELIDE
c.1962, Globetrotter
8-Day Wind
Metal: Brass
3.25H X 3.25W

PLATE 0903
RELIDE
c.1962, Grandeur & Elegance
8-Day Wind
Metal: Gold
8H X 7.25D

PLATE 0904
RELIDE
c.1962, Horoscope
8-Day Wind
Metal: Gold
9.25H X 7W

PLATE 0905
RELIDE
c.1962, Host Time
8-Day Wind, Luminous Dial
Metal: Black, Blue or Maroon
6.5W X 3.5L

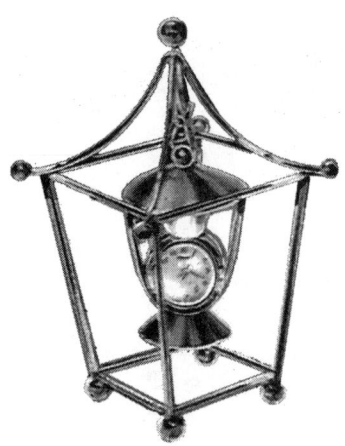

PLATE 0906
RELIDE
c.1962, Lantern
1-Day Wind
Metal: Brass
5.5H X 3W

PLATE 0907
RELIDE
c.1962, Miniature
8-Day Wind
Metal: Brass
2H X 1.25W

PLATE 0908
RELIDE
c.1962, Nocturne
8-Day Wind
Metal: Gold and Black
4.5H X 4D

PLATE 0909
RELIDE
c.1962, Popular Quadrille
1-Day Wind
Metal: Brass
4.75H X 3.5W

RELIDE · R.F.D.

PLATE 0910
RELIDE
c.1962, Rectangle Companion
8-Day Wind, Luminous Dial
Metal: Brass
5.5H X 3.5W

PLATE 0911
RELIDE
c.1962, Rippling Halo
8-Day Wind, Alarm, Luminous Dial
Metal: Brass
3.75H X 3.75W

PLATE 0912
RELIDE
c.1962, Star-Time
8-Day Wind
Metal: Gold and Silver
6H X 5.5W

PLATE 0913
RELIDE
c.1962, Versatile
8-Day Wind
Metal: Gold
5.5H X 4.75W

PLATE 0914
REVERE
c.1963, Carthage
AC Electric, Chime
Wood: Mahogany
10H X 7W

PLATE 0915
REX
c.1933
8-Day Wind, Alarm
Metal: Ivory, Brown or Chrome with Black Trim
6.5H X 6.25W

PLATE 0916
R.F.D.
c.1932, #930
1-Day Wind, Alarm
Metal: Green or Pink
5H X 4.5W

PLATE 0917
R.F.D.
c.1932, #925
8-Day Wind, Alarm
Metal: Nickel

PLATE 0918
R.F.D.
c.1933, #930
1-Day Wind, Alarm
Metal: Nickel

R.F.D. - ROYAL KENMORE

Plate 09c.19
R.F.D.
c.1935, #930A
AC Electric
Bakelite: Walnut

Plate 0920
R.F.D.
c.1935, #931
1-Day Wind, Alarm
Metal: Nickel

Plate 0921
R.F.D.
c.1935, #936 (Lux)
1-Day Wind, Alarm
Metal: Green, Blue, Rose or Lavender

Plate 0922
RIO
c.1942 (Ingraham)
1-Day Wind, Alarm
Metal: Black or Ivory

Plate 0923
ROYAL KENMORE
c.1929, Penn
AC-Electric
Wood: Walnut

Plate 0924
ROYAL KENMORE
c.1929, Princess Pat
AC-Electric, Alarm
Bakelite: Walnut

Plate 0925
ROYAL KENMORE
c.1930, Electric Utility
AC Electric, Alarm Option
Bakelite: Walnut
6H X 5.25W

Plate 0926
ROYAL KENMORE
c.1932, Anna-Belle
AC Electric
Metal: Blue, Green, Ivory or Pink
7.25 Square

Plate 0927
ROYAL KENMORE
c.1932, #901, Irene
AC Electric
Bakelite: Walnut
6H X 4.5W

ROYAL KENMORE · SEARS

PLATE 0928
ROYAL KENMORE
c.1932, #902, Vernamae
AC Electric
Metal: Brass
4.75H X 6.75W

PLATE 0929
ROYAL KENMORE
c.1932, #903, Evelyn
AC Electric
Bakelite, Walnut
7.25H X 5.5W

PLATE 0930
ROYAL KENMORE
c.1932, #905, Kenalarm Petite
AC Electric, Alarm
Bakelite: Walnut
7H X 4.5W

PLATE 0931
ROYAL KENMORE
c.1932, #906, Dowling
AC Electric, Day/Date
Bakelite: Walnut
7H X 5.75W

PLATE 0932
ROYAL KENMORE
c.1932, #908, Montgomery
AC Electric
Wood: Walnut
10.5H X 8.25W

PLATE 0933
ROYAL KENMORE
c.1932, #910, McDonald
AC Electric
Wood: Walnut
10.75H X 8.25W

PLATE 0934
ROYAL KENMORE
c.1933, Skyscraper
AC-Electric, Alarm
Bakelite: Brown
7.25H X 5.5W

PLATE 0935
SEARS
c.1959, #7128
8-Day Wind, Chimes
Wood: Walnut
7.25H X 7W X 4.5D

PLATE 0936
SEARS
c.1965, #7100
AC Electric, Alarm
Plastic: White
3H X 4W

SEARS · SEMCA

PLATE 0937
SEARS
c.1965, #7135
AC Electric, Alarm, Luminous Dial Optional
Plastic: Walnut
3.5H X 6.75W

PLATE 0938
SEARS
c.1965, #7194-97, Tradition
AC Electric, Alarm
Plastic: Beige, Walnut, Blue or Orange
4H X 6.5W

PLATE 0939
SEARS
c.1965, #7171, Franklin
AC Electric, Alarm
Wood: Cherry
4.5H X 5.5W

PLATE 0940
SEARS
c.1965, #7118-7121
AC Electric, Alarm, Luminous Dial
Plastic: Beige, Blue, White or Walnut
3.5H X 4.5W

PLATE 0941
SEMCA
c.1950, #1334
8-Day Wind
Metal: Gold Satin Finish
5.75H X 9W

PLATE 0942
SEMCA
c.1950, #6820
1-Day Wind, Alarm, Luminous Dial
Metal: Brass
3.25H

PLATE 0943
SEMCA
c.1952, #113
1-Day or 8-Day Wind, Alarm, Luminous Dial
Metal: Brass
2.25H X 2.25W

PLATE 0944
SEMCA
c.1952, #718
1-Day Wind, Alarm, Luminous Dial
Metal: Gold w/Pink, Blue, Crystal, Amethyst, Peridot or Topaz
3H X 3W

PLATE 0945
SEMCA
c.1952, #741
1-Day Wind, Alarm-Musical, Luminous Dial
Metal: Blue, Maroon, Walnut, Green or Ivory
5.5H X 4W

SEMCA

PLATE 0946
SEMCA
c.1952, #773
8-Day Wind, Alarm, Luminous Dial
Metal: Gold
4H X 2.75W

PLATE 0947
SEMCA
c.1952, #7852
8-Day Wind
Metal: Gold
5.25H X 5W

PLATE 0948
SEMCA
c.1955, #117
1-Day Wind, Alarm, Luminous Dial
Metal: Gold
2.25H X 2.25W

PLATE 0949
SEMCA
c.1955, #721
8-Day Wind, Alarm, Luminous Dial
Metal: Gold w/Pink, Blue or Crystal Baguettes
3H X 3W

PLATE 0950
SEMCA
c.1955, #737
1-Day Wind, Alarm, Luminous Dial
Metal: Brass
3.25H X 2.75W X 1.5D

PLATE 0951
SEMCA
c.1955, #744
1-Day Wind, Alarm, Luminous Dial
Metal: Ivory, Green or Blue
3H X 3W

PLATE 0952
SEMCA
c.1955, #780
8-Day Wind, Alarm, Luminous Dial
Metal: Brass
4.5H X 5.5W

PLATE 0953
SEMCA
c.1955, #790
8-Day Wind, Alarm, Luminous Dial
Metal: Brass
4.5H X 3.25W

PLATE 0954
SEMCA
c.1955, #795
8-Day Wind, Alarm
Metal: Brass
7.25H X 4.25W

SEMCA · SENTINEL

PLATE 0955
SEMCA
c.1955, #796
8-Day Wind, Alarm
Metal: Gold
3H X 4.25W

PLATE 0956
SEMCA
c.1955, #7866
8-Day Wind, Alarm, Luminous Dial
Metal: Brass
5.75H X 3.25W X 2D

PLATE 0957
SENTINEL
c.1950, #16, Sentinel Prince
1-Day Wind, Alarm
Metal: Ivory
3.25H X 3W

PLATE 0958
SENTINEL
c.1955, Capstan
8-Day Wind
Metal: Brass

PLATE 0959
SENTINEL
c.1955, Dapper
40-Hour Wind, Alarm, Luminous Dial
Plastic: Ivory

PLATE 0960
SENTINEL
c.1955, Dawn
8-Day Wind, Alarm, Luminous Dial
Metal: Ivory

PLATE 0961
SENTINEL
c.1955, Little Pal
40-Hour Wind, Alarm, Luminous Dial
Metal: Ivory

PLATE 0962
SENTINEL
c.1955, Pride
40-Hour Wind, Alarm
Metal: Brass

PLATE 0963
SENTINEL
c.1955
8-Day Wind
Metal: Brass

SENTRY

PLATE 0964
SENTRY
c.1957, #6750, Miniature
1-Day Wind, Alarm, Luminous Dial
Metal: Ivory w/Brass Trim
3.75H X 3W

PLATE 0965
SENTRY
c.1957, #6810
1-Day Wind, Alarm, Luminous Dial
Metal: Ivory
5.5H X 4W

PLATE 0966
SENTRY
c.1957, #6813
1-Day Wind, Alarm, Luminous Dial
Metal: Ivory w/Brass trim
4.5 Square

PLATE 0967
SENTRY
c.1957, #6961
8-Day Wind, Alarm, Luminous Dial
Metal: Ivory
4.5H X 4W

PLATE 0968
SENTRY
c.1957, #7062
AC Electric, Alarm, Luminous Dial
Plastic: Ivory or Pink
3.5 Square

PLATE 0969
SENTRY
c.1958, #7052
AC Electric, Alarm, Luminous Dial
Plastic: White
4H X 5W

PLATE 0970
SENTRY
c.1958, #6812
1-Day Wind, Alarm, Luminous Dial Optional
Metal: Ivory w/Brass trim
4.5 Square

PLATE 0971
SENTRY
c.1958, #6952, Old Reliable
8-Day Wind, Alarm, Luminous Dial Optional
Metal: Ivory
5.5H X 5W

PLATE 0972
SENTRY
c.1958, #7050, Spotlight
AC Electric, Luminous Dial Optional
Plastic: White or Blue
3.75H X 4.5W

SESSIONS

PLATE 0973
SESSIONS
c.1931, El Mode
AC Electric
Wood: Mahogany or Walnut
6.25 Square

PLATE 0974
SESSIONS
c.1931, Elwyn
AC Electric
Wood: Mahogany or Walnut
5.75H X 5W

PLATE 0975
SESSIONS
c.1931, #939, Octagon or Sparta
8-Day Wind, Alarm
Metal: Nickel or Cracked Green

PLATE 0976
SESSIONS
c.1932, #916M
AC Electric
Wood: Ivory, Black or Mahogany
5H X 4W

PLATE 0977
SESSIONS
c.1932, #958M
AC Electric
Wood: Mahogany or Black
8.5H X 6.75W

PLATE 0978
SESSIONS
c.1932, A
AC Electric
Bakelite: Mahogany
7H X 5.25W

PLATE 0979
SESSIONS
c.1932, Coronet
AC Electric
Wood: Mahogany
8.5H X 5.5W

PLATE 0980
SESSIONS
c.1932, Hamilton
8-Day Wind, Chimes
Wood: Mahogany
12H X 9.5W

PLATE 0981
SESSIONS
c.1932, Jefferson
8-Day Wind, Chimes
Wood: Mahogany
10.25H X 8.5W

SESSIONS

PLATE 0982
SESSIONS
c.1932, Standish
8-Day Wind, Chimes
Wood: Mahogany
12.5H X 8.75W

PLATE 0983
SESSIONS
c.1932, #29, Westminster
AC Electric, Chime
Wood: Mahogany
15H X 11W

PLATE 0984
SESSIONS
c.1933, #151, Cuckoo
AC Electric
Metal: Brass
12.75H X 10.25W

PLATE 0985
SESSIONS
c.1933, #238, Airplane
AC Electric
Metal: Brass Plated
10.5H X 17W

PLATE 0986
SESSIONS
c.1933, #159, 160, Coach
AC Electric
Metal: Brass
8.75H X 12.75W

PLATE 0987
SESSIONS
c.1933, #239A, 239B, Farm
AC Electric
Metal: Red, Green or Blue w/Ivory Tints
9H X 12W

PLATE 0988
SESSIONS
c.1933, #152, 153, New Coach
AC Electric, Alarm
Metal: Brass or Nickel Plated
7.5H X 17W

SESSIONS

PLATE 0989
SESSIONS
c.1933, #154, Ship
AC Electric
Metal: Brass Plated
11H X 12.25W

PLATE 0990
SESSIONS
c.1933, #162, Windmill
AC Electric
Metal: Brass Plated
13H X 11W

PLATE 0991
SESSIONS
c.1934, Gothic Design
8-Day Wind, Chimes
Wood: Walnut
10.5H X 8.75W

PLATE 0992
SESSIONS
c.1935, 80, Nordic
AC Electric or 8-Day Wind
Wood: Mahogany
8.5H X 7.75W

PLATE 0993
SESSIONS
c.1935, W
AC Electric
Wood: Walnut

PLATE 0994
SESSIONS
c.1935
8-Day Wind, Alarm
Wood: Mahogany
9H X 8W

PLATE 0995
SESSIONS
c.1936, Manley, Stanley
AC Electric or 1-Day Wind, Alarm
Wood: Mahogany or Maple w/Chrome Inlay
5.5H X 4.5W

PLATE 0996
SESSIONS
c.1936, Maxwell
AC Electric
Wood: Mahogany or Maple w/Chrome Inlay
5H X 6W

PLATE 0997
SESSIONS
c.1936, Monroe
AC Electric
Wood: Curley Maple

SESSIONS

PLATE 0998
SESSIONS
c.1936, Morgan
AC Electric
Wood: Ivory w/Green or Maple w/Black Trim

PLATE 0999
SESSIONS
c.1936, Nevel
AC Electric
Wood: Mahogany w/Chrome Inlay

PLATE 1000
SESSIONS
c.1936, Nixon
1-Day Wind, Alarm
Wood: Ivory w/Green Trim

PLATE 1001
SESSIONS
c.1936, Norman
AC Electric, Alarm
Wood: Mahogany or Maple with Chrome Inlay
5 Square

PLATE 1002
SESSIONS
c.1936
AC Electric
Onyx

PLATE 1003
SESSIONS
c.1936, Westminster
8-Day Wind w/Chimes, Alarm
Wood: Mahogany

PLATE 1004
SESSIONS
c.1936
AC Electric
Wood: Mahogany
8.5H X 10W

PLATE 1006
SESSIONS
c.1936
AC Electric
Wood: Mahogany, Maple
4.5H X 5.5W

PLATE 1007
SESSIONS
c.1936
AC Electric
Wood: Mahogany, Ivory or Red
5.25H X 6.25W

SESSIONS

PLATE 1007
SESSIONS
c.1936
AC Electric
Wood: Mahogany, Ivory or Red
5.25H X 6.25W

PLATE 1008
SESSIONS
c.1936, #287, W
AC Electric
Wood: Walnut w/Black Trim
7H X 6W

PLATE 1009
SESSIONS
c.1938, SK
AC Electric
Wood: Green or Ivory
7.75H X 6.75W

PLATE 1010
SESSIONS
c.1938, #279, A
AC Electric
Wood: Walnut w/Marquetry Inlay
7H X 11.75W

PLATE 1011
SESSIONS
c.1939, #439
AC Electric, Alarm
Wood: Walnut or Mahogany
4.5H X 6.5W

PLATE 1012
SESSIONS
c.1938, W
AC Electric
Wood: Walnut w/Marquetry Inlay

PLATE 1013
SESSIONS
c.1939, Stir-Up
8-Day Wind, Alarm
Metal: Nickel Plated

PLATE 1014
SESSIONS
c.1939
8-Day Wind, Alarm
Wood: Maple
5.5H X 5.5W

SESSIONS

PLATE 1015
SESSIONS
c.1939
AC Electric or 8-Day Wind, Chime
Wood: Mahogany
11.5H X 9.25W

PLATE 1016
SESSIONS
c.1939
AC Electric
Wood: Walnut

PLATE 1017
SESSIONS
c.1939
AC Electric
Wood: Walnut

PLATE 1018
SESSIONS
c.1940, #134, DeLuxe Airliner
AC Electric or 8-Day Wind
Bakelite: Mahogany w/Chrome Trim
9.5H X 20W

PLATE 10c.19
SESSIONS
c.1940, Yankee Clipper
AC Electric or 8-Day Wind
Wood: Walnut w/Chrome Trim
17H X c.19W

PLATE 1020
SESSIONS
c.1939
AC Electric
Metal: Nickel w/Black Trim

PLATE 1021
SESSIONS
c.1940, #297, 501, Capstan
8-Day Wind or AC Electric
Wood: Walnut
9H X 6.75W

PLATE 1022
SESSIONS
c.1940, #290
AC Electric, Alarm
Wood: Walnut
5.25H X 8.25W

SESSIONS

PLATE 1023
SESSIONS
c.1940, #294
AC Electric
Wood: Walnut
7H X 8.5W

PLATE 1024
SESSIONS
c.1940, #298, 358
AC Electric
Bakelite/Plaskon: Walnut or Ivory
4.5H X 5.5W

PLATE 1025
SESSIONS
c.1940
AC Electric
Wood: Walnut w/Black Trim
6H X 7W

PLATE 1026
SESSIONS
c.1940, Zephyr
AC Electric, Alarm
Wood: Walnut
7H X 9.75W

PLATE 1027
SESSIONS
c.1940
AC Electric
Wood: Mahogany
8.75H X 10.25L

PLATE 1028
SESSIONS
c.1940
AC Electric
Wood: Walnut w/Brass Trim
8H X 8W

PLATE 1029
SESSIONS
c.1940
AC Electric
Wood: Walnut
6.75H X 10.5W

PLATE 1030
SESSIONS
c.1940, Scottie
AC Electric
Wood: Walnut
6H

SESSIONS

PLATE 1031
SESSIONS
c.1941, #200, Airliner
AC Electric
Walnut Bakelite w/Chrome Trim
10H X 21W

PLATE 1032
SESSIONS
c.1941, Modern Cabinet Design
8-Day Wind or AC Electric
Wood: Mahogany
8.75H X 12.75W

PLATE 1033
SESSIONS
c.1941, Capitol Dome
AC Electric or 8-Day Wind
Chrome and Mahogany
12.5H X 8.5W

PLATE 1034
SESSIONS
c.1941, Moderne
AC Electric
Marble: Onyx

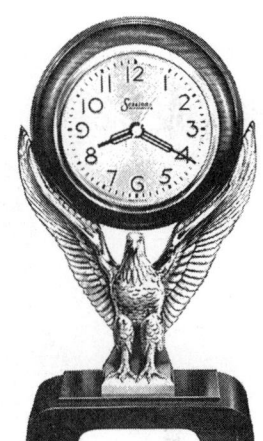

PLATE 1035
SESSIONS
c.1942, #135, 136, Golden Eagle
8-Day Wind or AC Electric
Walnut and Brass
10.5H X 6W

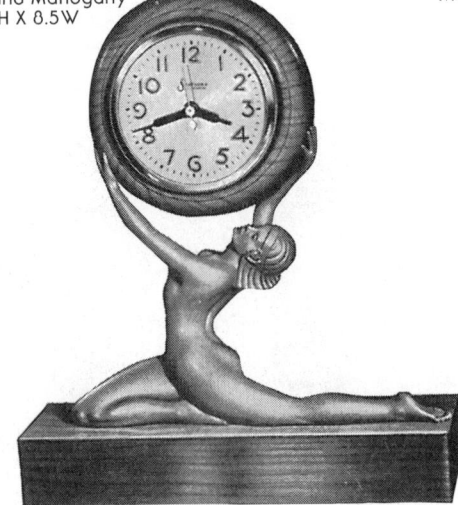

PLATE 1036
SESSIONS
c.1942, #139, 140, Golden Girl
8-Day Wind or AC Electric
Walnut and Brass
13H X 11W

PLATE 1037
SESSIONS
c.1942, #130, 131, Panther
8-Day Wind or AC Electric
Mahogany and Bronze
10H X 12.5W

SESSIONS

PLATE 1038
SESSIONS
c.1942, #827, Waterman Set
AC Electric
Wood: Walnut
6.5H X 11L

PLATE 1039
SESSIONS
c.1942, #132, 133, Winged Victory
8-Day Wind or AC Electric
Walnut and Brass
7.25H X c.19.5W

PLATE 1040
SESSIONS
c.1942, Shelf Clipper
AC Electric
Walnut and Brass
6.5H X 10W

PLATE 1041
SESSIONS
c.1942, #390
AC Electric
Wood: Walnut
4H X 7.75W

PLATE 1042
SESSIONS
c.1942, #394
AC Electric
Walnut and Brass
5H X 7.5W

PLATE 1043
SESSIONS
c.1942, #419, 432
AC Electric
Walnut and Brass
4.5H X 5.25W

PLATE 1044
SESSIONS
c.1942, #420
AC Electric
Walnut and Brass
9.5H X 10W

SESSIONS

PLATE 1045
SESSIONS
c.1942, #424
AC Electric
Bakelite/Plaskon: Ivory, White, Red or Walnut
4.5H X 5.75W

PLATE 1046
SESSIONS
c.1942, #434
AC Electric
Wood: Walnut
4.5H X 6W

PLATE 1047
SESSIONS
c.1942, #435
AC Electric
Wood: Walnut
5.5H X 8W

PLATE 1048
SESSIONS
c.1947, #4A, Pussyfooter
-Day Wind or AC Electric, Alarm, Luminous Dial Optional
Plaskon: Ivory
4.5H X 7.25W

PLATE 1049
SESSIONS
c.1948, Ballerina
AC Electric
Wood: Walnut w/Brass Plated Trim

PLATE 1050
SESSIONS
c.1948, Boy and Dog
AC Electric
Wood: Walnut w/Brass Plated Trim

PLATE 1051
SESSIONS
c.1948, Horseshoe
AC Electric
Metal: Bronze

PLATE 1052
SESSIONS
c.1949, Sailing Ship
AC Electric
Ceramic: Ivory
11.25H X 11W

PLATE 1053
SESSIONS
c.1949, #136
8-Day Wind or AC Electric
Wood: Mahogany
4.75H X 4.25W

SESSIONS

Plate 1054
SESSIONS
c.1949
8-Day Wind or AC Electric
Wood: Mahogany
5.75H X 4.5W

Plate 1055
SESSIONS
c.1949, Ship's Wheel
8-Day Wind or AC Electric
Wood: Mahogany
7.5H X 6.75W

Plate 1056
SESSIONS
c.1950, #134
AC Electric
Wood: Mahogany
6.75W

Plate 1057
SESSIONS
c.1949
AC Electric
Wood: Walnut
8H X 15W

Plate 1058
SESSIONS
c.1950, Occasional
AC Electric
Wood: Mahogany
4.75H X 8.25W

Plate 1059
SESSIONS
c.1951, Mak-A-Clock
AC Electric
Wood: Walnut

Plate 1060
SESSIONS
c.1951, Western Horse
AC Electric
Walnut Base w/Brass Plated Figures
11H X 17.5W X 5D

SESSIONS

PLATE 1061
SESSIONS
c.1951
AC Electric
Wood: Walnut w/Brass
6.75H X 23W

PLATE 1062
SESSIONS
c.1957
#73, Enchantment (Plastic); #75, Escort (Wood)
AC Electric, Alarm, Luminous Dial Optional
Plastic: Honey ; Wood: Maple
4.5H X 6.5L

PLATE 1063
SESSIONS
c.1956, Aquarius
AC Electric, Luminous Dial, Animated
Brass w/Painted Glass
11H X 9W

PLATE 1064
SESSIONS
c.1956, Bravo
AC Electric, Alarm
Wood: Mahogany
4H X 5W

PLATE 1065
SESSIONS
c.1956, Interlude
AC Electric, Luminous Dial
Wood: Mahogany

PLATE 1066
SESSIONS
c.1957, Connoisseur
AC Electric, Alarm
Chrome and White
6H X 8W

PLATE 1067
SESSIONS
c.1957, Pixie
AC Electric, Alarm, Luminous Dial Optional
Plastic: White

PLATE 1068
SESSIONS
c.1957, Sweetheart
AC Electric, Alarm, Luminous Dial Optional
Plastic: White

SESSIONS

Plate 1069
SESSIONS
c.1957, Tee Vee
AC Electric
Plastic: Mahogany

Plate 1070
SESSIONS
c.1960, #11501, Love Alarm
AC Electric, Alarm, Luminous Dial
Plastic: Pink or Blue
3.5H X 6.5W

Plate 1071
SESSIONS
c.1958, Bird
AC Electric, Animated, Luminous Dial
Plastic: Walnut or Onyx
10.5H X 7.5W X 4.75D

Plate 1072
SESSIONS
c.1958, Flying Cloud
AC Electric
Wood: Walnut w/Chrome Trim
14.75H X 17.75W

Plate 1073
SESSIONS
c.1958, Swinging Playmates
AC Electric, Animated, Luminous Dial
Plastic: Walnut or Onyx
10.5H X 7.5W X 4.75D

Plate 1074
SESSIONS
c.1962, Doze-On
AC Electric, Alarm, Luminous Dial Optional
Plastic: White, Pink or Blue
3.5H X 3.25W

Plate 1075
SESSIONS
c.1962, Shelton
AC Electric, Alarm, Luminous Dial
Wood: Mahogany or Cinnamon
4.5H X 4.75W

Plate 1076
SESSIONS
c.1963, Limelite
AC Electric, Alarm, Luminous Dial
Plastic: White, Yellow, Blue or Tan
5.5H X 6.5W

SESSIONS · SETH THOMAS

Plate 1077
SESSIONS
c.1962, Lenox
AC Electric, Alarm, Luminous Dial Optional
Wood: Walnut
4.25H X 6.25W

Plate 1078
SESSIONS
c.1962, Lorelei
AC Electric, Alarm, Luminous Dial Optional
Plastic: Pink, White or Blue
6.25W

Plate 1079
SESSIONS
c.1962, Sessionette
AC Electric, Alarm, Luminous Dial Optional
Plastic: White
3H X 3.5W

Plate 1080
SESSIONS
c.1963, Sessionglo
AC Electric, Alarm, Luminous Dial
Plastic: White, Pink or Blue
3H X 2.25D

Plate 1081
SETH THOMAS
c.1931, Durango
AC Electric
Onyx: Green, Pink, Yellow, Gold or Walnut
7H X 5.5W

Plate 1082
SETH THOMAS
c.1931, Gibson
AC Electric
Wood: Mahogany
6.25H X 5.25W

Plate 1083
SETH THOMAS
c.1931, Hour-glass
AC Electric
Wood: Mahogany
6.25H X 4.75W

Plate 1084
SETH THOMAS
c.1931, Nanking
AC Electric, Strike
Wood: Walnut
9.75H X 7W

SETH THOMAS

Plate 1085
SETH THOMAS
c.1931, Newton
AC Electric, Strike
Wood: Mahogany
8.25H X 6.25W

Plate 1086
SETH THOMAS
c.1931, Sonora
AC Electric, Alarm
Onyx
6.25H X 5W

Plate 1087
SETH THOMAS
c.1931, Stetson
AC Electric
Wood: Mahogany
6.5H X 5.25W

Plate 1088
SETH THOMAS
c.1931, Upson
AC Electric, Alarm
Wood: Mahogany
6.5H X 6W

Plate 1089
SETH THOMAS
c.1931, Westbury
AC Electric, Chime
Wood: Mahogany
10.25H X 8.25W

Plate 1090
SETH THOMAS
c.1933, Capstan, Ship's Wheel
AC Electric, Alarm
Wood: Mahogany
8H X 6.75W X 3D

Plate 1091
SETH THOMAS
c.1933, Crest
AC Electric
Wood: Mahogany
5.5H X 5W

Plate 1092
SETH THOMAS
c.1933, Dalesbury
AC Electric, Chime
Wood: Mahogany
10.5H X 8W X 5.75D

Plate 1093
SETH THOMAS
c.1933, Floret
AC Electric
Wood: Mahogany
5.25H X 5.5W

SETH THOMAS

PLATE 1094
SETH THOMAS
c.1933, Lotus
AC Electric
Marble: White
6.75H X 6.5W

PLATE 1095
SETH THOMAS
c.1933, Tabor
AC Electric
Wood: Mahogany
4.75H X 4.5W

PLATE 1096
SETH THOMAS
c.1933, Woodmont
AC Electric
Wood: Mahogany
6.5H X 5.5W

PLATE 1097
SETH THOMAS
c.1934, Boudoir
1-Day Wind
Wood: Mahogany w/Maple Inlay, Brass Feet

PLATE 1098
SETH THOMAS
c.1935, Plymouth
8-Day Wind, Hourly Chime, Alarm
Wood: Mahogany
9.25H X 5W

PLATE 1099
SETH THOMAS
c.1936
8-Day Wind, Strike
Wood: Mahogany
9.75H X 9W X 6D

PLATE 1100
SETH THOMAS
c.1939, Console
AC Electric, Striking
Wood: Mahogany w/Brass Trim

PLATE 1101
SETH THOMAS
c.1939, E-853, Echo (Luminous)
AC Electric, Alarm
Wood: Walnut w/Brass Trim
5.25H X 5.5W

PLATE 1102
SETH THOMAS
c.1939, E-853, Echo
AC Electric, Alarm
Wood: Walnut w/Brass Trim
5.25H X 5.5W

SETH THOMAS

PLATE 1103
SETH THOMAS
c.1940, Desk Set
8-Day Wind
Walnut and Black Bakelite
4.5H X 12W

PLATE 1104
SETH THOMAS
c.1956, Baxter
AC Electric
Wood: Mahogany w/Brass Trim
4.5H X 8.5W

PLATE 1105
SETH THOMAS
c.1940, E-884, Lee
AC Electric, Alarm
Plaskon: Ivory

PLATE 1106
SETH THOMAS
c.1942, Culver
AC Electric
Wood: Walnut
6 Square

PLATE 1107
SETH THOMAS
c.1947, Carlisle
AC Electric
Plastic: Black w/Brass Base
4.5H X 5W

PLATE 1108
SETH THOMAS
c.1948, Yukon
AC Electric
Metal: Brass
5.25H

PLATE 1109
SETH THOMAS
c.1951, Severa
1-Day Wind, Alarm
Wood: Mahogany w/Brass Trim
4H X 4W

PLATE 1110
SETH THOMAS
c.1952, Alcor
8-Day Wind, Alarm
Metal: Brass
7.5H X 6W

SETH THOMAS

PLATE 1111
SETH THOMAS
c.1952, Northbury
AC, Electric or 8-Day Wind, Chime
Wood: Mahogany
11H X 8.25W

PLATE 1112
SETH THOMAS
c.1952, Polaris
8-Day Wind, Alarm
Metal: Brass
6.75H X 5W

PLATE 1113
SETH THOMAS
c.1952, Vega
8-Day Wind, Alarm
Metal: Brass
5.5H X 5.75W

PLATE 1114
SETH THOMAS
c.1956, Cathay
AC Electric, Alarm, Luminous Dial Optional
Wood: Mahogany or Blonde
4.5 Square

PLATE 1115
SETH THOMAS
c.1956, Compass
AC Electric, Alarm
Wood: Mahogany w/Black or Black w/Walnut
4.25H X 5.75W

PLATE 1116
SETH THOMAS
c.1956, Penthouse
AC Electric
Wood: Cherry or Blonde
6.5H X 6.25W

PLATE 1117
SETH THOMAS
c.1956, Poise
AC Electric
Wood: Mahogany
5.25 Square

PLATE 1118
SETH THOMAS
c.1956, Rudder
Alarm
Wood: Walnut
6H X 6W

PLATE 1119
SETH THOMAS
c.1956, Sharon-Echo
AC Electric, Strike
Wood: Maple or Mahogany
6.25 Square

SETH THOMAS · SILVER

PLATE 1120
SETH THOMAS
c.1958, Leather Case
1-Day Wind, Alarm
Metal with Leather Case, Brass trim
3.75 Square

PLATE 1121
SETH THOMAS
c.1959, Wayne
AC Electric
Wood: Walnut
5.25H X 4.75W

PLATE 1122
SETH THOMAS
c.1963, Beverly
AC Electric, Alarm, Luminous Dial
Wood: Walnut or Mahogany
4.25H X 4.75W

PLATE 1123
SETH THOMAS
c.1963, Canewood
AC Electric, Alarm, Luminous Dial
Wood: Mahogany or Walnut
5H X 6W

PLATE 1124
SETH THOMAS
c.1963, Facer
40-Hour Wind, Alarm, Luminous Dial
Crystal
3H X 3W X 1.5D

PLATE 1125
SILVER
c.1937, #200, Silver Swingtime
AC Electric
Wood: Ivory or Walnut
8H X 7.75W

PLATE 1126
SILVER
c.1937, #50, Rotary (Lux)
1-Day Wind, Alarm
Metal: Ivory, Black or Brass
4H X 5W

PLATE 1127
SILVER
c.1937, #778 (Lux)
1-Day Wind, Alarm
Metal: Ivory or Green
4H X 7.25W

SILVERTONE · SUNBEAM

PLATE 1128
SILVERTONE
c.1932, #2812, DeLuxe (Lux)
AC Electric
Metal: Nickel, Black
6H X 6W

PLATE 1129
SILVERTONE
c.1932, #2813, DeLuxe (Lux)
AC Electric
Metal: Black, Nickel
4.75H X 4.25W

PLATE 1130
SPARTUS
c.1963, Time-O-Lite
AC Electric, Alarm
Metal: Brass, White
10.75H X 5.75W

PLATE 1131
SPARTUS
c.1962, Moon-Glo Planter
AC Electric, Alarm, Luminous Dial
Metal: Copper
9.25H X 14.5W

PLATE 1132
SUNBEAM
c.1958, Vari-Lite
AC Electric, Alarm
Plastic: White, Tan
4.25H X 6.5W

PLATE 1133
SUNBEAM
c.1958, #7081
AC Electric, Alarm, Luminous Dial
Plastic: Ivory
3.5H X 3W

PLATE 1134
SUNBEAM
c.1958, #7084
AC Electric, Alarm, Luminous Dial Optional
Plastic: Ivory

PLATE 1135
SUNBEAM
c.1965, Preferred, Slumberwood
AC Electric, Strike, Alarm, Luminous Dial
Plastic: Brown or Gold
6.5H X 3.25W

SUNBEAM · TELECHRON

PLATE 1136
SUNBEAM
c.1965, Design
AC Electric, Alarm, Luminous Dial
Plastic: Tan
3.25H X 3.75W

PLATE 1137
SUNBEAM
c.1965, Petite
AC Electric, Alarm
Plastic: Ivory
3H X 3.5W

PLATE 1138
SUNDBERG-FERAR
c.1965. #7190
AC Electric, Alarm, Luminous Dial
Plastic: White, Beige, Pink or Turquoise
4H X 6W

PLATE 1139
SUN-UP
c.1936, #6202, Gothic (Ingraham)
8-Day Wind, Alarm
Metal: Brown Lacquer with Copper Trim
5.5H X 4.5W

PLATE 1140
SUN-UP
c.1936, #6209 (Ingraham)
8-Day Wind, Alarm, Luminous Dial
Metal: Ivory or Black with Nickel Trim
5H X 5W

PLATE 1141
SUN-UP
c.1938, #8959, Octagon
1-Day Wind, Alarm
Metal: Rose, Green or Ivory
4.5H X 4.25W

PLATE 1142
SUN-UP
c.1938, #8961, Ultra-Modern
30-Hour Wind, Alarm
Metal: Ivory, Green, or Red
4.5H X 5.5W

PLATE 1143
TELECHRON
c.1928, #370, Clinton
AC Electric
Wood: Mahogany
6H X 5W

PLATE 1144
TELECHRON
c.1928, #402, Mantel
AC Electric
Metal: Bronze
7H X 8W

TELECHRON

PLATE 1145
TELECHRON
c.1929, #323, Petite
AC Electric
Wood: Ivory, Red or Green
6H X 5.5W

PLATE 1146
TELECHRON
c.1929, #431, Modernique (Frankl des.)
AC Electric
Metal: Machined Silver & Gold or Chrome w/ Purple & Black
7.75H X 5.75W

PLATE 1147
TELECHRON
c.1929, #522, Salem
AC Electric
Wood: Mahogany
7H X 7W

PLATE 1148
TELECHRON
c.1930, #523, Patricia
AC Electric
Wood: Ivory, Red or Green
8H X 7.25W

PLATE 1149
TELECHRON
c.1930, #524, Oxford
AC Electric
Wood: Mahogany
8.5H X 7.75W

PLATE 1150
TELECHRON
c.1930, #700, Electro-Alarm (Frankl Attr.)
AC Electric, Alarm, Illuminated Dial
Bakelite/Plaskon: Brown, Ivory or Green
7.5H X 5W

PLATE 1151
TELECHRON
c.1931, #326, Bruce
AC Electric
Wood: Mahogany w/Inlay
5.5H X 5.5W

PLATE 1152
TELECHRON
c.1931, #526, Bellevue
AC Electric
Wood: Mahogany and Burl Maple
7.25H X 7W

PLATE 1153
TELECHRON
c.1931, #530, Nottingham
AC Electric
Wood: Mahogany w/Inlay
9.75H X 6W

TELECHRON

PLATE 1154
TELECHRON
c.1931, #531, Lorraine
AC Electric
Wood: Mahogany and Burl Maple
8.5H X 7W

PLATE 1155
TELECHRON
c.1931, #602, Castleton
AC Electric
Wood: Mahogany
11.5H X 10W

PLATE 1156
TELECHRON
c.1931, #603, Jefferson
AC Electric
Wood: Mahogany
11.5H X 9.25W

PLATE 1157
TELECHRON
c.1931, #711, Telalarm
AC Electric, Alarm, Illuminated Dial
Metal: Alloy w/Black base
5H X 4.25W

PLATE 1158
TELECHRON
c.1932, #329, Colony
AC Electric
Wood: Mahogany

PLATE 1159
TELECHRON
c.1932, #532, Shelburne
AC Electric
Wood: Mahogany w/Lacewood
9H X 7W

PLATE 1160
TELECHRON
c.1932, #605, Waverly
AC Electric
Wood: Mahogany
11.5 X 8.5

PLATE 1161
TELECHRON
c.1932, #606, Winchester
AC Electric
Wood: Mahogany w/Satinwood
11.5H X 8.5W

PLATE 1162
TELECHRON
c.1932, 3A-51, Renault
AC Electric
Wood: Mahogany
5H X 3.5W

TELECHRON

PLATE 1163
TELECHRON
c.1932, 3F-51, Duke
AC Electric
Bakelite: Black
4.5H

PLATE 1164
TELECHRON
c.1932, R-930
AC Electric, Chime
Wood: Walnut
9.25H

PLATE 1165
TELECHRON
c.1933, 4F-51B, Telart
AC Electric
Metal/Bakelite: Chrome w/ Black Base
5.5H X 6.25W

PLATE 1166
TELECHRON
c.1933, 8B-03, Minitman
AC Electric, Cyclometer
Wood: Mahogany
6.5H X 4.25W

PLATE 1167
TELECHRON
c.1934, 7F-53, Telebell
AC Electric, Alarm
Metal/Bakelite/Plaskon: Nickel w/Black or Black w/Ivory
4.75H X 4.5W

PLATE 1168
TELECHRON
c.1934, 7B-01, Autolarm
AC Electric, Alarm, Luminous Dial
Bakelite: Walnut
6H X 4.75W

PLATE 1169
TELECHRON
c.1934, 3F-01, Commonwealth
AC Electric
Wood: Mahogany w/Chrome Trim
4.5H X 12W

PLATE 1170
TELECHRON
c.1934, 8B-01, Minitmaster
AC Electric, Cyclometer, Illuminated Dial
Bakelite: Black w/Brass Trim
6.5H X 4.5W

TELECHRON

PLATE 1171
TELECHRON
c.1934, 8B-05, New Minitmaster
AC Electric, Cyclometer, Illuminated Dial
Bakelite/Plaskon: Black or Ivory
6.5H X 4.25W

PLATE 1172
TELECHRON
c.1935, 4F-59, Attache
AC Electric, Alarm Optional
Metal: Brass or Chrome
5H X 5W

PLATE 1173
TELECHRON
c.1935, 4F-61, Pharoah
AC Electric
Wood: Mahogany
6.5H X 7.5W

PLATE 1174
TELECHRON
c.1936, 7F-63, Quacker
AC Electric, Alarm Optional ("Smug")
Plaskon: Black, Yellow or Blue with Orange Bill
5.75H X 6W

PLATE 1175
TELECHRON
c.1936, 3F-53, Daphne
AC Electric
Catalin: Ivory (Butterscotch), Black, Red, Green,
Rose Quartz or Clear
3.5H X 4.25W

PLATE 1176
TELECHRON
c.1936, 4F-63, Aztec
AC Electric, Alarm Optional
Metal: Brass or Chrome
5.5H X 5.5W

PLATE 1177
TELECHRON
c.1936, 4F-65, Luxor
AC Electric
Metal/Mirror: Chrome Base w/Brass Bezel
Blue, Silver or Lavender Mirror
6.5H X 7.5W

PLATE 1178
TELECHRON
c.1936, 7F-01, Announcer
AC Electric, Alarm, Illuminated Dial
Bakelite/Metal: Black Bakelite Case w/Metal Front
5.5H X 5W

PLATE 1179
TELECHRON
c.1936, 7F-03, Clarion
AC Electric, Alarm, Luminous Dial
Bakelite: Black
5.25H

TELECHRON

PLATE 1180
TELECHRON
c.1936, 7F-149, Sparkler
AC Electric, Alarm, Luminous Dial
Bakelite/Plaskon: Black, Ivory
4.75H

PLATE 1181
TELECHRON
c.1936, 7F-57, Airlarm
AC Electric, Alarm
Wood: Maple or Walnut
5.25 Square

PLATE 1182
TELECHRON
c.1936, 7F-65, Aladdin
AC Electric, Alarm, Luminous Dial
Bakelite/Plaskon: Black or Ivory

PLATE 1183
TELECHRON
c.1936, 7F-65, Deputy
AC Electric
Bakelite: Walnut or Ivory
4.5H

PLATE 1184
TELECHRON
c.1936, 7F-71, Gendarme
AC Electric, Alarm
Bakelite: Brown or Ivory
4.75H

PLATE 1185
TELECHRON
c.1936, 7F-73, Meadowlark
AC Electric, Alarm
Wood: Black or Cherry
5.5H

PLATE 1186
TELECHRON
c.1935, Pelicans
AC Electric
Chrome Figures w/Catalin Trim and Black Marble Base

PLATE 1187
TELECHRON
c.1936, 8B-09, Tribute (Teague des.)
AC Electric, Cyclometer
Wood: Walnut and Maple
4.25H X 8W

TELECHRON

Plate 1188
TELECHRON
c.1936, CF-363, Usher/CF-769, Constable (w/Alarm)
AC Electric, Alarm Optional, Luminous Dial
Bakelite/Plaskon: Black or Ivory
4H X 4.75W

Plate 1189
TELECHRON
c.1937, 4H-81, Statesman
AC Electric, Alarm Optional
Marble: White
6.5H X 6W

Plate 1190
TELECHRON
c.1937, 3F-67, Pageant
AC Electric
Bakelite/Plaskon: Ivory, Brown or Black w/Brass Trim
4.5H X 4.25W

Plate 1191
TELECHRON
c.1936, 5F-51, Doric
AC Electric
Wood: Walnut and Maple
8H X 7W

Plate 1192
TELECHRON
c.1938, 3H-78, Basque
AC Electric
Catalin: Ivory (Butterscotch) or Black
4.5H X 5W

Plate 1193
TELECHRON
c.1938, CH-783, Kleertone
AC Electric, Alarm
Catalin: Ivory (Butterscotch), Brown or Black
4.5H X 4.5W

Plate 1194
TELECHRON
c.1937, 4B-79, Olympic
AC Electric
Wood: Walnut and Maple
7H X 11.5W

Plate 1195
TELECHRON
c.1937, 8B-07, Baron (Teague Des.)
AC Electric, Cyclometer
Bakelite/Plaskon: Black, Ivory or Walnut
3.5H X 8W X 3.75D

TELECHRON

PLATE 1196
TELECHRON
c.1938, 8B-11, Granada (Teague Attr.)
AC Electric, Cyclometer
Bakelite: Brown or Black w/Maroon
3.75H X 8.25W X 3.75D

PLATE 1197
TELECHRON
c.1939, 3F-71, Coronado
AC Electric
Wood: Walnut
4.5H X 7.75W

PLATE 1198
TELECHRON
c.1939, 3H-73, Domino
AC Electric
Bakelite: Black or Walnut
4.5H

PLATE 1199
TELECHRON
c.1939, 3H-79, Croft
AC Electric, Alarm Optional
Bakelite: Walnut
4.5H X 4.5W

PLATE 1200
TELECHRON
c.1939, 3H-81, Virginian
AC Electric, Alarm Optional
Wood: Two-Tone
5.25H

PLATE 1201
TELECHRON
c.1939, 3H-83, Melbourne
AC Electric
Green Catalin w/Black Wood Base
5.5H X 6W

PLATE 1202
TELECHRON
c.1939, 4B-85, Cordova
AC Electric
Wood: Mahogany
7.5H X 3.25W

PLATE 1203
TELECHRON
c.1939, 4F-55, Airlux
AC Electric, Alarm Optional
Marble: White Onyx
5.25 Square

TELECHRON

PLATE 1204
TELECHRON
c.1939, 4F-67, Embassy
AC Electric
Metal: Chrome

PLATE 1205
TELECHRON
c.1939, 4F-73, Smartset
AC Electric
Wood: Walnut
6.5H X 7.25W

PLATE 1206
TELECHRON
c.1939, 4H-77, Deauville
AC Electric
Blue or Black Mirror
7H

PLATE 1207
TELECHRON
c.1939, 4H-83, Naples
AC Electric, Alarm Optional
Wood: Walnut
5.75H X 6.5W

PLATE 1208
TELECHRON
c.1939, 4H-91, Finesse
AC Electric
Wood, Faux Leather
6.5H X 8.25W

PLATE 1209
TELECHRON
c.1939, 4H-93, Highland
AC Electric, Optional Strike
Wood: Walnut
7H X 7W

PLATE 1210
TELECHRON
c.1939, 4H-95, Kendall
AC Electric
Wood: Mahogany
7H X 7W

PLATE 1211
TELECHRON
c.1939, 6B-01, Jubilee
AC Electric
Wood: Walnut
8.5H X 10.75W

PLATE 1212
TELECHRON
c.1939, 6B-03, Seville
AC Electric, Strike, Alarm
Wood: Walnut
8.5H X 11.75W

TELECHRON

Plate 1213
TELECHRON
c.1939, 6B-05, Picardy
AC Electric, Strike
Wood: Mahogany
8.5H X 11.75W

Plate 1214
TELECHRON
c.1939, 7H-77, Mirolarm
AC Electric, Alarm
Blue or Pink Mirror
5H

Plate 1215
TELECHRON
c.1939, 7H-79, Butler
AC Electric, Alarm, Luminous Dial Optional
Bakelite: Black or Walnut

Plate 1216
TELECHRON
c.1939, 7H-85, Attendant
AC Electric, Alarm, Luminous Dial Optional
Bakelite/Plaskon: Walnut w/Nickel or Ivory w/Gold
5H X 4.75W

Plate 1217
TELECHRON
c.1939, 8F-03, Explorer
AC Electric, Alarm
Wood: Walnut
6.25H

Plate 1218
TELECHRON
c.1940, 3H-89, Bancroft
AC Electric
Wood: Walnut
5.25H X 5.5W

Plate 1219
TELECHRON
c.1940, 4B-07, Harwich
AC Electric
Onyx: Ivory and Brown
6H X 10W

Plate 1220
TELECHRON
c.1940, 4B-153, Barclay
AC Electric
Onyx: Ivory and Brown
6.25H X 10.25W

TELECHRON

PLATE 1221
TELECHRON
c.1940, 7F-75, Mayfair
AC Electric, Alarm
Metal: Brass, Black Base
6.25H X 5.25W

PLATE 1222
TELECHRON
c.1940, 7H-109, Flotilla
AC Electric, Alarm
Metal: Brass and Black
6.75H X 7.5W

PLATE 1223
TELECHRON
c.1940, 7H-91, Secretary
AC Electric, Alarm, Luminous Dial Optional
Bakelite/Plaskon: Walnut or Ivory
4.25H X 5.25W

PLATE 1224
TELECHRON
c.1940, 7H-93, New Telalarm
AC Electric, Alarm, Luminous Dial Optional
Bakelite w/Brass or Nickel
5H X 4.74W

PLATE 1225
TELECHRON
c.1940, 7H-99, Steward
AC Electric, Alarm
Metal and Bakelite: Brass w/Walnut Bakelite
6.5H X 6W

PLATE 1226
TELECHRON
c.1940, CH-387, Somerset
AC Electric
Bakelite: Walnut
5.5H X 6W

PLATE 1227
TELECHRON
c.1941, 3H-97, Vassel
AC Electric
Wood: Walnut
5.5H X 5.75W

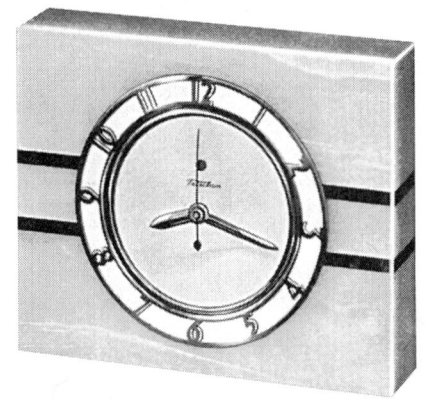

PLATE 1228
TELECHRON
c.1941, 4B-151, Stoneham
AC Electric
Onyx: Ivory and Brown
6H X 7.5W

PLATE 1229
TELECHRON
c.1941, 4B-155, Hampshire
AC Electric
Onyx: Ivory and Brown
6.5H X 9W

TELECHRON

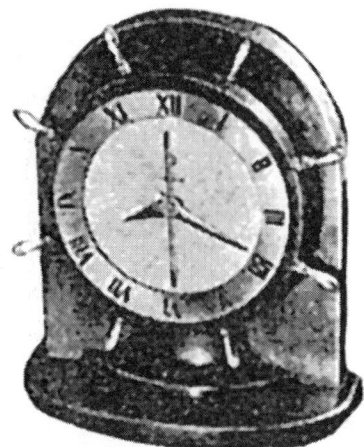

PLATE 1230
TELECHRON
c.1941, 4H-89, Vagabond
AC Electric
Wood: Walnut w/Brass
7.5H X 6.75W

PLATE 1231
TELECHRON
c.1941, 5H-57, Suave
AC Electric, Alarm
Bakelite: Walnut w/Brass
6.25H X 5.25W

PLATE 1232
TELECHRON
c.1941, 5H-59, Satellite
AC Electric
Metal: Brass
7H X 6.5W

PLATE 1233
TELECHRON
c.1941, 6B-13, Magnolia
AC Electric, Striking
Wood: Mahogany
7.5H X 9W

PLATE 1234
TELECHRON
c.1941, Conductor
AC Electric, Alarm
Bakelite/Plaskon: Brown or Ivory
5H X 5W

PLATE 1235
TELECHRON
c.1941, 7H-101, Imp
AC Electric, Alarm
Catalin: Ivory (Butterscotch), Rose or Brown
4.5H X 4.5W

PLATE 1236
TELECHRON
c.1941, 7H-113, Custodian
AC Electric, Alarm
Wood: Walnut
5H X 5W

PLATE 1237
TELECHRON
c.1941, 7H-115, Fortress
AC Electric, Alarm
Ivory Plaskon

PLATE 1238
TELECHRON
c.1941, 7H-117, Reporter
AC Electric, Alarm
Bakelite/Plaskon: Ivory or Brown
4.5H X 4.25W

TELECHRON

PLATE 1239
TELECHRON
c.1941, 7H-1c.19, Governor
AC Electric, Alarm
Wood: Stained Pine
5.5H X 5.25W

PLATE 1240
TELECHRON
c.1941, 7H-122, Serene
AC Electric, Alarm
Ivory Plaskon w/Clear or Blue Acrylic

PLATE 1241
TELECHRON
c.1941, 7H-89, Guest
AC Electric, Alarm
Wood: Faux Leather
6H X 6W

PLATE 1242
TELECHRON
c.1941, 8H-15, Instructor
AC Electric
Wood: Walnut
5.5H X 5.5W

PLATE 1243
TELECHRON
c.1941, 8H-17, Registrar
AC Electric, Calendar
Wood: Walnut
5H X 5.75W

PLATE 1244
TELECHRON
c.1942, 4H-97, Forum
AC Electric
Wood: Walnut
7.5H X 8W

PLATE 1245
TELECHRON
c.1946, 7H-125, Dispatcher
AC Electric, Alarm
Bakelite/Plaskon: Brown or Ivory
4.5H X 4.5W

PLATE 1246
TELECHRON
c.1949, 7H-149, Sparkler
AC Electric, Alarm, Illuminated Dial
Plastic: Ivory
4.5H X 4.75W

PLATE 1247
TELECHRON
c.1949, 3H-157, Yachtsman
AC Electric
Metal: Brass
6H X 7W

TELECHRON

PLATE 1248
TELECHRON
c.1948, 7H-133, Electric Executive
AC Electric
Wood: Walnut

PLATE 1249
TELECHRON
c.1941, 8B-13, Register
AC Electric, Cyclometer
Wood: Walnut
4H X 8.25W X 3.75D

PLATE 1250
TELECHRON
c.1948, 7H-137, Little Tel
AC Electric, Alarm
Plastic: Walnut or Ivory
3.5H X 4.25W

PLATE 1251
TELECHRON
c.1951, 3H-163, Swarthmore
AC Electric
Wood: Mahogany
9.25H X 6.5W X 3.25D

PLATE 1252
TELECHRON
c.1950, 7H-09, Nocturne
AC Electric, Alarm, Luminous Dial
Plastic: Ivory or Walnut
4.5H X 5W

PLATE 1253
TELECHRON
c.1950, 7H-153, Serene
AC Electric, Alarm, Luminous Dial
Plaskon: Ivory
3.5H X 4.5W

PLATE 1254
TELECHRON
c.1951, 3H-159, Suave
AC Electric
Clear Glass
5.5H X 5.5W

PLATE 1255
TELECHRON
c.1951, 7H-07, Everset
AC Electric, Alarm, Luminous Dial
Plastic: Ivory
3.75H X 4.75W

TELECHRON

PLATE 1256
TELECHRON
c.1951, 7H-141, Airlux
AC Electric, Alarm
Acrylic: Mahogany or Transparent w/Brass
5.25H X 6.5W

PLATE 1257
TELECHRON
c.1951, 7H-157, Colonnade
AC Electric, Alarm
Wood: Walnut
4.25H X 4.75W

PLATE 1258
TELECHRON
c.1951, 7H-161, Tempo
AC Electric, Alarm, Luminous Dial
Plastic: Ivory
3.5H X 4.5W

PLATE 1259
TELECHRON
c.1951, 7H-163, Kirkwood
AC Electric, Alarm, Luminous Dial
Wood: Mahogany

PLATE 1260
TELECHRON
c.1951, 7H-165, Coronado
AC Electric, Alarm
Wood: Walnut
4.75H X 7.25W

PLATE 1261
TELECHRON
c.1951, 7H-169, Guest
AC Electric, Alarm, Luminous Dial
Plastic: Ivory
4H X 4.75W

PLATE 1262
TELECHRON
c.1951, 7H-173, Tel-A-Glow
AC Electric, Alarm, Luminous Dial
Plastic: Ivory
4H X 5.25W

PLATE 1263
TELECHRON
c.1951, 7H-179, Tribute
AC Electric
Crystal w/Gold base

PLATE 1264
TELECHRON
c.1951, 7H-183, Imp
AC Electric, Alarm
Plastic: Ivory or Brown
3.75H X 5.25W

TELECHRON

PLATE 1265
TELECHRON
c.1951, 7H-185, Tiara
AC Electric, Alarm, Luminous Dial
Pink, Green or Blue
4.5H X 5.25W

PLATE 1266
TELECHRON
c.1951, 7H-187, Personality
AC Electric
Metal base w/Removeable Glass
(For Insertion of Photos, etc)

PLATE 1267
TELECHRON
c.1951, 7H-189, Alladin
AC Electric, Alarm, Luminous Dial
Plastic: Ivory
3.75H X 4.75W

PLATE 1268
TELECHRON
c.1952, 7H-c.199, Minstrel
AC Electric, Alarm
Plastic: Ivory
3.5H X 4.5W

PLATE 1269
TELECHRON
c.1952, 7HP-171, Bancroft
AC Electric, Alarm
Plastic: Ivory
4.5H X 5W

PLATE 1270
TELECHRON
c.1953, 7H-c.195, Mirolarm
AC Electric, Alarm
Plastic: Ivory w/Brass Trim
5H X 5.5W

PLATE 1271
TELECHRON
c.1953, 7H-c.197, Illuminette
AC Electric, Alarm, Luminous Dial
Plastic: Ivory w/Gold
4.5H X 5.25W

PLATE 1272
TELECHRON
c.1953, 7H-201, Telegrain
AC Electric, Alarm
Wood: Walnut
4.75H X 5W

PLATE 1273
TELECHRON
c.1953, 7H-207, Lullaby
AC Electric, Alarm, Luminous Dial
Plastic: Ivory
3.5H X 3.5W

TELECHRON

PLATE 1274
TELECHRON
c.1952, 2H-33, Ivy
AC Electric
Plastic: Red, Green, Grey or Yellow
6H X 8.5W

PLATE 1275
TELECHRON
c.1953, 7H-215, Decor
AC Electric, Alarm
Plastic: Beige
3.75H X 6W

PLATE 1276
TELECHRON
c.1953, 7H-209, Gracewood
AC Electric, Alarm
Wood: Mahogany, Maple or Blonde
4.25H X 3.75W

PLATE 1277
TELECHRON
c.1953, 7H-211, Dorm
AC Electric, Alarm, Luminous Dial Optional
Plastic: Ivory
3.5H X 4W

PLATE 1278
TELECHRON
c.1954, 8H-29, Telejour
AC Electric
Metal: Brass
5.75H X 5.75W

PLATE 1279
TELECHRON
c.1954, 2H-47, Telechoice
AC Electric
Plastic: White, Red or Yellow w/Chrome or Brown w/Brass
4.75H X 8W

PLATE 1280
TELECHRON
c.1955, 5H-69, Illumitime
AC Electric
Wood and Metal: Black and White
7.5H X 11W

TELECHRON · TIMETER

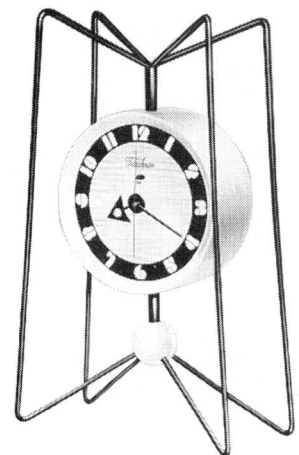

PLATE 1281
TELECHRON
c.1955, 5H-65, Outline
AC Electric
Wood: Maple w/Metal
14H X 6.5W

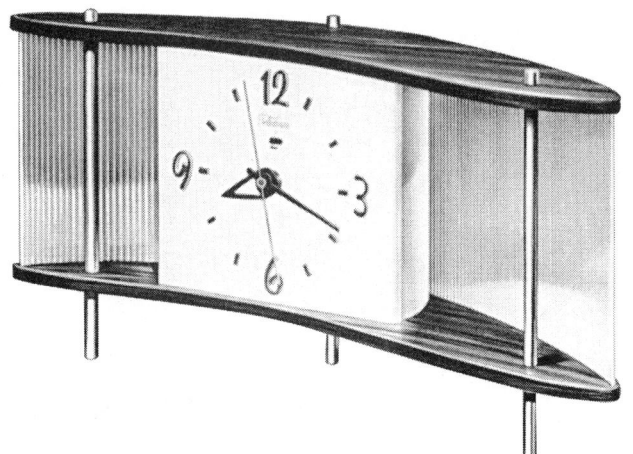

PLATE 1282
TELECHRON
c.1955, 5H-71, Panorama
AC Electric
Wood: Wanut w/Brass and Plastic
7.5H X 14W

PLATE 1283
TELECHRON
c.1955, 5H-67, Showpiece
AC Electric
Metal: Silver and Brass
13.5H X 6.25W

PLATE 1284
TELECHRON
c.1955, 7H-213, Perspective
AC Electric, Alarm
Plastic: Black w/Brass Trim
6H X 7W

PLATE 1285
TIME KING
c.1933, #160 (Ingraham)
1-Day Wind
Metal: Green, Blue, Pink or Black
6H

PLATE 1286
TIMEMASTER
c.1936, #910, New Timemaster (Ingraham)
1-Day Wind, Alarm
Metal: Chrome
5.25 Square

PLATE 1287
TIMETER
c.1934, #4601
AC Electric, Rotary
Metal: Black w/Chrome Trim

PLATE 1288
TIMETER
c.1934, #4602
AC Electric, Rotary
Wood: Walnut w/Marquetry Inlay

PLATE 1289
TIMETER
c.1934, #4603
AC Electric, Rotary
Metal: Chrome

TIMEX · USALITE

PLATE 1290
TIMEX
c.1954, Falcon
40-Hour Wind, Alarm, Luminous Dial Optional
Metal: Ivory
3.75H X 3.25W

PLATE 1291
TIMEX
c.1955, Radiolite
40-Hour Wind, Alarm, Luminous Dial
Metal: Walnut or Ivory
3.75H X 3.25W

PLATE 1292
TIMEX
c.1957, Falcon SW
40-Hour Wind, Alarm, Luminous Dial
Metal: Green, Ivory or Gold
3.75H X 3.25W

PLATE 1293
TIMEX
c.1957, Falcon, SW
40-Hour Wind, Alarm, Luminous Dial
Metal: Ivory or Green
3.75H X 3.25W

PLATE 1294
TUXEDO
c.1932, Tuxedo (Lux)
1 Day Wind, Alarm
Metal: Green, Gold or Bronze
5.25H X 6W

PLATE 1295
U.S. TIME CORP.
c.1950, Happalong Cassidy
1-Day Wind, Alarm
Metal: Red or Black

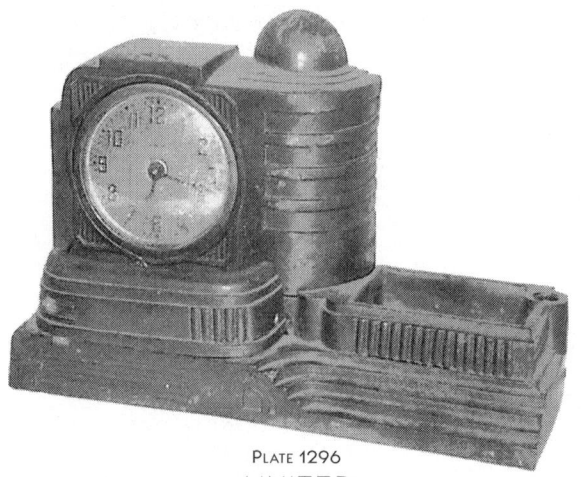

PLATE 1296
UNITED
c.1933, Futurist Desk Set (w/lamp, pen, inkwell)
AC Electric
Metal: Bronzed Spelter

PLATE 1297
USALITE
c.1932, #700, Atlas
AC Electric, Alarm
Metal: Nickel
9.25H X 4.75W X 4.25D

PLATE 1298
USALITE
c.1935, 12, Pequot
1-Day Wind
Catalin: Green, Amber
3H

USALITE · VIKING

PLATE 1299
USALITE
c.1935, #704, Modernistic
AC Electric
Metal: Silver and Black
9H X 5W X 3.25D

PLATE 1300
VICTOR
c.1931, #1110, One Day Intermittent
1-Day Wind, Alarm, Luminous Dial Optional
Metal: Green, Blue, Red or Nickel w/gold
6.25H

PLATE 1301
VICTOR
c.1931, #1135, One Day Intermittent
1 Day Wind, Alarm, Luminous Dial Optional
Metal: Nickel
7H

PLATE 1302
VIKING
c.1932, #851, Electro-Glo
AC Electric, Illuminated Dial
Metal: Black Base w/ Chrome
9.75H X 16.75W

PLATE 1303
VIKING
c.1932, #1400, Electro-Glo
AC Electric, Illuminated Dial
Metal: Black Base w/ Chrome
10H

PLATE 1304
VIKING
c.1932, #1600, Electro-Glo
AC Electric, Illuminated Dial
Metal: Black Base, Chrome
9H X 8.5W

PLATE 1305
VIKING
c.1933, Moon-Glo
AC Electric, Illuminated Dial
Metal: Foil Backed Glass on Chrome Base

PLATE 1306
VIKING
c.1934
8-Day Wind
Metal: Chrome
4.5H

WALTHAM

PLATE 1307
VIM
c.1930, #1201
1-Day Wind, Alarm, Luminous Dial
Metal: Green, Blue or Nickel
5.25H

PLATE 1308
WALTHAM
c.1925, #1207-8
8-Day Pocket Wind Movement
Wood: Walnut
11H X 10.5W X 3.5D

PLATE 1309
WALTHAM
c.1925, #1231-8, Nouveau
8-Day Pocket Wind Movement
Wood: Walnut
11H X 10.5W X 3.5D

PLATE 1310
WALTHAM
c.1932, #3013
1-Day Wind, Alarm
Metal: Gold or Blue
4.5H X 4.5W

PLATE 1311
WALTHAM
c.1932, #8300
40-Hour Wind
Wood: Mahogany
4.75H

PLATE 1312
WALTHAM
c.1939, #8574, Desk Set
AC Electric
Wood: Mahogany
5.75H X 8W

PLATE 1313
WALTHAM
c.1940, #663, Parker Pen and Pencil
AC Electric
Wood: Walnut
6H X 12W X 5.5D

PLATE 1314
WALTHAM
c.1940, #665, Parker Pen and Pencil
8-Day Wind
Wood: Walnut and Black
4.5H X 12W X 5.5D

WALTHAM

PLATE 1315
WALTHAM
c.1940, #666, Parker Pen and Pencil
40-Hour Wind
Wood: Walnut
5.5H X 14W X 5D

PLATE 1316
WALTHAM
c.1940, #3531, Parker Pen and Pencil
8-Day Wind, Alarm
Marble: Green, Cream or Walnut
6H X 12.5W

PLATE 1317
WALTHAM
c.1940, #1010, Cleopatra
AC Electric, Alarm
Wood: Black
6.5H X 8W X 4.5D

PLATE 1318
WALTHAM
c.1940, #1018
AC Electric, Alarm
Wood: Green
7H X 8W X 3.75D

PLATE 1319
WALTHAM
c.1940, #1857
8-Day Wind
Leather: Black, Pigskin or Blue
4H

PLATE 1320
WALTHAM
c.1940, #8558
AC Electric
Wood: Mahogany
8H X 10W

PLATE 1321
WALTHAM
c.1940, #644
8-Day Wind
Wood: Walnut
6.5H X 7.5W

PLATE 1322
WALTHAM
c.1940, #646
8-Day Wind
Mirror: Pink or Blue
5.5H X 7.5W

WALTHAM · WARD

PLATE 1323
WALTHAM
c.1940, #648
8-Day Wind
Marble: Black and Chrome
6.5H X 6.25W

PLATE 1324
WALTHAM
c.1940, #8581
8-Day Wind
Black Marble w/Blue Mirror & Chrome
6H X 6W

PLATE 1325
WARD
c.1934, #951, 908, 909, Waldorf (Ingraham)
1-Day Wind, Alarm
Metal: Black w/Nickel, Green w/Nickel or Walnut w/Copper
5H X 5W

PLATE 1326
WARD
c.1935, #903
1-Day Wind, Alarm
Metal: Green or Pink
4.25H X 3.5W

PLATE 1327
WARD
c.1936, #924
1-Day Wind, Alarm
Metal: Black
5.25H X 5.25W

PLATE 1328
WARD
c.1936, #925
1-Day Wind or AC Electric, Alarm, Luminous Dial Optional
Metal: Black w/Nickel, Grey w/Nickel or Ivory
5.25H X 5W

PLATE 1329
WARD
c.1936, #926, Round Modern (Lux)
1-Day Wind, Alarm
Metal: Green w/Brass or Black w/Nickel
5H X 4.5W

PLATE 1330
WARD
c.1936, #1051 (Lux)
1-Day Wind, Alarm
Metal: Ivory, Black or Green w/Gold trim
5H

PLATE 1331
WARD
c.1936, #1052 (Lux)
1-Day Wind, Alarm
Metal: Ivory or Green w/Gold Trim
4.5H X 5.25W

WARD

PLATE 1332
WARD
c.1936, #924, 972
1-Day Wind, Alarm
Metal: Grey w/Nickel or Ivory w/Gold
3.25H X 3.25W

PLATE 1333
WARD
c.1936, #947, 948, Square
1-Day Wind, Alarm
Metal: Black or Green
4.25H X 3.75W

PLATE 1334
WARD
c.1937, #925, 974
1-Day Wind, Alarm, Luminous Dial Optional
Metal: Black or Ivory
5.25H X 5W

PLATE 1335
WARD
c.1942, #1000, 1001
AC Electric, Alarm
Bakelite/Plaskon: Walnut or Ivory w/Gold trim
4.5H X 5.5

PLATE 1336
WARD
c.1942, #1002
AC Electric, Alarm, Luminous Dial
Plastic: Ivory w/Gold trim
4.5H X 5.5W

PLATE 1337
WARD
c.1950, #6880, Square Case
1-Day Wind, Alarm
Metal: Ivory
4.5H

PLATE 1338
WARD
c.1950, #6839, 6881, Round Case
1-Day Wind, Alarm, Luminous Dial Optional
Metal: Ivory
4.5H X 4.5W

PLATE 1339
WARD
c.1950, #6951, 6952
8-Day Wind, Alarm, Luminous Dial Optional
Metal: Ivory
5.5H X 4.5W

PLATE 1340
WARD
c.1950, #6953, 6954, Old Reliable
8-Day Wind, Alarm, Luminous Dial Optional
Metal: Ivory
5.5H X 5.25W

WARD · WASHINGTON ELECTRIC

PLATE 1341
WARD
c.1951, #7075
AC Electric, Alarm
Plaskon: Ivory
4.5S

PLATE 1342
WARD
c.1954, #7055
AC Electric, Alarm
Wood: Mahogany
4H X 5W

PLATE 1343
WARD
c.1954, #7237
8-Day Wind, Strike
Wood: Mahogany
7.5H X 8W

PLATE 1344
WARD
c.1954, #6951, 6952
8-Day Wind, Alarm, Luminous Dial Optional
Metal: Ivory
4.5H X 5W

PLATE 1345
WARD
c.1954, #7050, 7051
AC Electric, Alarm, Luminous Dial Optional
Plastic: Ivory or Walnut
4.5H X 3.75W

PLATE 1345
WARD
c.1958, #7145, Perky
AC Electric
Plastic: Chrome or Copper
7.5H X 7.5W

PLATE 1347
WARD
c.1951, #6885 (Ingraham)
1-Day Wind, Alarm
Metal: Ivory
7H X 5.5W

PLATE 1348
WASHINGTON ELECTRIC
c.1931, #20, 25, Gothic
AC Electric, Alarm
Bakelite: Walnut
7.25H X 5.5W

PLATE 1349
WASHINGTON ELECTRIC
c.1931, #5, Ronell
AC Electric
Bakelite: Walnut
5.5H X 5W

WATERBURY

PLATE 1350
WATERBURY
c.1931, #112, Current
AC Electric
Metal: Green, Pink Gold, Blue w/Gold or Black w/Silver
5.25H

PLATE 1351
WATERBURY
c.1931, #113, Coil
AC Electric, Alarm Optional
Bakelite: Mahogany or Walnut
7.25H

PLATE 1352
WATERBURY
c.1931, #114, Modernistic
AC Electric
Bakelite: Black w/Chrome
7H X 5.75W

PLATE 1353
WATERBURY
c.1931, #115, Mayflower
AC Electric, Alarm
Bakelite: Mahogany
6.75H X 5W

PLATE 1354
WATERBURY
c.1931, #119, Arcadia
AC Electric
Wood: Walnut
7.75H X 6.75W

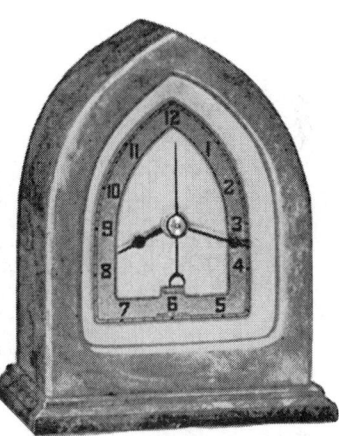

PLATE 1355
WATERBURY
c.1931, #120, Bryn Mawr
AC Electric
Metal: Green, Pink, Ivory or Blue
4.5H X 3.75W

← PLATE 1357
WATERBURY
c.1931
1-Day Wind, Alarm, Luminous Dial Optional
Metal: Nickel
6H

PLATE 1357 →
WATERBURY-INGERSOL
c.1931, Correct Time
(Sales Display Clock)
AC Electric
Wood: Mahogany
19H X 8.25W X 13.5D

WESTCLOX

PLATE 1358
WESTCLOX
c.1910, Big Ben
1-Day Wind, Alarm
Metal: Nickel Plated
5H

PLATE 1359
WESTCLOX
c.1927, Big Ben (Dreyfuss Des.)
1-Day Wind, Alarm
Metal: Nickel or Cracked Paint Finish:
Green, Blue or Rose

PLATE 1360
WESTCLOX
c.1931, Bantam
1-Day Wind, Alarm
Metal: Green
4.5H

PLATE 1361
WESTCLOX
c.1931, Leg
1-Day Wind
Metal: Nickel Plated
7H

PLATE 1362
WESTCLOX
c.1931, Roman Arch Design
8-Day Wind, Alarm
Bakelite: Walnut
5.25H X 5.5W

PLATE 1363
WESTCLOX
c.1931, Modernistic Design
8-Day Wind, Alarm
Bakelite: Walnut
5.25H X 5.5W

PLATE 1364
WESTCLOX
c.1931, Big Ben
AC Electric, Alarm
Wood: Mahogany
5.75H X 5.5W

PLATE 1365
WESTCLOX
c.1931, Ben Hur
1-Day Wind, Alarm
Metal: Nickel, Blue, Green or Red
4.5H

PLATE 1366
WESTCLOX
c.1931, America
1-Day Wind, Alarm
Metal: Nickel, Blue, Green or Red
6.25H

WESTCLOX

PLATE 1368
WESTCLOX
c.1931, #401, La Salle Series
1-Day Wind, Alarm
Metal: Dura Alloy
3.25H X 3.25W

PLATE 1369
WESTCLOX
c.1931, #402, La Salle Series
1-Day Wind, Alarm
Metal: Dura Alloy
3.25H X 3.5W

PLATE 1370
WESTCLOX
c.1931, #403, La Salle Series
1-Day Wind, Alarm
Metal: Dura Alloy
3.25H X 2.25W

PLATE 1371
WESTCLOX
c.1931, #404, La Salle Series
1-Day Wind, Alarm, Luminous Dial
Metal: Dura Alloy
3.25H

PLATE 1372
WESTCLOX
c.1931, #405, La Salle Series
1-Day Wind, Alarm, Luminous Dial
Metal: Dura Alloy w/Black
3.25H

PLATE 1373
WESTCLOX
c.1931, #406, La Salle Series
1-Day Wind, Alarm, Luminous Dial
Metal: Dura Alloy w/Gold, Black
3.25H

PLATE 1374
WESTCLOX
c.1931, Big Ben (Dreyfuss Des.)
1-Day Wind, Alarm, Luminous Dial Optional
Metal: Nickel
3.25H

PLATE 1375
WESTCLOX
c.1931, Tom Thumb
1-Day Wind, Alarm
Metal: Green
2.5H

PLATE 1376
WESTCLOX
c.1931, Big Ben (Dreyfuss Attr.)
AC Electric, Alarm, Luminous Dial Optional
Wood: Mahogany
5.25H X 4.5W

WESTCLOX

PLATE 1377
WESTCLOX
c.1931, Que-Tee
AC Electric
Bakelite: Mahogany
6.5H X 4.75W

PLATE 1378
WESTCLOX
c.1931, Big Ben (Dreyfuss Des.)
1-Day Wind, Alarm, Luminous Dial Optional
Metal: Black w/Nickel or Ivory w/Gold
5.25H X 4W

PLATE 1379
WESTCLOX
c.1931, Baby Ben (Dreyfss Des.)
1-Day Wind, Alarm, Luminous Dial Optional
Metal: Black w/Nickel or Walnut w/Copper
3.25H

PLATE 1380
WESTCLOX
c.1933, Big Ben (Dreyfuss Des.)
1-Day Wind, Alarm, Luminous Dial Optional
Metal: Black w/Nickel or Ivory w/Gold
5.25H X 4W

PLATE 1381
WESTCLOX
c.1933, Baby Ben (Dreyfuss Des.)
1-Day Wind, Alarm, Luminous Dial Optional
Metal: Ivory w/Gold or Black w/Nickel
3.25H

PLATE 1382
WESTCLOX
c.1934, Dura
1-Day Wind, Alarm
Metal: Dura Silver Alloy

PLATE 1383
WESTCLOX
c.1934, #827, Silent Night
AC Electric, Alarm
Metal: Ivory w/Gold Trim
5.25H

PLATE 1384
WESTCLOX
c.1934, #865, Andover
AC Electric
Metal: Nickel w/Blue Glass
6.25H

WESTCLOX

PLATE 1385
WESTCLOX
c.1934, #868, Orb
AC Electric, Alarm
Metal: Black w/Gold Trim
5.5H

PLATE 1386
WESTCLOX
c.1934, #873, Bachelor
AC Electric, Alarm
Bakelite/Plaskon: Brown, Ivory or Black w/Brass
4.75H X 5W

PLATE 1387
WESTCLOX
c.1934, Siesta
1-Day Wind or AC Electric, Alarm
Metal: Black w/Nickel

PLATE 1388
WESTCLOX
c.1934, Modern Square
1-Day Wind, Alarm
Metal: Black w/Nickel trim
4.25H X 4.25W

PLATE 1389
WESTCLOX
c.1934, Fortune
1-Day Wind, Alarm, Luminous Dial Optional
Metal: Black w/Nickel Trim
4.5H X 4.5W

PLATE 1390
WESTCLOX
c.1934, #814, 815, Country Club
AC Electric, Alarm, Luminous Dial
Metal: Black w/Nickel or Ivory w/Gold
4.75 Square

PLATE 1391
WESTCLOX
c.1935, #828, Ben Bolt
AC Electric, Alarm
Metal: Black w/Nickel Trim
4.5H

PLATE 1392
WESTCLOX
c.1935, #812, American
AC Electric, Alarm, Luminous Dial Optional
Metal: Black w/Nickel Trim
4H

PLATE 1393
WESTCLOX
c.1935, #846, Greenwich
AC Electric, Alarm
Wood: Walnut
5.25H

WESTCLOX

PLATE 1394
WESTCLOX
c.1935, #850, Ben Franklin
AC Electric, Alarm
Bakelite: Black w/Brass Trim
5.25H X 7.25W

PLATE 1395
WESTCLOX
c.1936, #944, New Bantam
1-Day Wind, Alarm
Metal: Green w/Black Base
4.75H

PLATE 1396
WESTCLOX
c.1936, #953, Tide
1-Day Wind, Alarm
Metal: Black w/Nickel Trim
4.75H X 4.75W

PLATE 1397
WESTCLOX
c.1936, Bingo
1-Day Wind, Alarm
Metal: Ivory or Walnut

PLATE 1398
WESTCLOX
c.1938, #959, 960, Spur
1-Day Wind or AC Electric, Alarm, Luminous Dial Optional
Metal: Black w/Nickel trim
4.75H X 4.75W

PLATE 1399
WESTCLOX
c.1940, S5-F, Logan
AC Electric
Metal: Ivory w/Brass Trim

PLATE 1400
WESTCLOX
c.1938, Leland
1-Day Wind
Metal: Chrome Base and Frame w/Smoke Glass

PLATE 1401
WESTCLOX
c.1939, #871, S5-G, Pittsfield
AC Electric, Alarm
Metal/Plaskon: Brass w/Ivory Bezel
5.75H

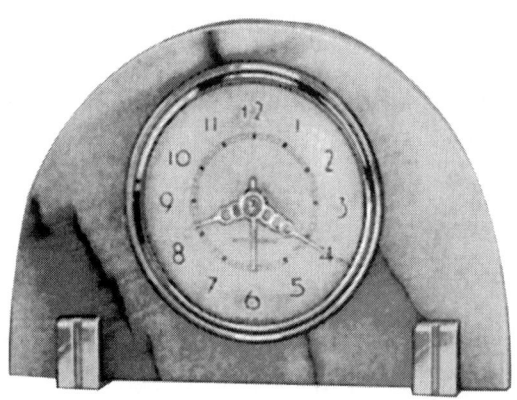

PLATE 1402
WESTCLOX
c.1939
AC Electric
Marble: Onyx w/Brass Trim

WESTCLOX

PLATE 1403
WESTCLOX
c.1939
AC Electric
Wood: Walnut w/Burl Maple

PLATE 1404
WESTCLOX
c.1939
AC Electric
Wood: Walnut

PLATE 1405
WESTCLOX
c.1939, Big Ben (Dreyfuss Des.)
AC Electric, Alarm
Metal: Black w/Nickel Trim or Ivory w/Gold
5.5H

PLATE 1406
WESTCLOX
c.1939, Big Ben (Dreyfuss Des.)
AC Electric, Alarm, Luminous Dial
Metal: Black w/Nickel Trim or Ivory w/Gold
5.5H

PLATE 1407
WESTCLOX
c.1939, Baby Ben (Dreyfuss Des.)
AC Electric, Alarm, Luminous Dial Optional
Metal: Black w/Nickel Trim or Ivory w/Gold
3.5H

PLATE 1408
WESTCLOX
c.1939
AC Electric
Metal: Ivory

PLATE 1409
WESTCLOX
c.1941, #987, Shelby
1-Day Wind, Alarm
Bakelite/Plaskon: Ivory or Walnut
4.5H X 5W

PLATE 1410
WESTCLOX
c.1948, General
1-Day Wind, Alarm, Luminous Dial Optional
Metal: Ivory w/gold trim
4.75 Square

PLATE 1411
WESTCLOX
c.1948, #74-3, Clock of Tomorrow
AC Electric, Alarm
Metal: Brass
5.5H X 4.5W

WESTCLOX

PLATE 1412
WESTCLOX
c.1948, #904, 907, Moonbeam
AC Electric, Alarm (w/Flashing Light), Luminous Dial Opt.
Plastic: Ivory w/Brass
5.5H X 6.5W

PLATE 1413
WESTCLOX
c.1948, S7-H, Sphinx
AC Electric, Alarm
Wood: Walnut

PLATE 1414
WESTCLOX
c.1949, Big Ben (Dreyfuss Des.)
1 Day Wind, Alarm, Luminous Dial Optional
Metal: Ivory w/Gold trim or Black w/Nickel trim
5.75H X 5.5W

PLATE 1415
WESTCLOX
c.1949, Baby Ben (Dreyfuss Des.)
1-Day Wind, Alarm, Luminous Dial Optional
Metal: Ivory w/Gold trim or Black w/Nickel trim
3.5H

PLATE 1416
WESTCLOX
c.1950, #943, Ardmore
AC Electric
Plastic: Walnut
5 Square

PLATE 1417
WESTCLOX
c.1950, #980
AC Electric, Alarm
Metal: Ivory w/Gold trim
5 Square

PLATE 1418
WESTCLOX
c.1950, Big Ben
AC Electric, Alarm, Luminous Dial Optional
Walnut w/Gold trim
5.25H X 5W

PLATE 14c.19
WESTCLOX
c.1950, #960, 962, Barry
AC Electric, Alarm
Metal: Black or Ivory
4.75H X 4.25W

PLATE 1420
WESTCLOX
c.1951, Bantam
AC Electric, Alarm, Luminous Dial
Plastic: Ivory
4H X 3.5W

WESTCLOX

Plate 1421
WESTCLOX
c.1957, Tide (Flamingo)
AC Electric, Alarm, Luminous Dial
Plastic: Pink or Yellow
3.25H X 4W

Plate 1422
WESTCLOX
c.1956, #656, 692, Sheraton
AC Electric, Alarm, Luminous Dial Optional
Wood: Mahogany or Maple
4.5H

Plate 1423
WESTCLOX
c.1955, Big Ben
1-Day Wind or AC Electric, Alarm, Luminous Dial Optional
Metal: Ivory w/Gold or Black w/Nickel
5H X 4.75W

Plate 1424
WESTCLOX
c.1955, Baby Ben
1-Day Wind, Alarm, Luminous Dial Optional
Metal: Ivory w/Gold or Black w/Nickel
3.5H

Plate 1425
WESTCLOX
c.1956, Glendale
AC Electric
Plastic: White
5.75H X 7.75W

Plate 1426
WESTCLOX
c.1957, Ellsworth
AC Electric, Alarm
Plastic: Grey or Red
4H X 6.75W

Plate 1427
WESTCLOX
c.1957, Piper
AC Electric, Alarm, Luminous Dial Optional
Metal: Ivory or Black
3H

WESTCLOX

PLATE 1428
WESTCLOX
c.1958, Lace
AC Electric, Alarm, Luminous Dial Optional
Plastic: White, Pink or Blue
6H X 7W

PLATE 1429
WESTCLOX
c.1962, Legend
Wind or Alarm
Wood: Walnut w/Brass
4H

PLATE 1430
WESTCLOX
c.1962, New Dune
1-Day Wind, Alarm, Luminous Dial
Metal: Brass
3.25H

PLATE 1431
WESTCLOX
c.1962, Dynamic
AC Electric, Alarm
Plastic: White or Pink
4.25H X 10.5W

PLATE 1432
WESTCLOX
c.1962, Drowse
AC Electric, Alarm, Luminous Dial
Plastic: Tan, Green or Pink
3.75H

PLATE 1433
WESTCLOX
c.1962, Award
AC Electric, Alarm, Luminous Dial
Wood: Walnut w/Brass
4.25H

PLATE 1434
WESTCLOX
c.1965, Double Bell
1-Day Wind, Alarm, Luminous Dial
Metal: Brass
4.75H

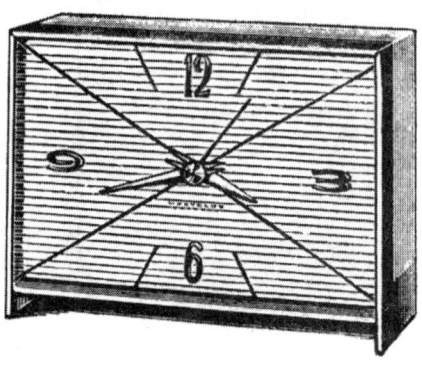

PLATE 1435
WESTCLOX
c.1962, Isotron
DC Electric
Metal: Brass, Silver
4.5H X 6.25W

WESTCLOX

PLATE 1436
WESTCLOX
c.1962, Big Ben
Day Wind or AC Electric, Alarm, Luminous Dial Optional
Metal: Ivory w/Brass or Black w/Nickel Trim
4.5H

PLATE 1437
WESTCLOX
c.1962, Baby Ben
1-Day Wind or AC Electric, Alarm, Luminous Dial Optional
Metal: Ivory w/Brass or Black w/Nickel Trim
4.5H 3.75H"

PLATE 1438
WESTCLOX
c.1965
1-Day Wind, Alarm, Luminous Dial
Metal: Beige
4.5H

PLATE 1439
WESTCLOX
c.1965, Quiet Tick
1-Day Wind, Alarm, Luminous Dial Optional
Plastic: Tan
4H

PLATE 1440
WESTCLOX
c.1965
AC Electric or 1-Day Wind, Alarm, Luminous Dial
Plastic: Grey or White
4H X 4W

PLATE 1441
WESTINGHOUSE
c.1932, WM611-68A, Nelson
AC Electric, Alarm
Metal: Black Suede w/Chrome Trim
4.75H X 6.25W X 1.5D

PLATE 1442
WESTINGHOUSE
c.1932, WM611-51AB, 52AG, 53AR, Magnus
AC Electric, Alarm
Metal: Blue, Green or Rose
6.25H X 5W

PLATE 1443
WESTINGHOUSE
c.1932, WM611-56A, Cunard
AC Electric, Alarm
Metal: Black w/Nickel Trim
4.5H X 4W

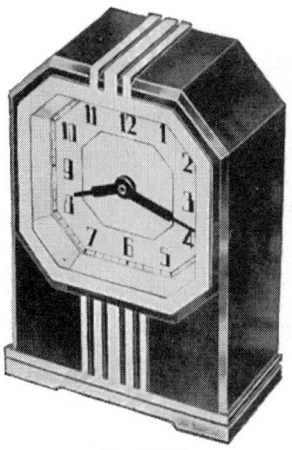

PLATE 1444
WESTINGHOUSE
c.1932, WM611-63T, Futurist
AC Electric
Metal: Black w/Gold Trim
5.5H X 4W

SECTION TWO

WEATHER METERS AND GUIDES

APPLIANCE SWITCHES

TIMERS

AIRGUIDE

PLATE 1457
AIRGUIDE
c.1934
Hygrometer
Metal: Black w/Chrome
3.5 Square

PLATE 1458
AIRGUIDE
c.1939, Air Condition Indicator
Hygrometer and Thermometer
Wood: Walnut w/Chrome
7.75H X 2.75W

PLATE 1459
AIRGUIDE
c.1940, Forecast Barometer
Barometer and Thermometer
Bakelite: Black w/Chrome
5H X 4.75W

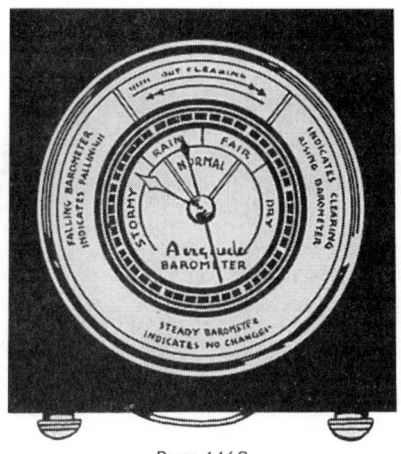

PLATE 1460
AIRGUIDE
c.1940, York
Barometer
Bakelite: Black w/Chrome trim
4.75 Square

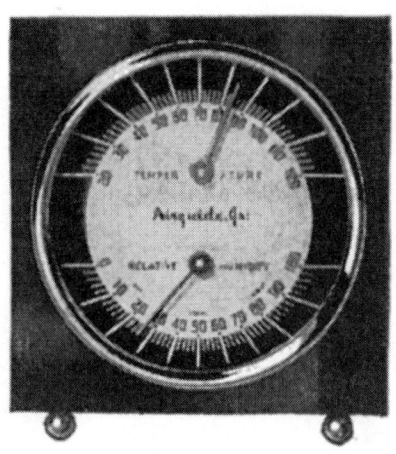

PLATE 1461
AIRGUIDE
c.1940, Tempid Teller
Barometer (or Hygrometer) and Thermometer
Bakelite: Black w/Chrome trim
3.5H X 3.25W

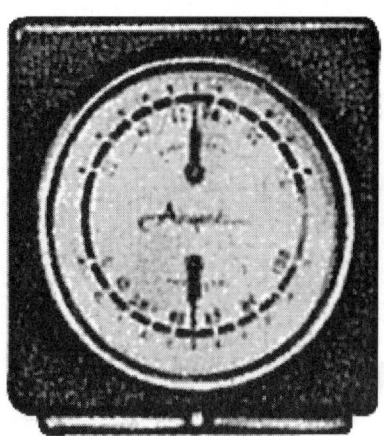

PLATE 1462
AIRGUIDE
c.1954, Argyle
Hygrometer and Thermometer
Plastic: Black
3.5H X 3.25W

PLATE 1463
AIRGUIDE
c.1942, 3-In-1 Airguide
Barometer, Hygrometer and Thermometer
Bakelite: Black w/Chrome Trim
5.5H X 9.5W X 2.25D

PLATE 1464
AIRGUIDE
c.1956, Corsair
Barometer, Hygrometer and Thermometer
Metal: Brass
5.25H X 9.5W

AIRGUIDE

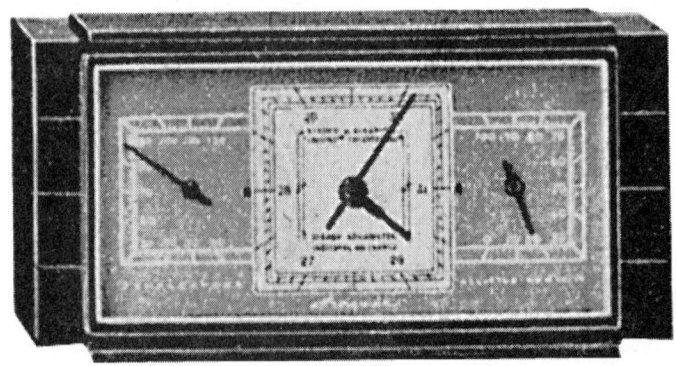

PLATE 1465
AIRGUIDE
c.1951, Princeton Air Pilot
Barometer, Hygrometer and Thermometer
Plastic: Grey
4H X 7.5W X 2D

PLATE 1466
AIRGUIDE
c.1954, Princeton Air Pilot
Barometer, Hygrometer and Thermometer
Plastic: Grey
4H X 7.5W X 2D

PLATE 1467
AIRGUIDE
c.1956, Princeton Air Pilot
Barometer, Hygrometer and Thermometer
Plastic: Grey
4H X 7.25W X 2D

PLATE 1468
AIRGUIDE
c.1957, Corsair
Hygrometer and Thermometer
Plastic: Grey
3H X 5.5W

PLATE 1469
AIRGUIDE
c.1963, Director
Barometer, Hygrometer and Thermometer
Metal: Aluminum
4.75H X 9.5W X 2D

PLATE 1470
AIRGUIDE
c.1963, Princeton
Barometer, Hygrometer and Thermometer
Metal: Grey w/Brass Base
4H X 8W X 1.75D

AIRGUIDE - BUGLE BOY

Plate 1472
AIRGUIDE
c.1963, Sherwood
Barometer, Hygrometer and Thermometer
Wood: Fruitwood w/Brass Trim
5.5H X 9.25W X 2.5D

Plate 1472
AIRGUIDE
c.1963, Zonar Comfort Coordinator
Hygrometer, Thermometer and Suggested Best Temperature
Metal
3.75H X 5.75W X 1.75D

Plate 1473
AIR-O-METER
c.1938
Hygrometer and Thermometer
Metal
3" Diameter

Plate 1474
BUGLE BOY
c.1936 (Lux)
1-Day Wind w/Thermometer, Alarm
Metal: Ivory with Green or Red Trim

Plate 1475
BUGLE BOY
c.1937, Thermometer Alarm (Lux)
44-Hour Wind w/Thermometer, Alarm
Metal: Green or Ivory
5.25H X 4.5W

Plate 1476
BUGLE BOY
c.1940, Smart Dome (Lux)
30 Hour Wind, Rotary w/Thermometer, Alarm
Metal: Ivory or Bronze

Plate 1477
BUGLE BOY
c.1939, 4-In-1 Calendar (Lux)
30-Hour Wind, Thermometer, Calendar, Alarm
Metal: Ivory or Bronze
7.75H

Plate 1478
BUGLE BOY
c.1940, Cloisonne Modern
30 Hour Windup, Thermometer, Alarm
Bakelite/Plaskon: Ivory or Mahogany
6.5H X 4.5W

BUGLE BOY - DELUXE

Plate 1479
BUGLE BOY
c.1940, Globe
8-Day Windup, Thermometer, Alarm
Metal: Ivory w/Brass or Black w/Chrome
5.75H X 5.25W

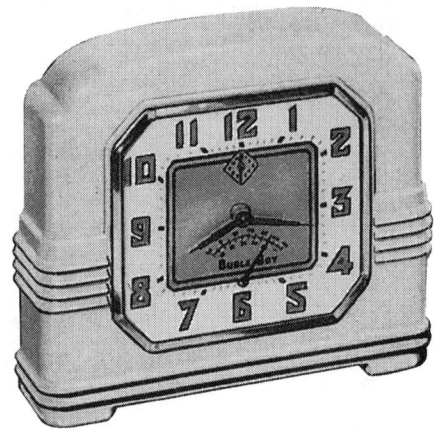

Plate 1480
BUGLE BOY
c.1940, Thermometer Alarm
30-Hour Wind, Thermometer, Alarm
Metal: Brown, Green or Ivory
7.5H X 6.25W

Plate 1481
BUGLE BOY
c.1951, Sunrise
40-Hour Wind, Thermometer, Alarm
Plastic: Ivory
4.5H X 4.25W

Plate 1482
CLOCK-TROLA
c.1933, Radio Switch
AC Electric Clock w/Appliance Switch
Bakelite, Walnut
7H X 7.5W

Plate 1483
DELUXE
c.1938, Minute Call (Footed)
AC Electric, Clock, Timer w/Alarm
Metal: White, Ivory, Green or Red
6.5H X 5W

Plate 1484
DELUXE
c.1939, Thermo-Alarm
1-Day Wind Clock w/Alarm and Thermometer
Metal: Ivory w/Brass trim
4.5H X 5.5W

Plate 1485
DELUXE
c.1940, Thermo-Alarm
1-Day Wind Clock w/Alarm, Thermometer
Metal: Ivory
4H X 7.25L

Plate 1486
DELUXE
c.1942
Thermometer
Metal
3.5W

EVERHOT · GILBERT

PLATE 1488
EVERHOT
c.1950, Appliance Timer
AC Electric Clock w/Appliance Switch, Alarm
Metal: Baked Enamel

PLATE 1489
FLEX-SEAL
c.1942, Flex-Seal Timer
Timer w/Alarm
Plastic: Black

PLATE 1490
GENERAL ELECTRIC
c.1930, TM8-30
AC Electric, Alarm, Appliance Timer
Metal: Chrome Housing w/Black Bakelite Trim
7.5H X 8.5W

PLATE 1491
GENERAL ELECTRIC
c.1939, 7F-64, Utility Timer
AC Electric Clock, Timer w/Alarm
Bakelite/Plaskon: Black or Ivory
5.25H

PLATE 1492
GENERAL ELECTRIC
c.1939, 8B-52, Voyager
AC Electric Clock w/Appliance Switch
Bakelite: Walnut
6.25H

PLATE 1493
GENERAL ELECTRIC
c.1949, Chef
AC Electric Clock w/Timer
Plastic: White
5.75H X 5.75W X 2.75D

PLATE 1494
GENERAL ELECTRIC
c.1949, Select-O-Switch
AC Electric, Clock w/Appliance Switch
Wood: Mahogany
5.25H X 6.5W X 2.75D

PLATE 1495
GENERAL ELECTRIC
c.1950, 8H-66, Little Chef
AC Electric Clock, Timer w/Alarm
Plastic: White
3.75H X 4W

PLATE 1496
GILBERT
c.1933, Highlander
40-Hour or 8-Day wind, Hygrometer/Thermometer
Metal: Ivory, Brown, Green or Black w/Chrome
5H X 6W

HAVLIN · JASON

PLATE 1497
HAVLIN
c.1930, Time Switch Clock
AC Electric Clock w/Appliance Switch
Bakelite: Walnut
6 H

PLATE 1498
HULL
c.1940, Desk Thermometer
Thermometer
Bakelite: Black w/Chrome trim
3 Square

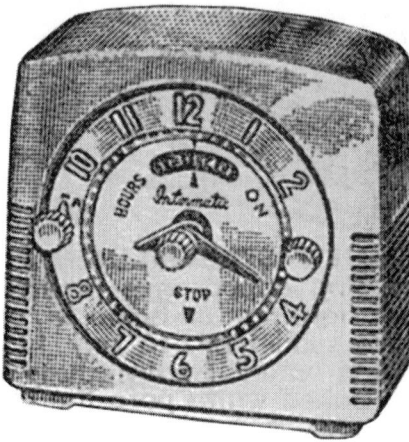

PLATE 1499
INTERMATIC
c.1958, A401, Clock-Timer
AC Electric Clock w/Appliance Switch
Plastic: Green
4.5H X 4.75W

PLATE 1500
INTERMATIC
c.1958, A211, Time-All
AC Electric, Appliance Timer
Plastic: Grey
4H X 5W

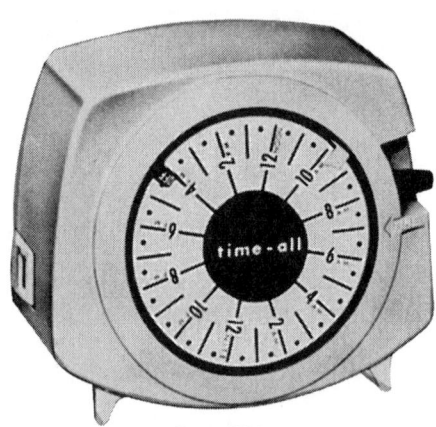

PLATE 1501
INTERMATIC
c.1963, Time-All
AC Electric, Appliance Timer
Plastic
4H X 5W

PLATE 1502
JASON
c.1962, Executive
Barometer and Thermometer
Wood: Walnut w/Brass
6 X 7

PLATE 1503
JASON
c.1962, Consultant
Barometer and Thermometer
Wood: Mahogany or Maple w/Brass
7W

PLATE 1504
JASON
c.1962, Diplomat
Barometer, Hygrometer and Thermometer
Wood: Fruitwood
8W

PLATE 1505
JASON
c.1962, VIP
Barometer and Hygrometer
Wood: Walnut w/Brass
7W

PLATE 1506
KLOK-TENNA
c.1930, Klok-Tenna
AC Electric Clock w/Radio Aerial
Bakelite: Walnut

PLATE 1507
LUX
c.1933, Thermo-Squire
1-Day Wind Clock w/Alarm and Thermometer
Metal: Black and Nickel
4H X 3.75W

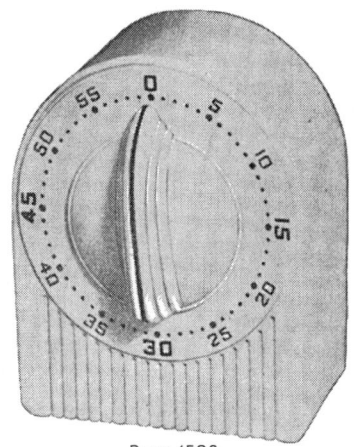

PLATE 1508
LUX
c.1949, Minute-Minder
Minute Timer w/Alarm
Metal: White
3.5H X 2.75W

PLATE 1509
LUX
c.1949, Minute-Minder
Minute Timer w/Alarm
Metal, White
5H X 3.75W

PLATE 1510
LUX
c.1963, Minute Minder
Minute Timer w/Alarm
Plastic: White

PLATE 1511
NATIONAL CALL
c.1938, Kitchenette (Lux)
1-Day Windup Clock w/Alarm and Thermometer
Metal: Ivory w/ Red, Green or Black
5H

PLATE 1512
NEW HAVEN
c.1931, Switchman
AC Electric Clock w/Appliance Switch
Bakelite: Walnut
4.75H X 4.75W

PLATE 1513
NEW HAVEN
c.1935, Switchman
AC Electric Clock w/Appliance Switch
Bakelite: Walnut
4.75H X 4.75W

NEW HAVEN · RELIDE

PLATE 1514
NEW HAVEN
c.1957
Wind, Minute Timer w/Alarm
White
3 Diameter

PLATE 1515
NUTONE
c.1942, Weather Man
Door Chime w/Airguide Hygrometer and Thermometer
Metal: Ivory w/Brass Bell Tubes

PLATE 1516
PILOT
c.1942, Desk Thermometer
Thermometer
Bakelite: Mahogany
3.5H

PLATE 1517
PILOT
c.1942, Mate
Mechanical: Thermometer
Metal: Brass
3 Dial

PLATE 1518
PILOT
c.1942, Ship's Wheel
Barometer
Metal: Brass
7 Diameter

PLATE 1519
PILOT
c.1942, Weather Man
Barometer
Metal: Brass
5.25 Diameter

PLATE 1520
PRESTO
c.1963, Long-Ring Minute Minder
Minute Timer w/Alarm
Plastic: Ivory and Black

PLATE 1521
RACINE
c.1929, Automatic Time Switch
8-Day Wind Clock w/Appliance Switch
Metal: Black

PLATE 1522
RELIDE
c.1962, L'Heure Book Clock
1-Day Wind, Alarm w/Thermometer
Metal w/Leather: Black, Walnut or Red
3.75H X 3W X 1D

RELIDE · SETH THOMAS

PLATE 1523
RELIDE
c.1962, Satellite
8-Day Wind
Clock, Thermometer and Barometer
Metal: Gold
8.25H X 7D

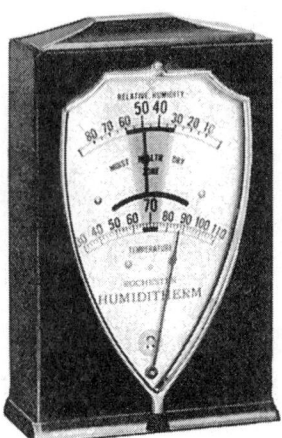

PLATE 1524
ROCHESTER
c.1934, Humiditherm
Hygrometer and Thermometer
Metal: Black w/Chrome
5.5H X 3.75W

PLATE 1525
ROYAL KENMORE
c.1932, Radiolarm Petite
AC Electric Clock w/Radio Switch
Bakelite: Walnut
6H X 4.5W

PLATE 1526
SELSI
c.1940, Admiral
Barometer w/Waltham Clock
Wood: Mahogany
8H X 18W X 5D

PLATE 1527
SELSI
c.1940, Forecaster
Barometer, Hygrometer and Thermometer
Wood: Mahogany or Walnut
4H X 8.5W

PLATE 1528
SESSIONS
c.1940, Combination Set
AC Electric Clock w/Barometer and Thermometer
Wood: Walnut w/Brass Trim
7H X 11.5W X 2.25D

PLATE 1529
SETH THOMAS
c.1940, Anchor Bookend Set
8-Day Wind Clock w/Barometer
Metal: Brass
6.5H X 5W

SESSIONS · SWIFT & ANDERSON

Plate 1530
SESSIONS
c.1940, Kloxit
Minute Timer w/Alarm
Metal: White, Red, Black or Ivory w/Chrome Trim
4.25H X 3.5W

Plate 1531
STELLAR
c.1962, General
Barometer, Hygrometer and Thermometer
Metal: Brass
8W

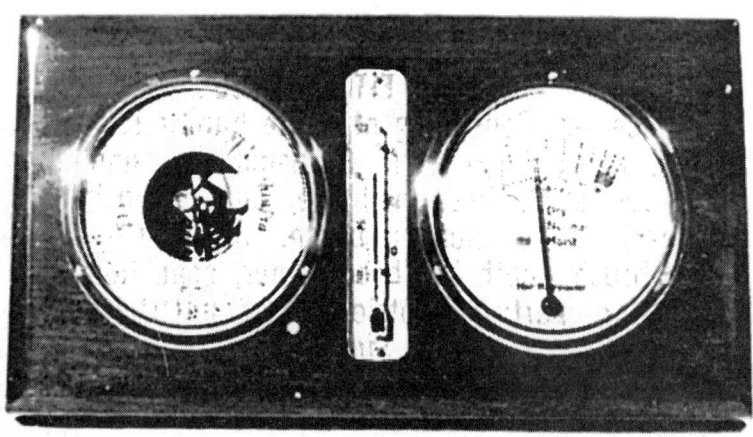

Plate 1532
STELLAR
c.1962, Weather Station
Barometer, Hygrometer and Thermometer
Wood: Walnut w/Brass
5H X 6W

Plate 1533
SUN-UP
c.1936, Automatic (Lux)
1-Day Wind, Thermometer, Alarm
Metal: Black, Green or Ivory
4.5H X 4W

Plate 1534
SUN-UP
c.1936 (Lux)
44-Hour Wind w/Thermometer, Alarm
Metal: Black or Green w/Nickel
4.5H X 4W

Plate 1535
SUN-UP
c.1936 (Lux)
44-Hour Wind w/Thermometer, Alarm
Metal: Black or Green
5.5H X 4.5W

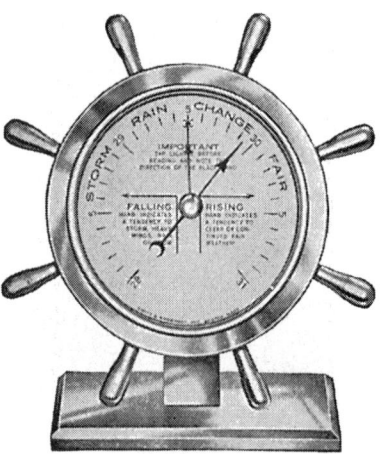

Plate 1536
SWIFT & ANDERSON
c.1940, Ship Wheel Barometer
Barometer
Metal: Bronze
5H X 5W

SWIFT & ANDERSON

PLATE 1537
SWIFT & ANDERSON
c.1940, Ship Wheel (2 Unit Set)
Barometer and Thermometer
Metal: Bronze or Chrome
5.25H X 8.5W

PLATE 1538
SWIFT & ANDERSON
c.1942, Desk Penometer
Barometer and Thermometer
Wood: Mahogany w/Brass Trim

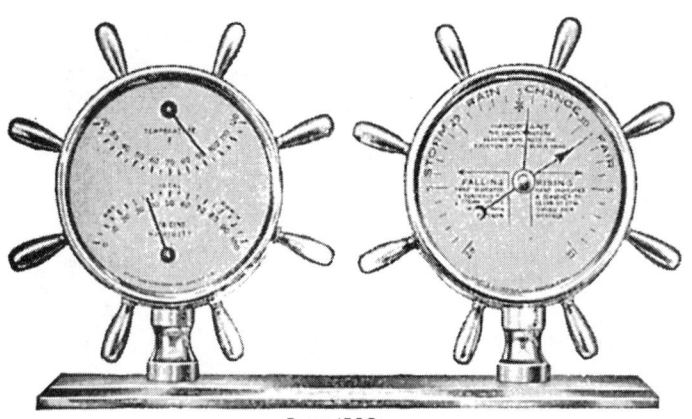

PLATE 1539
SWIFT & ANDERSON
c.1940, Ship Wheel (3 Unit Set)
Barometer, Hygrometer and Thermometer
Metal: Bronze
5.25H X 8.5W

PLATE 1540
SWIFT & ANDERSON
c.1940, American Combination
Barometer, Hygrometer and Thermometer
Bakelite: Black w/Chrome trim
4.5H X 8.5W

PLATE 1541
SWIFT & ANDERSON
c.1940, Biometer
Hygrometer and Thermometer
Bakelite: Black w/Chrome Trim
4H X 3W

PLATE 1542
SWIFT & ANDERSON
c.1940
Forecaster Barometer
Wood: Walnut
5.5H

PLATE 1543
SWIFT & ANDERSON
c.1940, Marine Design Barometer
Barometer
Metal: Brass
4.5H X 4W

SWIFT & ANDERSON

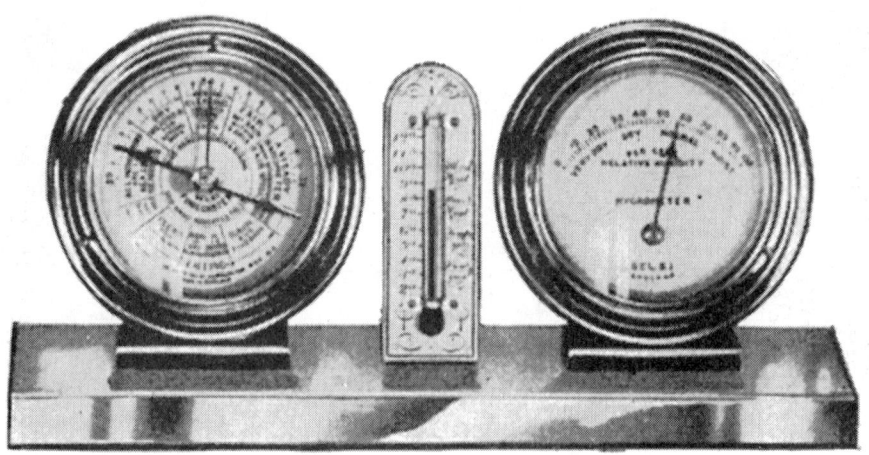

PLATE 1545
SWIFT & ANDERSON
c.1942, Desk Weather Station
Barometer, Hygrometer and Thermometer
Metal: Brass
8.5W

PLATE 1546
SWIFT & ANDERSON
c.1940, New Capstan
Barometer and Compass
Wood: Mahogany
8H X 4.75W

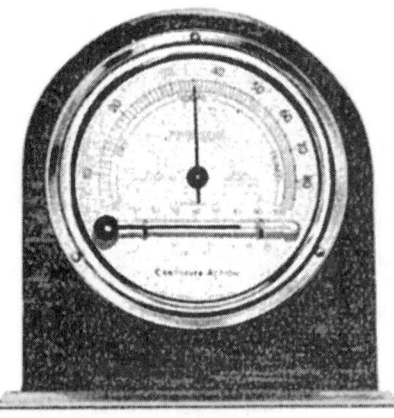

PLATE 1547
SWIFT & ANDERSON
c.1942, Biometer
Hygrometer and Thermometer
Wood: Mahogany w/Brass
5H X 4.75W

PLATE 1548
SWIFT & ANDERSON
c.1957, Fisherman
Barometer
Wood: Walnut
5H X 5W

PLATE 1549
SWIFT & ANDERSON
c.1957, Chelmsford
Barometer and Thermometer
Wood: Walnut
5H X 6W

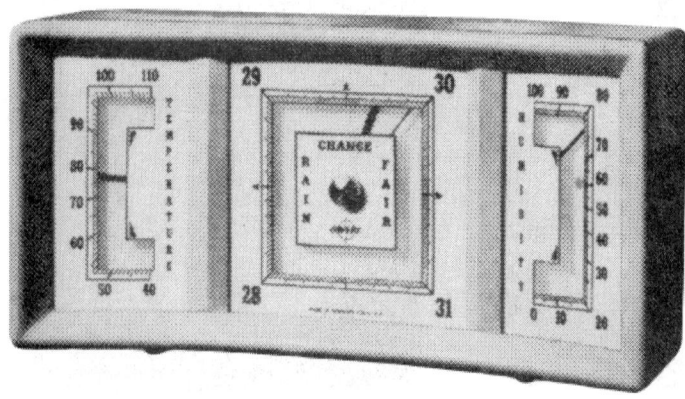

PLATE 1550
SWIFT & ANDERSON
c.1957, Comet
Barometer, Hygrometer and Thermometer
Plastic: Grey or Ivory
2.25H X 6.75W X 3.25D

PLATE 1551
SWIFT & ANDERSON
c.1956, Sherwood
Barometer, Hygrometer and Thermometer
Wood: Fruitwood w/Brass
9.25W

SWIFT & ANDERSON

PLATE 1552
SWIFT & ANDERSON
c.1956, Lowell
Barometer, Hygrometer and Thermometer
Wood: Mahogany or Maple w/Brass
4.75H X 8.5W X 2D

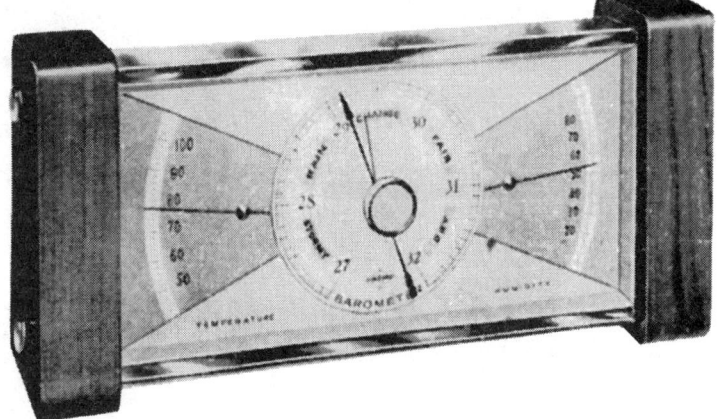

PLATE 1553
SWIFT & ANDERSON
c.1963, Sierra
Barometer, Hygrometer and Thermometer
Wood: Cherry w/Brass
4.5H X 10.25W

PLATE 1554
SWIFT & ANDERSON
c.1957, Huntsman
Barometer
Wood: Walnut
5H X 5W

PLATE 1555
SWIFT & ANDERSON
c.1957, German Barometer
Barometer
Wood: Walnut w/Brass
85mm Diameter

PLATE 1556
SWIFT & ANDERSON
c.1957, Windlass
Barometer or Hygrometer/Thermometer
Metal: Brass
5H

PLATE 1557
SWIFT & ANDERSON
c.1963, Chatham
Barometer
Wood & Metal: Mahogany and Brass
5H X 5W X 2D

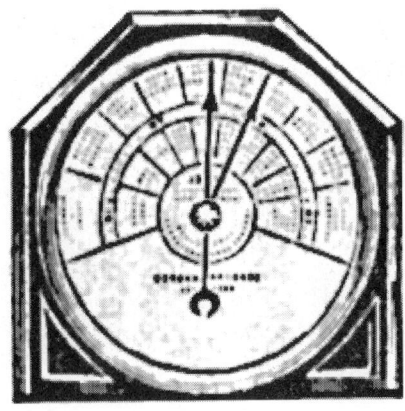

PLATE 1558
TAYLOR
c.1931
Barometer
Bakelite: Walnut

PLATE 1559
TAYLOR
c.1938, Baroguide (Teague Des.)
Barometer
Bakelite: Black w/Chrome Trim
5H X 5W

TAYLOR

PLATE 1560
TAYLOR
c.1938, Humiguide (Teague Attr.)
Hygrometer and Thermometer
Bakelite: Black w/Chrome Trim
6H X 4W

PLATE 1561
TAYLOR
c.1939, Combination Weather Stand
Barometer and Thermometer
Wood: Mahogany or Walnut
7H X 5.5W X 2.5D

PLATE 1562
TAYLOR
c.1939, Marlboro Stormguide
Barometer
Wood: Walnut w/Gold trim
4.5H X 6W

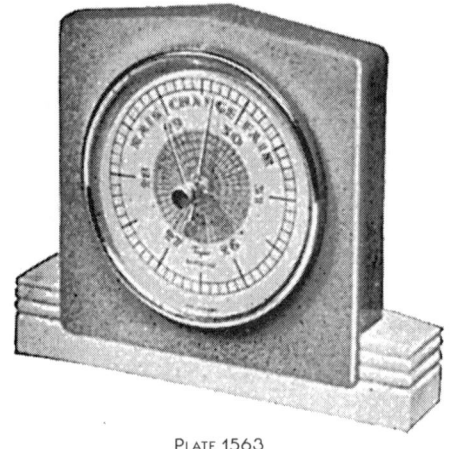

PLATE 1563
TAYLOR
c.1940, Fleetwood Baroguide
Barometer or Hygrometer
Catalin: Blue or Green w/White (Butterscotch) Base
5H X 5W

PLATE 1564
TAYLOR
c.1939, Clyde Stormoguide
Barometer
Wood: Mahogany w/Brass
6H X 6.75W

PLATE 1565
TAYLOR
c.1940, Ashton
Hygrometer and Thermometer
Plastic: Ivory
3.25 Square

PLATE 1566
TAYLOR
c.1940, Argyle
Barometer, Hygrometer and Thermometer
Bakelite: Black w/Chrome Trim
5.25H X 8.5W X 2.5D

PLATE 1567
TAYLOR
c.1940, Belmont Humiguide
Hygrometer and Thermometer
Metal: Lacquer
4.25H X 5.25W

TAYLOR

PLATE 1568
TAYLOR
c.1940, Darien
Barometer
Catalin: Translucent Ivory
3.25H

PLATE 1569
TAYLOR
c.1940, Fairfax Stormoguide
Barometer
Bakelite: Black w/Chrome Trim
5 Square

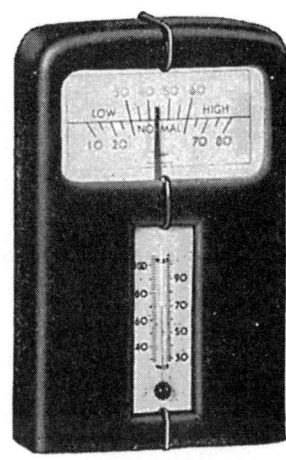

PLATE 1570
TAYLOR
c.1940, Hampton Humiguide
Hygrometer and Thermometer
Bakelite: Black
5.75H X 3.5W

PLATE 1571
TAYLOR
c.1940, Fairmont Stormguide
Barometer, Hygrometer and Thermometer
Bakelite: Black w/Chrome Trim
5H X 7.75W

PLATE 1572
TAYLOR
c.1940, Winton Combination
AC Electric, New Haven Clock w/Barometer
Bakelite: Black w/Chrome Trim
5H X 7.75W

PLATE 1573
TAYLOR
c.1940, Fisherman's Barometer
Barometer
Plastic: Black w/Snap-On Lid and Chrome Trim
3.5 Square

PLATE 1574
TAYLOR
c.1940, Kenmore Baroguide
Barometer
Metal: Bronze
3.5H X 6.5W

TAYLOR

PLATE 1575
TAYLOR
c.1940, Renwick Baroguide
Barometer
Wood: Ivory w/Bronze Trim
3.5 H

PLATE 1576
TAYLOR
c.1940, Stratford Stormoguide
Barometer
Wood: Black Lacquer w/Chrome Trim
6H X 5W

PLATE 1577
TAYLOR
c.1940, Ultra Humiguide
Hygrometer
Wood: Walnut
5.5 Square

PLATE 1578
TAYLOR
c.1940, Tremont Combination
Barometer, Hygrometer and Thermometer
Wood: Walnut w/Gold Trim
11.75 W

PLATE 1579
TAYLOR
c.1940, Warwick Stormoguide
Barometer
Wood: Mahogany w/Brass
5H X 7.5W

PLATE 1580
TAYLOR
c.1940, Voyager Baroguide
Barometer
Wood: Walnut w/Brass
6.75 Diameter

PLATE 1581
TAYLOR
c.1940, Yacht Stormoguide
Barometer
Metal: Brass
6.5 Diameter

PLATE 1582
TAYLOR
c.1940, Yacht Stormoguide
Barometer
Wood, Walnut w/Brass
6.5 Diameter

TAYLOR

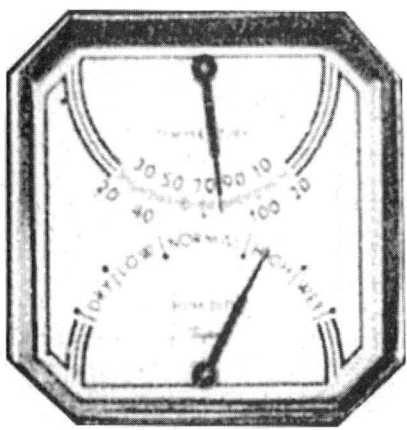

PLATE 1583
TAYLOR
c.1942, Combination
Hygrometer and Thermometer
Bakelite: Black w/Chrome
3.25 Square

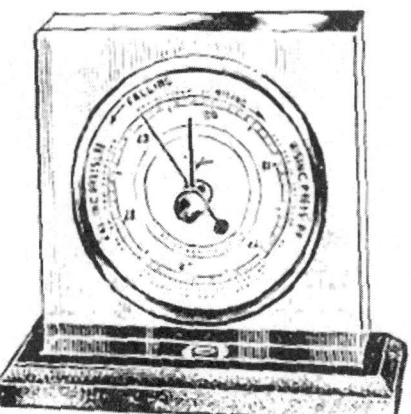

PLATE 1584
TAYLOR
c.1950, Baroguide
Barometer
Acrylic: Clear Top, Gold Base
5H X 4W

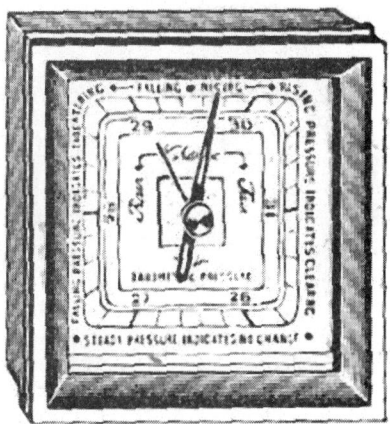

PLATE 1585
TAYLOR
c.1950, Baroguide
Barometer
Plastic: Ivory w/Gold Trim
4 Square

PLATE 1586
TAYLOR
c.1947, Humidiguide
Barometer, Hygrometer and Thermometer
Metal: Ivory w/Chrome Trim
5H X 7.75W

PLATE 1587
TAYLOR
c.1951, Combo Stormoguide
Barometer, Hygrometer and Thermometer
Bakelite: Black w/Chrome
5.25H X 8W X 2.25D

PLATE 1588
TAYLOR
c.1959, Combo Stormoguide
Barometer, Hygrometer and Thermometer
Wood: Dark or Blonde
6.5H X 10.25W

PLATE 1589
TAYLOR
c.1963, Ambassador
Barometer, Hygrometer and Thermometer
Wood: Mahogany w/Brass
5.5H X 9W

TAYLOR · TELECHRON

PLATE 1590
TAYLOR
c.1963, Aquila
Barometer, Hygrometer and Thermometer
Wood: Mahogany w/Brass
5H X 10.75W

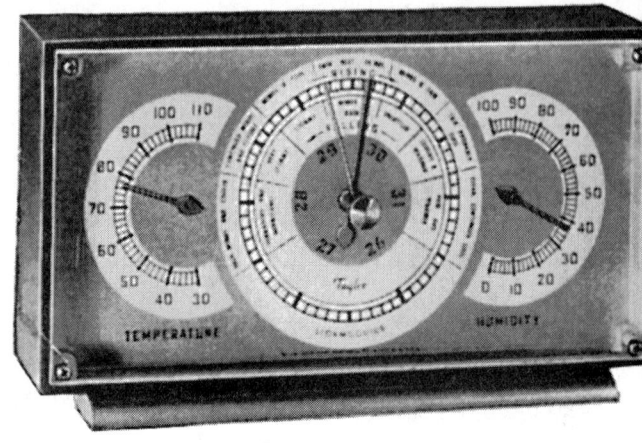

PLATE 1591
TAYLOR
c.1963, Consul
Barometer, Hygrometer and Thermometer
Wood: Gold Lacquer
3.5H X 7W

PLATE 1592
TAYLOR
c.1963, Fremont
Barometer, Hygrometer and Thermometer
Wood: Walnut w/Brass
5H X 8W

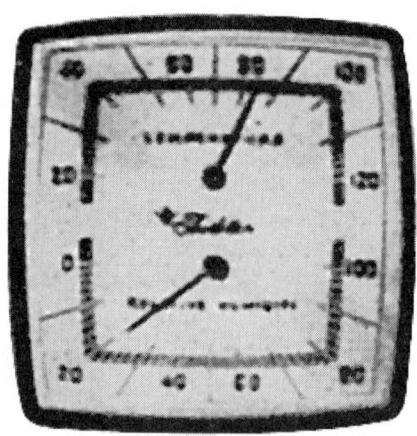

PLATE 1593
TAYLOR
c.1965, Combination
Hygrometer and Thermometer
Plastic: Grey
3.75 Square

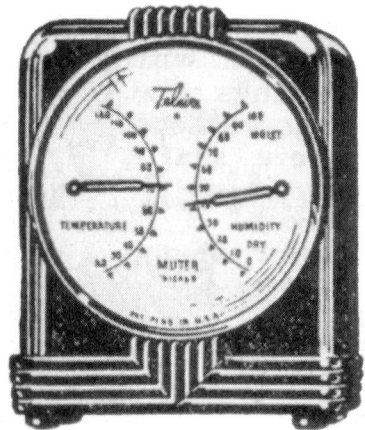

PLATE 1594
TELAIRE
c.1935, Telaire
Hygrometer and Barometer
Bakelite: Brown or Black

PLATE 1595
TELECHRON
c.1939, 8B-51, Controlla
AC Electric, Clock w/Appliance Switch
Bakelite: Walnut

PLATE 1596
TELECHRON
c.1939, 8B-53, Organizer
AC Electric, Clock w/Appliance Switch
Bakelite: Walnut
6.25H X 5.25W X 3.5D

TELECHRON · TORK·TIME

PLATE 1597
TELECHRON
c.1947, 8HA-55, Selector
AC Electric, Clock w/Appliance Switch, Alarm
Bakelite, Walnut
5.5H X 5.25W

PLATE 1598
TELECHRON
c.1947, 8HA-61, Switch Alarm
AC Electric, Clock w/Radio Switch
Bakelite: Walnut
5 Square

PLATE 1599
TELECHRON
c.1948
AC Electric Clock w/Timer and Alarm
Plastic: White
3.5H

PLATE 1600
TEMP ALERT
c.1942, Air Pilot
Barometer and Thermometer
Metal: Ivory
3.25 H

PLATE 1601
TEMP ALERT
c.1942, Bath Thermometer
Thermometer
Pink or Blue
3.25 Diameter

PLATE 1602
TEL·TRU
c.1940, Desk Thermometer
Thermometer
Plaskon: Ivory w/Chrome Trim
3 H

PLATE 1603
THERMODEX
c.1942, Fountain Pen
Pen w/Thermometer Base
Bakelite: Black or Walnut

PLATE 1604
TIME LITE
c.1929
Electric Time Switch
1-Day Wind Clock w/Appliance Switch
Metal: Bronze

PLATE 1605
TORK·TIME
c.1929
Time Clock
AC Electric Clock w/Appliance
Switch

TOWER · WESTINGHOUSE

PLATE 1606
TOWER
c.1954
Hygrometer and Thermometer
Plastic: Black or Ivory
4.5 Square

PLATE 1607
TOWER
c.1954
Barometer
Plastic: Black or Ivory
4.5 Square

PLATE 1608
TOWER
c.1954
Indoor/Outdoor Thermometer
Plastic: Black or Ivory
4.5 Square

PLATE 1609
WALTHAM
c.1939, Combination
AC Electric Clock w/Barometer
Wood: Walnut w/Silver
5.5H X 13W

PLATE 1610
WALTHAM
c.1940, Barometer Set
AC Electric Clock and Barometer
Wood: Mahogany w/Brass
8H X 18W

PLATE 1611
WARD
c.1941
Barometer and Thermometer
Metal, Grey
3.5H

PLATE 1612
WESTCLOX
c.1952, Switch Alarm
AC Electric Clock w/Appliance Switch
Metal: Ivory
5H X 4.75W

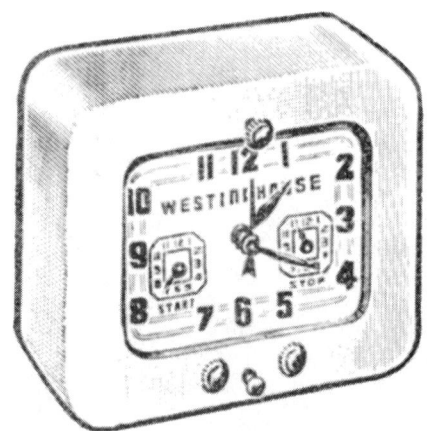

PLATE 1613
WESTINGHOUSE
c.1950, Appliance Timer
AC Electric Clock w/Appliance Switch and Alarm
Metal: Baked White Enamel
4.25H X 5.25W

APPENDIX NO. 1
MARKET VALUES: CLOCKS

Plate #	Brand Name	Year	Model No.	Model Name	Variation(s)	Value	Page
0001	Aldine	1930	9212		Mahogany	75	17
0002	Aristocrat	1951	6828	Minuet	Red	50	17
					Blue	50	17
0003	Aristocrat	1951	6844	Fleetwood	Ivory	90	17
					Black	100	17
0004	Artcraft	1931			Green	70	17
					Rose	70	17
0005	Autodex	1940	700	Clock Index	Walnut	125	17
0006	Autodex	1940	701	Clock Index	Mahogany	125	17
0007	Autodex	1940	702	Clock Calindex	Walnut	125	17
0008	Barr	1938		Digital	Ivory	125	17
0009	Belmont	1932	2820	Boudoir	Blue	250	17
					Green	200	17
					Lavender	350	17
					Ivory	150	17
0010	Bugle Boy	1934	2460	Modernistic	Brown w/Chrome Trim	200	18
0011	Bugle Boy	1936	6207		Green	50	18
					Green w/ Luminous Dial	60	18
					Black	40	18
					Black w/Luminous Dial	50	18
					Copper	60	18
					Copper w/Luminous Dial	70	18
0012	Bugle Boy	1937	1800	Octagon	Rose	90	18
					Green	80	18
					Ivory	70	18
0013	Bugle Boy	1939	1652		Black w/Chrome	100	18
					Ivory w/Brass	75	18
0014	Bugle Boy	1939	1655		Ivory	100	18
					Green	125	18
0015	Bugle Boy	1939	1656	Claridge	Ivory	60	18
					Pink	70	18
					Green	60	18
0016	Bugle Boy	1939	1657		Ivory	50	18
					Red	60	18
					Green	65	18
0017	Bugle Boy	1939	1658		Ivory	125	18
					Maroon	150	18
					Green	150	18
0018	Bugle Boy	1939	1659	Commander	Ivory w/Brass	75	18
					Grey w/Chrome	85	18
0019	Bugle Boy	1939			Ivory	50	19
					Green	60	19
					Coral	75	19
0020	Bugle Boy	1939	1650, 1651		Ivory	75	19
					Green	90	19
					Red	95	19
0021	Bugle Boy	1940	5154	Defender	Black	60	19
					Green	50	19
0022	Bugle Boy	1940	5155	Non-Tip	Ivory	70	19
					Green	80	19
					Coral	90	19
0023	Bugle Boy	1940	5156	Landscape	Ivory	100	19
					Green	125	19

Plate #	Brand Name	Year	Model No.	Model Name	Variation(s)	Value	Page
0024	Bugle Boy	1940	5157	Dome Style Rotary	Ivory	300	19
					Antique Bronze	325	19
0025	Bugle Boy	1940	5162	Round Thin	Ivory	75	19
					Black	100	19
0026	Bugle Boy	1940	8916	Footed Octagon	Ivory	90	19
					Green	100	19
					Mahogany	80	19
0027	Bugle Boy	1940	8917	Chum	Ivory w/Tan Base	100	19
					Black w/Tan Base	125	19
0028	Bugle Boy	1940	8918	Gabled Top	Ivory	60	20
					Black	80	20
0029	Bugle Boy	1940	8920	Console	Ivory	50	20
					Black	60	20
0030	Bugle Boy	1940	8922	Valley Brook	Ivory	100	20
					Green	125	20
					Blue	135	20
0031	Bugle Boy	1940	8923	Fireside (Animated)	Ivory	125	20
					Green	150	20
					Blue	160	20
0032	Bugle Boy	1940	8925	Horsehoe	Chrome	125	20
0033	Bugle Boy	1941	7568	4-In-1 Calendar	Chrome	375	20
0034	Bugle Boy	1941	7574	The Flag Waves		125	20
0035	Bugle Boy	1942	5202	Stylized Square	Ivory	70	20
					Black	60	20
					Brown	50	20
0036	Bugle Boy	1942	5204	Thin Streamlined	Ivory	75	20
					Brown	50	20
0037	Bugle Boy	1942	6581		Ivory	60	21
					Ivory w/Luminous Dial	75	21
					Black	75	21
					Black w/Luminous Dial	90	21
0038	Bugle Boy	1951	3463	Swinging Girl		175	21
0039	Bugle Boy	1951	3464	Swinging Playmates		200	21
0040	Bugle Boy	1951	3535	Fireball	Ivory	50	21
					Black	60	21
0041	Bugle Boy	1951	3576	Home Sweet Home		175	21
0042	Bugle Boy	1951	3581	Bank Clock	Ivory	250	21
0043	Bulova	1935	1209	Skyscraper	Walnut and Maple	250	21
0044	Cheiftan	1940		Executive	Walnut	100	21
0045	Chelsea	1947	7382	Manhattan	Walnut	40	21
0046	Chelsea	1947	7383	Clinton	Bronze	100	22
0047	Chelsea	1947	7384	Alden	Brass	50	22
0048	Clinton	1955	1		Gold	40	22
0049	Clinton	1955	2		Black and Gold	40	22
0050	Clinton	1955	6		Silver and Gold	75	22
0051	Clinton	1955	7		Green	40	22
					Blue	40	22
					Red	40	22
					Tan	40	22
0052	Clinton	1955	14	Cigarette Holder	Gold	60	22
0053	Comet	1930			Nickel	75	22
					Nickel w/Luminous Dial	90	22
0054	Comet	1930	1264, 1265		Nickel	65	22
					Nickel w/Luminous Dial	75	22
0055	Connecticut	1932			Walnut	75	23
0056	Connecticut	1932			Black	50	23
0057	Connecticut	1932	52, 53		Black	75	23
					Ivory	95	23
0058	Cutey	1929			Ivory	40	23
					Green	50	23
					Pink	55	23
0059	DeLuxe	1931	194	Pendulette	Green	200	23
					Blue	200	23
					Pink	210	23
					Lavender	250	23
0060	DeLuxe	1932		Organ Grinder	Brass	300	23
					Green	325	23
					Blue	325	23
					Pink	325	23

Plate #	Brand Name	Year	Model No.	Model Name	Variation(s)	Value	Page
0061	Deluxe	1932	151	Gothic	Mahogany	90	23
0062	DeLuxe	1932	167	Junior	Green	125	23
					Blue	135	23
					Pink	135	23
0063	Deluxe	1932	337, 437	Boudoir, Desk	Black w/Nickel	100	23
0064	DeLuxe	1932	582		Brass	65	24
					Green	75	24
					Blue	75	24
					Pink	75	24
0065	Deluxe	1932	1781	Gothic	Mahogany	90	24
0066	Deluxe	1932	1782	Elite	Mahogany	90	24
0067	Deluxe	1932	1783	Doric	Mahogany	110	24
0068	Deluxe	1934	432		Walnut	150	24
0069	DeLuxe	1938	951		Ivory	90	24
					Green	100	24
					Black	100	24
0070	DeLuxe	1938	954		Ivory	50	24
0071	DeLuxe	1938	1054		Ivory w/Gold	75	24
					Black w/Nickel	110	24
0072	DeLuxe	1939	1660	Skyline	Ivory w/Gold	90	24
					Black w/Gold	100	24
					Walnut w/Gold	80	24
0073	Deluxe	1939	8591		Chrome plated	150	25
0074	Deluxe	1939	8595			125	25
0075	DeLuxe	1939	8606			135	25
0076	Deluxe	1940	688, 689		Chrome	150	25
0077	Deluxe	1940	8568		Walnut	100	25
0078	Deluxe	1940	5806	Swinging	Chrome	250	25
0079	Deluxe	1942		Esquire	Ivory	60	25
					Ivory w/Luminous Dial	70	25
					Black	80	25
					Black w/Luminous Dial	90	25
0080	DeLuxe	1942	1052		Ivory	75	25
					Black	100	25
0081	Dinson	1951	6852	Jeweled	Gold	85	25
0082	Dinson	1952	6834		Ivory	50	26
0083	Duokron	1932	535, 536		Green	85	26
					Blue	85	26
					Ivory	75	26
					Red	90	26
0084	Edwards & Co.	1937		Tower	Walnut and Maple	125	26
0085	Elexa	1941			Brass and Black	65	26
0086	Elexa	1941			Black and Clear	85	26
0087	Eltime	1932	2835	B	Nickel	75	26
0088	Eltime	1934	46107, 6605	Utility	Walnut	175	26
					Walnut w/Luminous Dial	195	26
0089	Eltime	1934	4628, 4828	Dresser	Chrome w/Black	325	26
					Chrome w/White	300	26
0090	Empress	1932	3505	Empress	Crystalline Green	150	26
					Crystalline Black	150	26
					Crystalline Ivory	130	26
					Crystalline Pink	175	26
0091	Fashion	1931		Easel	Rose	100	27
					Green	95	27
					Blue	95	27
0092	Forestville	1962	3300	Tambourine		45	27
0093	Gable	1933			Black	80	27
0094	General Electric	1930	604	Brittany	Mahogany	75	27
0095	General Electric	1931	3F-54	Super Hostess	Green w/Chrome	125	27
0096	General Electric	1931	3F-56	Vogue	Copper w/Black	110	27
					Chrome w/Black	125	27
0097	General Electric	1931	3F-60	Fleet	Green	110	27
					Ivory	100	27
					Black	90	27
0098	General Electric	1931	7F-52	Morning Star	Black	125	27
					Ivory	140	27

Plate #	Brand Name	Year	Model No.	Model Name	Variation(s)	Value	Page
0099	General Electric	1931	7F-56	Radium Vendette	Ivory	125	27
					Ivory w/Luminous Dial	150	27
					Black	100	27
					Black w/Luminous Dial	110	27
0100	General Electric	1931	7F-58	Lumalarm	Black	150	28
					Ivory	175	28
0101	General Electric	1932	5		Mahogany	60	28
0102	General Electric	1932	28		Mahogany	70	28
0103	General Electric	1932	52	Petite	Black	150	28
0104	General Electric	1932	57		Black	150	28
0105	General Electric	1932	7F-62	Englewood	Mahogany	65	28
0106	General Electric	1933	8B-02	Executive	Brown w/Brass Face	250	28
					Black w/Silver Face	300	28
0107	General Electric	1934	3F-58	Secretary	Mahogany with Marquetry Inlay	80	28
0108	General Electric	1935	3F-64	Wellfleet	Green	90	28
					Ivory	80	28
					Black	80	28
0109	General Electric	1935	4F-60	Rex	Blue Mirror w/Chrome Bezel	250	29
0110	General Electric	1935	7F-52	Morning Star	Ivory	125	29
					Ivory w/Luminous Dial	130	29
					Black	100	29
					Black w/Luminous Dial	110	29
0111	General Electric	1935	8B-04	New Executive	Black	350	29
					Walnut	300	29
0112	General Electric	1936	3F-70	Park Avenue	Zebrawood w/Black Trim	150	29
0113	General Electric	1936	4F-52	Debutante	Chrome	110	29
					Brass	100	29
0114	General Electric	1936	4F-58	Lotus	Chrome w/Black Bakelite	325	29
0115	General Electric	1936	4F-62	Blue Night	Blue Mirror	250	29
0116	General Electric	1936	4F-64	Blue Night	Blue Mirror	200	29
0117	General Electric	1936	4F-66	Blue Night	Blue Mirror	225	29
0118	General Electric	1936	5F-50	Mirage	Ivory reverse painted glass	225	30
					Black reverse painted glass	250	30
0119	General Electric	1936	7F-60	Morning Glory	Mahogany	75	30
0120	General Electric	1936	7F-70	Overseer	Mahogany	85	30
0121	General Electric	1936	7F-72	Heralder	Black	100	30
					Mahogany	75	30
0122	General Electric	1936	8B-06	Budgeteer	Mahogany w/Brass	125	30
0123	General Electric	1937	3F-72	Brevet	Mahogany	60	30
0124	General Electric	1937	3F-74	Duncan	Black	75	30
					Blue	125	30
0125	General Electric	1937	3H-78	Basque	Butterscotch Catalin	250	30
					Black Catalin	275	30
0126	General Electric	1937	3H-80	Morgan	Mahogany	70	30
0127	General Electric	1937	4H-68	Tuileres	Blue Mirror	275	31
					Peach Mirror	325	31
0128	General Electric	1937	5F-54	Salon	White w/Silver	325	31
0129	General Electric	1937	5F-56	Soiree	White w/Silver	325	31
0130	General Electric	1937	5F-58	Ecstacy	Cobalt Mirror	225	31
					Light Blue-Grey Mirror	250	31
0131	General Electric	1937	7F-74	Heralder	Black Bakelite with Brass Trim	150	31
0132	General Electric	1937	7F-76	Geneva	Cobalt Mirror	150	31
					Light Blue-Grey Mirror	175	31
					Silver Mirror	125	31
0133	General Electric	1937	7H-82	Sophist	Mahogany	100	31
0134	General Electric	1938	5F-60	Ecstacy	Cobalt Mirror	125	31
					Light Blue-Grey Mirror	150	31
0135	General Electric	1938	5H-64	Lorraine	Blue Mirror	125	31
					Peach Mirror	150	31
0136	General Electric	1938	6H-02	Alencon	Blue Mirror	400	32
					Peach Mirror	500	32
0137	General Electric	1938	7H-86	Warburton	Tortoise Catalin	300	32
					Alabaster Catalin	325	32
0138	General Electric	1938	7H-88	Dawning	Cobalt Mirror	125	32
					Light Blue-Grey Mirror	150	32
0139	General Electric	1938	7H-90	Eldorado	Blue Mirror	275	32
					Peach Mirror	325	32

Plate #	Brand Name	Year	Model No.	Model Name	Variation(s)	Value	Page
0140	General Electric	1939	3H-88	World's Fair	Walnut	150	32
0141	General Electric	1939	3H-90	Norfolk	Striped Veneer with Back base	175	32
0142	General Electric	1939	3H-92	New Lorraine	Striped Veneer with Back base	150	32
0143	General Electric	1939	4H-72	Breton	White	425	32
0144	General Electric	1939	4H-78	Ballard	Brass	80	32
0145	General Electric	1939	4H-80	Tuscan	Walnut and Zebrawood	150	33
0146	General Electric	1939	4H-84	Athens	Walnut	75	33
0147	General Electric	1939	7H-78	Acorn	Black	90	33
					Walnut	75	33
0148	General Electric	1939	7H-80	Julep	Pink Catalin	350	33
					Ivory Catalin	225	33
0149	General Electric	1939	7H-92	Circe	White w/Silver	425	33
0150	General Electric	1939	7H-94	Sergeant	Ivory	110	33
					Ivory w/Luminous Dial	125	33
					Black	100	33
					Black w/Luminous Dial	110	33
0151	General Electric	1939	7H-95	Colonade	2-Tone	125	33
0152	General Electric	1939	8H-76	Ithaca	Black	80	33
					Walnut	60	33
0153	General Electric	1940	3H-152	Sherwood	Mahogany	75	33
0154	General Electric	1940	3H-158	Gay	Walnut	65	34
0155	General Electric	1940	7H-98	Corporal	Ivory	60	34
					Brown	50	34
0156	General Electric	1940	7H-102	Ashby	Blue Mirror	115	34
					Peach Mirror	140	34
0157	General Electric	1940	7H-104	Hesperas	White	95	34
0158	General Electric	1940	7H-110	Orpheus	Brass	100	34
0159	General Electric	1940	7H-112	Gallant	Brass	70	34
0160	General Electric	1941	3H-98	Navigator	Ivory	75	34
					Walnut	75	34
0161	General Electric	1941	3H-154	Saddle		60	34
0162	General Electric	1941	3H-156	Narcissus	White	90	34
0163	General Electric	1941	3H-162	Thrill	Walnut	100	35
0164	General Electric	1941	3H-164	Bounty	Walnut	45	35
0165	General Electric	1941	3H-166	Nimbus	Walnut and Maple	65	35
0166	General Electric	1941	4H-76	Sampson	Walnut	175	35
0167	General Electric	1941	7H-106	Morning Glory	Nickel	75	35
0168	General Electric	1941	7H-118	Troubador	Walnut	60	35
					Ivory	75	35
0169	General Electric	1941	7H-120	Modern	Walnut	50	35
0170	General Electric	1941	8H-14	Almanac	Mahogany	70	35
0171	General Electric	1942	6B-14	Winthrop	Mahogany	75	35
0172	General Electric	1942	8B-10	Framingham	Walnut	125	36
0173	General Electric	1946	7H-132	Brisk	Mahogany w/Black	60	36
0174	General Electric	1946	7H-134	Helper	Ivory	150	36
0175	General Electric	1947	7H-136	Gay Hour	Butterscotch Catalin	175	36
0176	General Electric	1947	7H-138	Chipper	Walnut	95	36
0177	General Electric	1947	7H-142	Contact	Faux Leather	60	36
0178	General Electric	1947	7H-160	Heralder	Ivory	80	36
					Ivory w/Luminous Dial	85	36
0179	General Electric	1947	7H-164	Beau	Walnut	50	36
0180	General Electric	1948	7H-196	New Heralder	Ivory	80	36
0181	General Electric	1949	3H-176	Geneva	Mahogany	65	37
					Birch	75	37
0182	General Electric	1949	3H-180	Voyager	Brown Catalin	125	37
0183	General Electric	1949	6B-20	Ridgefield	Mahogany	75	37
0184	General Electric	1949	7H-154	Chantilly	Ivory	65	37
0185	General Electric	1949	7H-166	Morning Glory	Silver and Brass	80	37
0186	General Electric	1949	7H-170	Morning Star	Ivory	50	37
0187	General Electric	1949	7H-170	Morning Star	Ivory	40	37
0188	General Electric	1950	7H-174	The Informer	Ivory	35	37
0189	General Electric	1950	7H-180	The Chipper	Ivory	45	37
0190	General Electric	1950	7H-190	Gay	Ivory	35	38
0191	General Electric	1951		Repeater	Ivory	50	38
0192	General Electric	1951	7H-116	Orderly	Ivory	65	38
					Walnut	50	38
0193	General Electric	1951	7H-188	Candlewick	Mahogany	40	38

Plate #	Brand Name	Year	Model No.	Model Name	Variation(s)	Value	Page
0194	General Electric	1951	7H-192	Wink	Ivory	30	38
0195	General Electric	1951	7H-194	Nudger	Ivory	25	38
0196	General Electric	1951	7H-198	Lumalarm	Ivory	40	38
0197	General Electric	1951	7H-204	Tweed	Brass	30	38
0198	General Electric	1951	7H-208	Riser	Ivory	20	39
0199	General Electric	1951		Clansman	White	20	39
0200	General Electric	1953	7H-213	Perspective	Black w/Gold Trim	225	39
0201	General Electric	1953	7H-220	Starter	Ivory	15	39
0202	General Electric	1953		Woodsman	Mahogany	20	39
0203	General Electric	1954	5H-70	Higgins Glass	Handblown Higgins Glass	750	39
0204	General Electric	1954	7H-216	Brite-Dial	Black	30	39
0205	General Electric	1954	7H-217	Telecrat	Ivory	20	39
0206	General Electric	1954	7H-224	Partner	Gold	25	39
0207	General Electric	1954	7H-228	Architect	Mahogany	20	39
0208	General Electric	1954	7H-232	Caller	White	20	40
0209	General Electric	1954	7H-226	Urban	Ivory	20	40
0210	General Electric	1955	7H-215	Decor	Birch	25	40
0211	General Electric	1955	7H-225	Luminary	Ivory	15	40
0212	General Electric	1955	7H-236	Revelation	Walnut	75	40
0213	General Electric	1955		Versatile	Red	60	40
					Yellow	55	40
					White	50	40
					Walnut	40	40
0214	General Electric	1956	2H-103	Cupboard	Red	45	40
					Yellow	40	40
					White	25	40
					Walnut	20	40
0215	General Electric	1956	7H-204	Tweed	Brass	20	40
0216	General Electric	1956	7H-223	Room-Mate	Ivory	10	40
0217	General Electric	1956	7H-233	Circlewood	Mahogany	20	41
0218	General Electric	1957		Galaxy	Pink	40	41
0219	General Electric	1957		Keynote	White	20	41
					Yellow	35	41
					Red	40	41
0220	General Electric	1957		Radial	Tan	20	41
0221	General Electric	1957		Snooz-Alarm	Grey	10	41
0222	General Electric	1958		Concord	Mahogany	20	41
0223	General Electric	1958		Chorus	Mahogany	30	41
0224	General Electric	1958		Little Snooz	Grey	10	41
0225	General Electric	1958		Scope	Grey	50	41
0226	General Electric	1958		Tempo	Ivory	20	42
0227	General Electric	1958		Trend	Red	40	42
					Black	20	42
0228	General Electric	1958		Tune Alarm	Mahogany	50	42
0229	General Electric	1958		Twinkle	Mahogany	35	42
0230	General Electric	1958		Twinkle	Mahogany	15	42
0231	General Electric	1958		Warbler	Mahogany	15	42
0232	General Electric	1958		Lumalarm	Ivory	30	42
0233	General Electric	1960		Royal Snooz	Tan	25	42
0234	General Electric	1960		Snooze	White	10	42
0235	General Electric	1960		Snooze	Mahogany	40	43
0236	General Electric	1960		Soft Tick	Ivory	30	43
0236	General Electric	1960		Wakewood	Blond	20	43
					Mahogany	15	43
0238	General Electric	1960	7381K	Atomic	Pink	100	43
0239	General Electric	1960		Twin Bell	Brass	25	43
0240	General Electric	1960			Ivory	20	43
0241	General Electric	1960			White	10	43
0242	Gilbert	1931			Brass	110	43
0243	Gilbert	1931			Green	50	43
					Blue	60	43
					Red	60	43
0244	Gilbert	1931			Green	60	44
					Blue	70	44
					Red	70	44

Plate#	Brand Name	Year	Model No.	Model Name	Variation(s)	Value	Page
0245	Gilbert	1931			Green	60	44
					Green w/Luminous Dial	70	44
					Blue	70	44
					Blue w/Luminous Dial	75	44
					Red	70	44
					Red w/Luminous Dial	75	44
					Nickel	70	44
					Nickel w/Luminous Dial	75	44
0246	Gilbert	1932	605		Black and Nickel	150	44
0247	Gilbert	1932	414		Black and Nickel	90	44
0248	Gilbert	1932				75	44
0249	Gilbert	1932			Green	90	44
					Blue	95	44
					Rose	95	44
0250	Gilbert	1932			Green	80	44
					Blue	80	44
					Rose	85	44
0251	Gilbert	1933			Green	50	44
					Blue	60	44
					Rose	65	44
0252	Gilbert	1933			Green	50	44
					Blue	60	44
					Red	60	44
0253	Gilbert	1934		Salute	Green	70	45
					Blue	75	45
					Pink	80	45
0254	Gilbert	1934			Mahogany	75	45
0255	Gilbert	1934	940, 941		Green	75	45
					Pink	85	45
0256	Gilbert	1934		Mogul	Chrome and Black	200	45
					Ivory or Black	125	45
0257	Gilbert	1934			Green	65	45
					Blue	70	45
					Pink	75	45
0258	Gilbert	1935			Green	70	45
					Blue	75	45
					Pink	80	45
0259	Gilbert	1936			Ivory	45	45
					Nickel	125	45
0260	Gilbert	1936			Green w/Ivory	90	45
0261	Gilbert	1937	947, 968		Black	70	45
					Black w/Luminous Dial	75	45
					Green	60	45
					Green w/Luminous Dial	65	45
0262	Gilbert	1938	956	Little Gilbert	Ivory w/Gold	60	46
					Black w/Nickel	75	46
0263	Gilbert	1938	908, 909		Ivory w/Gold	90	46
					Black w/Nickel	125	46
0264	Gilbert	1939	1202, 1203		Ivory w/Gold	75	46
					Rust w/Gold	80	46
					Green w/Nickel	95	46
0265	Gilbert	1939			Rose	70	46
					Green	60	46
					Black	60	46
					Ivory	50	46
0267	Gilbert	1939			Rose	90	46
					Green	80	46
					Ivory	60	46
0268	Gilbert	1940		Calender	Black	150	46
0269	Gilbert	1940		Charlie McCarthy	Ivory	350	46
0270	Gilbert	1940			Mahogany	75	46
0271	Gilbert	1941	982		Ivory	65	47
					Black	75	47
0272	Gilbert	1942	333		Ivory	50	47
0273	Gilbert	1942		Bell	Ivory	60	47
					Ivory w/Luminous Dial	70	47
					Black	70	47
					Black w/Luminous Dial	80	47

Plate#	Brand Name	Year	Model No.	Model Name	Variation(s)	Value	Page
0274	Gilbert	1942		Modern	Ivory	50	47
					Black	60	47
0275	Gilbert	1942			Ivory	75	47
					Black	75	47
0276	Gilbert	1947			Ivory	30	47
0277	Gilbert	1948			Ivory	35	47
0278	Gilbert	1949		Trophy	Ivory w/Gold	25	47
					Ivory w/Gold w/Luminous Dial	30	47
0279	Gilbert	1950			Ivory	80	47
					Ivory w/Luminous Dial	85	47
					Black w/Chrome	150	47
					Black w/Chrome w/Luminous Dial	160	47
0280	Gilbert	1951		Sovereign	Ivory	75	48
					Ivory w/Luminous Dial	85	48
0281	Gilbert	1952			Ivory	30	48
					Ivory w/Luminous Dial	35	48
0282	Gilbert	1962	1265	Sprite	Ivory	50	48
					Black	70	48
					Green	65	48
					Pink	65	48
0283	Gilbert	1962	1266	Vanguard	Ivory	20	48
					Ivory w/Luminous Dial	25	48
					Black	30	48
					Black w/Luminous Dial	35	48
					Green	30	48
					Green w/Luminous Dial	35	48
					Pink	30	48
					Pink w/Luminous Dial	35	48
0284	Gilbert	1962		Nite-Glo	Ivory	20	48
0285	Gilbert	1962		Square Model	Ivory	25	48
0286	Gilbert	1962		Startime	Ivory	20	48
					Ivory w/Luminous Dial	25	48
					Black	30	48
					Black w/Luminous Dial	35	48
					Green	30	48
					Green w/Luminous Dial	35	48
					Pink	30	48
					Pink w/Luminous Dial	35	48
0287	Gilbert	1962			Ivory	40	48
					Green	50	48
					Tan	40	48
0288	Gilbert	1965		Coronet	Nickel	25	48
0289	Gold Shield	1942	World Time			50	49
0290	Gordon	1938	1076		Black	125	49
0291	Haddon	1962	156	Linear	24k Gold	150	49
0292	Haddon	1962	705	Vision	24k Gold	100	49
0293	Hamilton	1934	S-402	Sangamo	Alabaster w/Black & Green	225	49
0294	Hamilton	1935	S404	Sangamo Skyscraper	Various Exotic Veneers	200	49
0295	Hammond	1931		Old Dutch		125	49
0296	Hammond	1931		Petite		100	49
0297	Hammond	1931		Octagon	White Onyx	150	49
0298	Hammond	1931		Boudoir	Black & White Onyx	175	50
0299	Hammond	1931		Double Director	Black & White Onyx	225	50
0300	Hammond	1931		Arcadia	Mahogany	125	50
0301	Hammond	1931		Knickerbocker		125	50
0302	Hammond	1931		Melody	Black & White Onyx	250	50
0303	Hammond	1931		Columbia	Mahogany	225	50
0304	Hammond	1931		Duchess	White & Green Onyx	225	50
0305	Hammond	1931		Avondale	Walnut	100	50
0306	Hammond	1931		Skyline	Black & White Onyx	350	50
0307	Hammond	1931		Parisian	Green Onyx	125	51
0308	Hammond	1931		Valencia	Rance & Black	150	51
0309	Hammond	1931		Double Executive	Green Onyx	225	51
0310	Hammond	1931		Ruff	White Onyx	110	51
0311	Hammond	1931		Seneca	Green & Black Onyx	200	51
0312	Hammond	1931		Beacon	Walnut	125	51
					Black	150	51

Plate #	Brand Name	Year	Model No.	Model Name	Variation(s)	Value	Page
0313	Hammond	1931		Glenmora	Walnut	150	51
0314	Hammond	1931		Gregory/Calender	Black	175	51
					Walnut	150	51
0315	Hammond	1931		Logan	Walnut	90	51
0316	Hammond	1931		Oakwood	Walnut	110	52
0317	Hammond	1931		Sherwood	Mahogany	100	52
0318	Hammond	1931			Mahogany	95	52
0319	Hammond	1931			Mahogany	95	52
0320	Hammond	1931			Mahogany	150	52
0321	Hammond	1932		Firefly	Walnut	90	52
					Ivory	110	52
					Green	125	52
					Black	125	52
0322	Hammond	1932			Walnut	90	52
0323	Hammond	1932			Walnut	125	52
0324	Hammond	1933		Gloria	Chrome w/Green Face	175	52
					Chrome w/Pink Face	175	52
0325	Hammond	1934		Tower-Modernistic	Silver and Black	250	53
0326	Hammond	1934		Grenadier	Chrome w/Black	150	53
0327	Hammond	1934		Paris	Brown	75	53
					Black	95	53
					Ivory	90	53
0328	Hammond	1934		Polo Alarm	Chrome	140	53
0329	Hammond	1936		Falcon	Brown	75	53
					Black	90	53
0330	Hammond	1936		Modern Firefly	Ivory	125	53
					Black	125	53
0331	Hammond	1937		Empress	Black & Chrome w/Blue Mirror	350	53
0332	Hammond	1937		Firefly?	Ivory	110	53
0333	Hammond	1938		Tripoli	Mahogany	125	53
0334	Hammond	1938		Aurora	Burl Maple	175	54
					Orientalwood	200	54
0335	Hammond	1938		Chancellor	Walnut	125	54
0336	Hammond	1938		Courtier	Walnut	125	54
0337	Hammond	1938		Diplomat	Redwood	125	54
					Maple	135	54
0338	Hammond	1939		Regent	White	90	54
0339	Hammond	1939		Edgemont	Chrome	125	54
0340	Hammond	1939			Blue Mirror	250	54
0341	Hammond	1939		Asbury	Ivory w/Gold	95	54
					Black w/Chrome	110	54
0342	Hammond	1939		Cathay	Ivory	100	54
0343	Hammond	1940			Green	110	55
0344	Hammond	1940			Blue Mirror	275	55
0345	Hammond	1940			Blue Mirror	225	55
0346	Hammond	1941			White Onyx	100	55
0347	Hammond	1941			White Onyx	150	55
0348	Hammond	1941		Arc of Time	White Onyx	125	55
0349	Hammond	1941		Dayton	Mahogany	125	55
0350	Hammond	1941		Fantasy	Ivory	75	55
0351	Hammond	1941		Mentor	Mahogany	75	55
0352	Hammond	1941		Luna	Mahogany	65	56
0353	Hammond	1941		Pilot	Walnut	90	56
0354	Hammond	1941		Riviera	Satin Gold	150	56
0355	Harmony House	1946	7076		Walnut	25	56
					Ivory	30	56
0356	Harmony House	1951	7086		Mahogany	50	56
0357	Harmony House	1951	7029, 7032	Modern	Mahogany	40	56
					Mahogany w/Luminous Dial	45	56
0358	Harmony House	1951	7048, 7056	Precision	Mahogany	30	56
					Mahogany w/Luminous Dial	35	56
					Ivory	35	56
					Ivory w/Luminous Dial	40	56
					Black	40	56
					Black w/Luminous Dial	45	56

Plate#	Brand Name	Year	Model No.	Model Name	Variation(s)	Value	Page
0359	Harmony House	1951	7063, 7064	Junior	Pink	40	56
					Pink w/Luminous Dial	45	56
					Ivory	30	56
					Ivory w/Luminous Dial	35	56
					Sky Blue	40	56
					Sky Blue w/Luminous Dial	45	56
0360	Harmony House	1952	7011, 7012	Extra Thin	Ivory	50	56
					Ivory w/Luminous Dial	55	56
0361	Harmony House	1953	7110		Ivory	15	57
0362	Harmony House	1953	7013, 7014	square design	Ivory	20	57
					Ivory w/Luminous Dial	25	57
0363	Harmony House	1954	7040	Modern	Ivory	40	57
					Pink	50	57
					Blue	50	57
0364	Harmony House	1954	7035, 7036	Designer	Ivory	20	57
					Ivory w/Luminous Dial	25	57
0365	Harmony House	1959	7068	Daisy Boutique	Ivory	25	57
0366	Harmony House	1959	7069		Ivory	20	57
0367	Harmony House	1959	7070		Gold	20	57
0368	Harmony House	1959	7082		Ivory	20	57
					Beige	25	57
0369	Harmony House	1959	7151	Add-a-Nap	White	20	57
0370	Harmony House	1959	7155	Add-a-Nap	Mahogany	15	58
0371	Harmony House	1959	7107, 7108		Ivory	15	58
					Ivory w/Luminous Dial	20	58
0372	Harmony House	1959	7140, 7141	shadow box crystal	Ivory	40	58
					Ivory w/Luminous Dial	45	58
					White	40	58
					White w/Luminous Dial	45	58
					Pink	60	58
					Pink w/Luminous Dial	65	58
0373	Havlin	1930		Kennerly	Walnut	60	58
0374	Havlin	1930		Mary Lou	Walnut	65	58
0375	Havlin	1931	1033		Walnut	70	58
0376	Havlin	1931	1038		Walnut	60	58
0377	Havalarm	1932		Havalarm Delux	Walnut	90	58
0378	Herman Miller	1931	4018		Mahogany	250	58
0379	Herman Miller	1931	4197		Mahogany	225	59
0380	Herman Miller	1933	TR410	Rohde Des.	Mahogany	1000	59
0381	Herman Miller	1933	TR410	Rohde Des.	Mahogany w/Illuminated Dial	1200	59
0382	Herman Miller	1931	4776		Walnut	1500	59
0383	Herman Miller	1931	4784		Mahogany	1750	59
0384	Herman Miller	1931	5187		Mahogany	250	59
0385	Herman Miller	1933		Square (Rohde Des.)	Chrome	400	59
0386	Herman Miller	1936			Walnut	1500	59
0387	Herman Miller	1936			White	1500	59
					Black	1750	60
0389	Herman Miller	1936			Walnut	2200	60
0390	Herschede	1932	2053	French Gothic Style	Mahogany	225	60
0391	Herschede	1932	6046	Sheraton	Mahogany w/Maple	325	60
0392	Herschede	1932	6078	Sheraton-Colonial	Mahogany	325	60
0393	Herschede	1933	2005	Colonial	Mahogany	300	60
0394	Herschede	1933	2011	Gothic	Mahogany	300	60
0395	Herschede	1933	2013	Sheraton-Colonial	Mahogany	225	60
0396	Herschede	1933	2023	Gothic	Mahogany	250	61
0397	Herschede	1933	2035	Colonial	Walnut w/Redwood	300	61
0398	Herschede	1933	2041	Moderne	Rosewood w/Green catalin	325	61
0399	Herschede	1933	2047	Sheraton-Colonial	Maple	325	61
0400	Herschede	1933	2051	Louis XVI	Walnut w/Satinwood inlay	425	61
0401	Herschede	1933	3002	Gothic	Mahogany	175	61
0402	Herschede	1933	3004	Colonial	Mahogany	175	61
0403	Herschede	1933	6002	Sheraton	Brass finials	350	61
0404	Herschede	1933	6012	Gothic	Mahogany	300	61
0405	Herschede	1933	6016	Gothic	Mahogany	300	62
0406	Herschede	1933	6018	Georgian	Mahogany w/Maple	275	62
0407	Herschede	1933	6020	Louis XIV	Walnut	300	62
0408	Herschede	1933	6028	Chippendale	Mahogany	300	62

Plate#	Brand Name	Year	Model No.	Model Name	Variation(s)	Value	Page
0409	Herschede	1933	6040	Gothic	Mahogany	275	62
0410	Herschede	1933	6062	Moderne	Amboyna w/Ivory	425	62
0411	Herschede	1963	2177	Warren	Cherry	65	62
0412	Howard	1939	5468	Mariner	Chrome	150	62
0413	Howard	1939	5469	Horseshoe-Good Luck	Chrome	175	62
0414	Howell Lamp	1957	797	Future	Black	125	63
					Blue	125	63
0415	Howell Lamp	1957	800	Embassy	Blue	100	63
					White	100	63
0416	Howell Lamp	1957	1617	Musicale	White	100	63
					Black	100	63
0417	Howell Lamp	1957	801	Moderne	Pink	125	63
					Blue	125	63
0418	Imperial	1947		Zephyr	Black w/Ivory Fins	275	63
					Ivory w/Red Fins	325	63
0419	Ingersol	1931	10		Mahogany	100	63
0420	Ingersol	1931	15		Mahogany	110	64
0421	Ingersol	1931	20		Mahogany	125	64
0422	Ingersol	1931	30		Mahogany	110	64
0423	Ingersol	1931	35		Mahogany	150	64
0424	Ingersol	1931	40		Mahogany	175	64
0425	Ingersol	1931	150		Mahogany	110	64
0426	Ingersol	1931	151		Mahogany	115	64
0427	Ingersol	1931	250		Mahogany	110	64
0428	Ingersol	1931	251		Mahogany	110	64
0429	Ingersol	1931		Photo Traveler	Blue	60	65
					Red	60	65
					Pink	60	65
					Tan	60	65
					Green	60	65
0430	Ingersol	1931		Traveler	Blue	50	65
					Red	50	65
					Pink	50	65
					Tan	50	65
					Green	50	65
0431	Ingersol	1933		Pilot	Black	60	65
0432	Ingersol	1934	420	Mickey Mouse	Red	400	65
					Green	450	65
0433	Ingersol	1934			Black	80	65
0434	Ingersol	1934	426	Dollar	Chrome	65	65
0435	Ingersol	1934		Big Bad Wolf	Red	250	65
0436	Ingersol	1934			Teal w/Brass	225	65
0437	Ingersol	1936	2122		Green w/Chrome	90	65
					Black w/Chrome	110	65
0438	Ingersol	1936	2123		Green	75	66
					Black	75	66
0439	Ingersol	1936	2147		Green	70	66
0440	Ingersol	1936	2148	Daintie	Green	75	66
					Brass	70	66
0441	Ingersol	1936	2149	Daybreak	Chrome w/Black	90	66
					Ivory w/Gold	70	66
0442	Ingersol	1936	2150	Petite	Chrome w/Brass	75	66
					Black w/Chrome	90	66
0443	Ingersol	1936	2482	Measuring Tape	Black w/Chrome	175	66
					Copper w/Chrome	150	66
0444	Ingersol	1936	2482R	Gable	Black w/Chrome	90	66
0445	Ingersol	1947	6828, 6830		Red	60	66
					Red w/Luminous Dial	65	66
					Green	60	66
					Green w/Luminous Dial	65	66
					Grey	50	66
					Grey w/Luminous Dial	55	66
					Blue	60	66
					Blue w/Luminous Dial	65	66
0446	Ingersol	1947			Ivory	50	66
					Green	65	66
					Navy	65	66
					Yellow	65	66
					Mahogany	50	66

Plate #	Brand Name	Year	Model No.	Model Name	Variation(s)	Value	Page
0447	Ingersol	1949	414	AMI	Ivory	45	67
					Ivory w/Luminous Dial	50	67
					Green	60	67
					Green w/Luminous Dial	65	67
					Navy	60	67
					Navy w/Luminous Dial	65	67
					Mahogany	45	67
					Mahogany w/Luminous Dial	50	67
0448	Ingersol	1951		Sunrise	White	40	67
0449	Ingraham	1930		Cathedral	Mahogany	175	67
0450	Ingraham	1930		Colonial	Mahogany	250	67
0451	Ingraham	1930		Elton	Mahogany	100	67
0452	Ingraham	1932		Classic	Green	90	67
					Blue	90	67
					Ivory	80	67
0453	Ingraham	1932			Pink	75	67
					Green	75	67
					Blue	75	67
0454	Ingraham	1932			Mahogany	250	67
0455	Ingraham	1932			Mahogany	350	67
0456	Ingraham	1932		Automatic	Black	100	68
					Black w/Luminous Dial	110	68
					Chrome	90	68
					Chrome w/Luminous Dial	95	68
					Green	100	68
					Green w/Luminous Dial	115	68
0457	Ingraham	1933		Ace	Black	100	68
					Chrome	90	68
					Green	110	68
0458	Ingraham	1933		Ace Luminous	Black	110	68
					Chrome	95	68
					Green	115	68
0459	Ingraham	1933		Ace	Ivory	90	68
					Green	100	68
					Black	100	68
					Chrome	95	68
0460	Ingraham	1933		Commander	Walnut	125	68
0461	Ingraham	1933		Magic	Black	75	68
					Ivory	65	68
					Chrome	125	68
0462	Ingraham	1933		Modern	Black & Nickel	175	68
					Black & Nickel w/Lum. Dial	200	68
					Walnut and Copper	150	68
					Walnut & Copper w/Lum. Dial	165	68
0463	Ingraham	1933		Modern	Black w/ Nickel	90	68
					Black w/ Nickel w/Lum. Dial	100	68
					Green w/Nickel	95	68
					Green w/Nickel w/Lum. Dial	105	68
					Ivory w/Gold	85	68
					Ivory w/Gold w/Lum. Dial	90	68
0464	Ingraham	1933			Mahogany	250	68
0465	Ingraham	1933			Walnut	110	69
0466	Ingraham	1933			Chrome	350	69
0467	Ingraham	1933			Mahogany	125	69
0468	Ingraham	1934		Non-Tip Base	Blue w/Nickel	175	69
					Green w/Nickel	175	69
0469	Ingraham	1934		Commander	Chrome	150	69
					Black w/Chrome	150	69
0470	Ingraham	1934			Walnut	135	69
0471	Ingraham	1935		Calais	Mahogany	175	69
0472	Ingraham	1935		Timemaster	Chrome and Black	125	69
					Chrome & Black w/Lum. Dial	135	69
0473	Ingraham	1935		Stylewood	Walnut with Marquetry Inlay	125	69
0474	Ingraham	1935			Black w/Gold trim	60	70
					Ivory w/Gold trim	50	70
0475	Ingraham	1935	SC-323		Walnut	150	70
0476	Ingraham	1935	SD-321		Walnut	125	70

Plate#	Brand Name	Year	Model No.	Model Name	Variation(s)	Value	Page
0477	Ingraham	1936		Bullet	Black	100	70
					Rose	125	70
					Green	125	70
					Ivory	100	70
0478	Ingraham	1936		Claridge	Ivory	150	70
					Black	175	70
0479	Ingraham	1936		Dover	Walnut	150	70
0480	Ingraham	1936		Gothic	Walnut	225	70
0481	Ingraham	1936		Meteor	Black	75	70
					Ivory	65	70
					Rose	85	70
					Green	85	70
0482	Ingraham	1936		Penguin	Black w/ Nickel	175	70
					Green w/Nickel	175	70
					Ivory w/Gold	150	70
0483	Ingraham	1936	SSC-3	Self-Starting Upright	Walnut	150	71
0484	Ingraham	1936		Victory	Nickel	90	71
					Nickel w/Luminous Dial	100	71
					Black	95	71
					Black w/Luminous Dial	105	71
0485	Ingraham	1936		X-Ray/Round	Green	70	71
					Green w/Luminous Dial	75	71
					Nickel	90	71
					Nickel w/Luminous Dial	95	71
0486	Ingraham	1936		X-Ray/Square	Black w/ Nickel	75	71
					Pink w/ Nickel	80	71
					Green w/Nickel	80	71
					Ivory w/Gold	65	71
0487	Ingraham	1936		X-Ray/Square Lum.	Black w/Nickel	80	71
					Green w/Nickel	85	71
					Pink w/Nickel	85	71
					Ivory w/Gold	70	71
0488	Ingraham	1936			Black w/Nickel	70	71
					Green w/Nickel	75	71
					Pink w/Nickel	75	71
					Ivory w/Gold	65	71
0489	Ingraham	1936			Black	60	71
					Green	65	71
					Pink	65	71
0490	Ingraham	1936			Mahogany	125	71
0491	Ingraham	1936	SSD-1		Walnut	250	71
0492	Ingraham	1936			Ivory w/Nickel	100	72
					Green w/Nickel	125	72
					Black w/Nickel	135	72
0493	Ingraham	1937		Fireball	Black	60	72
					Black w/Luminous Dial	65	72
					Ivory	50	72
					Ivory w/Luminous Dial	55	72
0494	Ingraham	1937		Gable	Black and Chrome	150	72
0495	Ingraham	1937		Modern	Ivory	40	72
					Ivory w/Luminous Dial	45	72
0496	Ingraham	1937		Penguin	Black w/Nickel	150	72
					Green w/Nickel	150	72
0497	Ingraham	1937	2-3W	Radio	Walnut w/Green Inlay	750	72
					Walnut w/Red Inlay	800	72
0498	Ingraham	1937	D-157	Skyscraper	Walnut	375	72
0499	Ingraham	1937	C-154		Walnut	175	72
0500	Ingraham	1937			Blue	75	72
					Pink	75	72
					Green	75	72
0501	Ingraham	1937			Ivory	30	73
					Black	25	73
0502	Ingraham	1937			Black w/ Nickel	125	73
					Green w/Nickel	115	73
					Ivory w/Gold	100	73
0503	Ingraham	1938		Arcade	Black	90	73
					Rose	90	73
					Ivory	85	73
					Green	90	73

Plate #	Brand Name	Year	Model No.	Model Name	Variation(s)	Value	Page
0504	Ingraham	1938		Eagle	Ivory w/Yellow	110	73
					Ivory w/Yellow w/Lum. Dial	115	73
					Ivory w/Walnut	110	73
					Ivory w/Walnut w/Lum. Dial	115	73
0505	Ingraham	1938		Fleetwood	Black	100	73
					Ivory	90	73
					Green	110	73
					Chrome	150	73
0506	Ingraham	1938		Master	Chrome	60	73
0507	Ingraham	1938		Radium	Nickel	95	73
0508	Ingraham	1938		Victorian	Black	90	73
					Black w/Luminous Dial	100	73
					Ivory	80	73
					Ivory w/Luminous Dial	90	73
0509	Ingraham	1938	SSD-3	World's Fair	Mahogany	250	73
0510	Ingraham	1938	A-210		Walnut	125	74
0511	Ingraham	1938	SSD-2		Walnut	275	74
0512	Ingraham	1938		X-Ray	Black	75	74
					Ivory	65	74
					Green	80	74
0513	Ingraham	1938		X-Ray Luminous	Black	80	74
					Ivory	70	74
					Green	85	74
0514	Ingraham	1938			Ivory w/Gold	75	74
0515	Ingraham	1938			Walnut	150	74
0516	Ingraham	1938			Black w/Nickel	85	74
					Black w/Nickel w/Lum. Dial	90	74
					Green w/Nickel	90	74
					Green w/Nickel w/Lum. Dial	95	74
					Ivory w/Gold	80	74
					Ivory w/Gold w/Lum. Dial	85	74
0517	Ingraham	1939		Cadet	Ivory	90	74
					Black	110	74
					Walnut	90	74
					Coral	125	74
					Nickel	175	74
0518	Ingraham	1939		Cascade	Ivory	75	74
					Green	90	74
					Nickel	150	74
0519	Ingraham	1939		Classic	Blue	100	75
					Green	100	75
					Ivory	80	75
					Nickel	150	75
0520	Ingraham	1939		Guard	Black	75	75
					Walnut	60	75
					Ivory	65	75
0521	Ingraham	1939		Mayfair	Walnut	135	75
0522	Ingraham	1939		Overland	Black	70	75
					Pink	75	75
					Green	75	75
					Ivory	60	75
0523	Ingraham	1939		Salute	Rose	75	75
					Green	75	75
					Blue	80	75
0524	Ingraham	1939		Sentry	Black	125	75
					Brown	110	75
					Ivory	110	75
					Chrome	90	75
0525	Ingraham	1939		Skyline	Black	110	75
					Ivory	90	75
					Rose	125	75
					Brown	90	75
					Chrome	190	75
0526	Ingraham	1939		York	Walnut	125	75
0527	Ingraham	1939	SA-12		Green Catalin	250	75
					Yellow Catalin	225	75
0528	Ingraham	1939			Black w/Chrome	50	76
					Ivory w/Gold	40	76

Plate #	Brand Name	Year	Model No.	Model Name	Variation(s)	Value	Page
0529	Ingraham	1939			Walnut	75	76
0530	Ingraham	1939		Upright	Walnut	100	76
0531	Ingraham	1939			Green w/Nickel	85	76
					Ivory w/Gold	75	76
0532	Ingraham	1939			Walnut	125	76
0533	Ingraham	1939			Walnut	125	76
0534	Ingraham	1939			Walnut	150	76
0535	Ingraham	1939			Black	75	76
					Black w/Luminous Dial	80	76
					Ivory	65	76
					Ivory w/Luminous Dial	70	76
0536	Ingraham	1939			Black	75	76
					Ivory	65	76
0537	Ingraham	1940		Chilton	Black	90	77
					Black w/Luminous Dial	100	77
					Ivory	80	77
					Ivory w/Luminous Dial	90	77
0538	Ingraham	1940		Miracle-Tone	Walnut w/Green Inlay	275	77
					Walnut w/Red Inlay	300	77
0539	Ingraham	1940		Two-In-One	Nickel	80	77
0540	Ingraham	1940	SD-180		Walnut	70	77
0541	Ingraham	1940			Walnut	90	77
0542	Ingraham	1940			Walnut	110	77
0543	Ingraham	1940	SSD-4		Walnut w/Green Inlay	275	77
					Walnut w/Red Inlay	300	77
0544	Ingraham	1940			Walnut	250	77
0545	Ingraham	1940			Nickel	90	77
					Ivory	75	77
0546	Ingraham	1940			Black	80	78
					Ivory	70	78
0547	Ingraham	1940			Walnut	85	78
					Maple	110	78
0548	Ingraham	1941		Ace Skyscraper	Walnut	150	78
0549	Ingraham	1941		Beacon	Ivory	60	78
					Black	70	78
					Nickel	75	78
0550	Ingraham	1941		Commander	Ivory w/Gold	75	78
					Ivory w/Gold w/Luminous Dial	85	78
0551	Ingraham	1941		Federal	Black	75	78
					Ivory	65	78
0552	Ingraham	1941		New Rite-Vu	Ivory	70	78
					Brown	65	78
					Gold	75	78
					Nickel	125	78
0553	Ingraham	1941		New Time Ball Clock	Chrome w/Black	250	78
					Gold w/Black	225	78
0554	Ingraham	1941		Wakemaster	Black	45	78
					Black w/Luminous Dial	50	78
					Ivory	35	78
					Ivory w/Luminous Dial	40	78
0555	Ingraham	1941			Ivory	60	79
					Black	70	79
0556	Ingraham	1941			Walnut	70	79
0557	Ingraham	1941			Walnut	100	79
0558	Ingraham	1941			Black	75	79
					Green	70	79
					Ivory	60	79
0559	Ingraham	1941			Walnut	150	79
0560	Ingraham	1941			Walnut	125	79
0561	Ingraham	1941			Walnut	125	79
0562	Ingraham	1941			Gold	100	79
					Nickel	110	79
0563	Ingraham	1941			Butterscotch Catalin	225	79
					Brown Catalin	250	79
					Green Catalin	275	79
0564	Ingraham	1942		Antique Replica	Walnut	50	80
0565	Ingraham	1942		Broadcast	Ivory	65	80

Plate#	Brand Name	Year	Model No.	Model Name	Variation(s)	Value	Page
0566	Ingraham	1942		Midget	Nickel	85	80
					Ivory	70	80
					Black	85	80
0567	Ingraham	1942		Modern	Walnut	125	80
0568	Ingraham	1942		Utility Alarm	Ivory	40	80
0569	Ingraham	1942			Ivory	75	80
					Black	85	80
0570	Ingraham	1942			Ivory	60	80
					Black	70	80
0571	Ingraham	1942			Walnut	60	80
0572	Ingraham	1942			Walnut	75	80
0573	Ingraham	1946		Sentinel	Ivory	60	81
0574	Ingraham	1947			Ivory	50	81
0575	Ingraham	1948		Belle-alarm	Ivory w/gold	40	81
					Ivory w/gold w/Luminous Dial	45	81
0576	Ingraham	1948		Night 'n' Day	Ivory w/gold trim	60	81
					Ivory w/gold w/Luminous Dial	65	81
0577	Ingraham	1948		Yearling	Ivory	110	81
					Brown	110	81
0578	Ingraham	1949		Ace	Ivory w/Gold	60	81
0579	Ingraham	1949		Guard	Black	75	81
					Walnut	60	81
					Ivory	70	81
0580	Ingraham	1949			Ivory	45	81
					Ivory w/Luminous Dial	50	81
0581	Ingraham	1950		Sentinel	Ivory	35	81
0582	Ingraham	1950		Sentinel	Ivory	40	82
0583	Ingraham	1950		Princess	Ivory	60	82
0584	Ingraham	1950			Walnut	110	82
0585	Ingraham	1951		Roy Rogers	Green	225	82
					Sky Blue	250	82
					Walnut	200	82
					Tan	225	82
0586	Ingraham	1957		Eagle	Ivory	60	82
					Brown	50	82
0587	Jefferson	1956		Golden Hour	Gold	100	82
0588	Jefferson	1956		Golden Helm	Gold	150	82
					Chrome	175	82
0589	Jefferson	1956		Golden Secret	Gold	250	82
0590	Jefferson	1963			Chrome	75	82
0591	Jefferson	1963			Black	75	83
0592	Jewelite	1963			Gold	110	83
0593	Klok-Tenna	1930		Klok Tenna	Walnut	150	83
0594	Lackner	1935		Neon Glo	Butterscotch Catalin	1200	83
					Brown Catalin	1500	83
					Red Catalin	1700	83
					Green Catalin	1500	83
0595	Lackner	1935		Neon Glo	Maple	100	83
0596	Lackner	1938		Pedestal	Brown	600	83
					Black	750	83
0597	Lackner	1939		Nassau	Walnut	850	83
0598	Lackner	1941			Walnut w/Acrylic	450	83
0600	Lawson	1932		Zephyr	Brass w/Nickel	750	84
					Copper w/Nickel	900	84
0601	Lawson	1933	215		Walnut w/Brass	225	84
0602	Lawson	1934		Moderne Desk	Copper w/Brass	350	84
0603	Lawson	1934		Pyramid	Copper	350	84
0604	Lawson	1939	303	Streamline	Bronze	200	84
0605	Lawson	1935	480	Futurist	Brass and Bronze	400	84
0606	Lectrolarm	1932			Walnut	125	85
0607	Lincoln	1932		Gothic No.1	Mahogany	80	85
0608	Lincoln	1932		No. 80	Walnut	75	85
0609	Lincoln	1932		B	Walnut	95	85
0610	Lincoln	1932		No.490	Mahogany	125	85
0611	Lincoln	1932		No.191	Walnut	225	85
0612	Louis	1956		La Moderne	Black	400	85
0613	Lux	1930			Green	90	85
					Blue	90	85
					Nickel	100	85

Plate #	Brand Name	Year	Model No.	Model Name	Variation(s)	Value	Page
0614	Lux	1930			Nickel	125	86
0615	Lux	1930			Green	100	86
					Rose	100	86
0616	Lux	1930			Ivory	110	86
					Rose	125	86
0617	Lux	1930			Orchid	150	86
					Green	115	86
					Rose	125	86
0618	Lux	1931		Chilton	Ivory	90	86
					Brown	80	86
0619	Lux	1932			Nickel	110	86
0620	Lux	1933	70		Black and Nickel	125	86
0621	Lux	1933	71	Gothic	Black and Nickel	125	86
0622	Lux	1933	72		Mahogany	60	86
0623	Lux	1933	74		Black and Nickel	75	87
0624	Lux	1933		DeLuxe	Walnut	60	87
0625	Lux	1933		Patriot	White	60	87
0626	Lux	1935		Tape Measure	Brass	125	87
0627	Lux	1933		Gong	Chrome	150	87
0628	Lux	1938		Vendome Alarm	Ivory	125	87
					Blue	150	87
					Green	160	87
					Maroon	150	87
0629	Lux	1938		Spinning Wheel	Ivory	125	87
					Green	150	87
					Black	125	87
					Maroon	150	87
0630	Lux	1938		Streamline	Ivory	75	87
					Black	100	87
					Green	110	87
					Maroon	110	87
					Rose	125	87
0631	Lux	1939		Apollo	Ivory	90	87
					Green	100	87
					Black	125	87
0632	Lux	1939		Chatham	Ivory w/Brass trim	75	88
0633	Lux	1939		Chatham	Mahogany	60	88
0634	Lux	1939		Modern Eight	Green w/Chrome	160	88
					Black w/ Chrome	150	88
0635	Lux	1941	948	Esquire/Round	Ivory	60	88
					Black	75	88
					Green	65	88
0636	Lux	1941	907	Esquire/Square	Ivory	65	88
					Black	75	88
					Pink	75	88
					Beige	65	88
0637	Lux	1940	949	Utopia	Ivory	65	88
					Black	80	88
					Green	70	88
0638	Lux	1941	978		Ivory	75	88
					Black	80	88
					Tan	75	88
0639	Lux	1942	336	Symphony	Walnut	125	88
0640	Lux	1942		Pyramid	Ivory	125	89
					Black	150	89
0641	Lux	1947			Ivory	60	89
					Black	75	89
0642	Lux	1951	323		Green	65	89
					Tan	60	89
0643	Lux	1962	243		Ivory w/Gold	60	89
0644	Lux	1962	240	Wren	Ivory	40	89
0645	Lux	1962	385		Ivory	30	89
0646	Lux	1962	995	Occasional Calender	Black	40	89
0647	Lux	1962		Gabriel	Brass	40	89
0648	Lux	1965		Conquerer	Ivory	40	89
0649	Lyceum	1940			Green	35	90
					Blue	35	90

Plate#	Brand Name	Year	Model No.	Model Name	Variation(s)	Value	Page
0650	Lyceum	1940			Pink	40	90
					Green	35	90
					Blue	35	90
0651	Lyceum	1940			Blue	35	90
					Black	35	90
					Green	35	90
0652	Manning-Bwmn	1932	907		Green w/Chrome	250	90
0653	Manning-Bwmn	1934	911		Walnut	150	90
0654	Marlboro	1932		Easel	Green	100	90
					Rose	110	90
0655	Mastercrafters	1955	9	La Moderne	Mahogany	75	90
0656	Mastercrafters	1955	47	Flying Cloud	Walnut	125	90
0657	Mastercrafters	1960	49	Starlight	Gold	110	90
0658	Mastercrafters	1955	4740	Waterfall	Gold	175	91
0659	Mastercrafters	1955	244	Dorell	Gold	110	91
0660	Mastercrafters	1955	913	Estate	Gold	75	91
0661	Mastercrafters	1955	425	Frell	Walnut	125	91
0662	Mastercrafters	1955	506	Benler	Walnut	125	91
0663	Mastercrafters	1955	830	Dean	Gold	75	91
0664	Mastercrafters	1955	272	Fireplace	Walnut	150	91
0665	Mastercrafters	1955	551	Swinging Playmates	Walnut	200	91
					Onyx	225	91
0666	Mastercrafters	1955	920	Merry-Go-Round	Walnut	225	91
					Onyx	250	91
0667	Mastercrafters	1963	1907	Country Church	White	50	92
					Gold	60	92
0668	Mastercrafters	1963	2074	Pot Belly	Black	60	92
0669	Mastercrafters	1963	2254, 2255		Black	75	92
0670	Match King	1936		Imperial	Chrome	325	92
0671	McCracken	1933			Chrome	110	92
0672	National Call	1930	8501		Chrome	90	92
					Green	100	92
					Blue	100	92
					Rose	110	92
0673	National Call	1930	8517		Mahogany	110	92
					Blue	125	92
					Green	125	92
0674	National Call	1932	8513	Monterey	Green	90	92
					Rose	95	92
0675	National Call	1932	8542	Patriot	Green	65	92
					Blue	65	92
					Rose	75	92
					Black	70	92
0676	National Call	1932	8601	Thin	Green	75	93
					Blue	75	93
					Rose	80	93
					Black	80	93
0677	National Call	1932	8645		Walnut or Black	125	93
0678	National Call	1932	8650		Walnut	125	93
0679	National Call	1934	8533	thin model new style	Black w/Nickel	150	93
0680	National Call	1936	8501	Jubilee Special	Green	90	93
					Green w/Luminous Dial	100	93
					Blue	90	93
					Blue w/Luminous Dial	100	93
					Rose	100	93
					Rose w/Luminous Dial	110	93
					Black	100	93
					Black w/Luminous Dial	110	93
0681	National Call	1936	8550		Ivory	65	93
0682	National Call	1936	8508	Modern Square	Ivory	100	93
					Ivory w/Luminous Dial	110	93
0683	National Call	1938	8501		Ivory w/Gold	80	93
					Black w/Nickel	100	93
					Red w/Nickel	100	93
					Green w/Nickel	100	93
					Blue w/Nickel	100	93
0684	National Call	1938	8577		Walnut	125	93

Plate#	Brand Name	Year	Model No.	Model Name	Variation(s)	Value	Page
0685	National Call	1940	8578, 8580		Black	125	94
					Ivory	110	94
0686	National Call	1940	8583		Ivory	50	94
0687	National Call	1940			Black	90	94
					Coral	100	94
0688	National Call	1951	7066, 7067	Belle-Alarm	Ivory	40	94
					Ivory w/Luminous Dial	45	94
0689	National Call	1951	7317	Home Sweet Home	Ivory	175	94
					Walnut	175	94
0690	National Call	1952	7322	Skipper	Brass	150	94
0691	National Call	1951	7361	Rancho	Walnut	125	94
0692	National Call	1953	7066		Ivory	125	94
					Ivory w/Luminous Dial	45	95
0693	National Call	1953	7004	Utility	Ivory	40	95
0694	National Call	1953	7344		Mahogany	30	95
0695	National Call	1953	7171, 7172		Mahogany	25	95
0696	National Call	1954	7044		Ivory	45	95
0697	National Call	1954	7134		Mahogany	35	95
0698	National Call	1954	7300	Waterfall	Walnut	175	95
0699	National Call	1954	7377	Ballerina	Mahogany	200	95
0700	National Call	1954	7095		Ivory	50	95
0701	National Call	1957	7034, 7033		Ivory	20	96
					Ivory w/Luminous Dial	25	96
0702	National Call	1959	7040		Brass	20	96
0703	National Call	1959	7028, 7049	Pedestal Base	Ivory	20	96
					Ivory w/Luminous Dial	25	96
0704	New Haven	1928		Specialty	Brass	150	96
0705	New Haven	1929		Nouveau	Brass	125	96
0706	New Haven	1930		Art Alarm	Walnut 4.25H	90	96
					Walnut 2.75H	110	96
0707	New Haven	1930		Tat-Too Junior	Green	100	96
					Green w/Luminous Dial	105	96
					Blue	100	96
					Blue w/Luminous Dial	105	96
0708	New Haven	1930		Abbey Artlarm	Mahogany	125	96
					Mahogany w/Luminous Dial	135	96
0709	New Haven	1930		Library	Green Catalin	250	96
0710	New Haven	1930		Gothic Easel	Mahogany	200	97
0711	New Haven	1930		Eldon	Mahogany w/Maple	125	97
0712	New Haven	1930		Electric Tatoo	Nickel w/Black	125	97
0713	New Haven	1930		Eureka	Nickel w/Black	75	97
0714	New Haven	1930		Good Cheer	Mahogany	75	97
0715	New Haven	1930		Lantern	Copper	175	97
0716	New Haven	1930		Pownal	Green Catalin	250	97
0717	New Haven	1931		Pandora	Mahogany	150	97
0718	New Haven	1931		Ideal	Nickel	110	97
					Brass	100	97
					Ivory	90	97
0719	New Haven	1931			Green	110	98
0720	New Haven	1931		Artlarm Octagon	Green	100	98
					Green w/Luminous Dial	110	98
					Red	120	98
					Red w/Luminous Dial	130	98
0721	New Haven	1931		Artlarm Square	Green	60	98
					Green w/Luminous Dial	65	98
					Blue	60	98
					Blue w/Luminous Dial	65	98
0722	New Haven	1931			Nickel	75	98
					Nickel w/Luminous Dial	80	98
0723	New Haven	1931		Cloister	Mahogany	225	98
0724	New Haven	1931		Don Garcia	Cream	120	98
0725	New Haven	1931		Don Pio Pico	Cream w/Black	125	98
0726	New Haven	1931		Don Santee	Cream w/Black	175	98
0727	New Haven	1931		Elwood	Mahogany	65	98
0728	New Haven	1931		Grenadier	Mahogany	75	99
0729	New Haven	1931		Inca	Mahogany	75	99
0730	New Haven	1931		Mentor	Mahogany	110	99

Plate#	Brand Name	Year	Model No.	Model Name	Variation(s)	Value	Page
0731	New Haven	1931		Palas	Green w/Black	150	99
0732	New Haven	1931		Penrose	Mahogany	100	99
0733	New Haven	1931		Preston	Green w/Black	225	99
0734	New Haven	1931			Mahogany	100	99
0735	New Haven	1931			Orchid	150	99
					Green	125	99
					Rose	125	99
0736	New Haven	1931			Walnut 3.5H	135	99
					Walnut 5.25H	125	99
0737	New Haven	1931			Nickel	75	100
0738	New Haven	1932		Don Louis	Onyx	125	100
0739	New Haven	1932		Don Pedro	Onyx	125	100
0740	New Haven	1932		Tattoo	Nickel w/Black	125	100
0741	New Haven	1932		Burton	Walnut	150	100
0742	New Haven	1932			Nickel	90	100
0743	New Haven	1932		Colored Glass	Various Colors	150+	100
0744	New Haven	1932			Green w/Brass	125	100
0745	New Haven	1932			Nickel w/Black	125	100
0746	New Haven	1932		Den	Green w/Black	150	101
0747	New Haven	1933	25		Black w/Gold	275	101
0748	New Haven	1933	56		Catalin and Onyx	225	101
0749	New Haven	1933	124		Walnut	75	101
					Black	90	101
0750	New Haven	1933	4604		Black	80	101
0751	New Haven	1933	4606		Chrome	125	101
0752	New Haven	1933	4608		Mahogany	125	101
0753	New Haven	1933	4609	Stylis	Mahogany	275	101
0754	New Haven	1933		Adare	Gold and Chrome	250	101
0755	New Haven	1933			Black w/Nickel	125	102
					Black w/Nickel w/Lum. Dial	135	102
					Green w/Nickel	100	102
					Green w/Nickel w/Lum. Dial	110	102
					Rose w/Nickel	100	102
					Rose w/Nickel w/Lum. Dial	110	102
0756	New Haven	1933		Geometric-3 Tier	Walnut w/Maple	200	102
0757	New Haven	1933		Geometric-Round	Walnut w/Maple	225	102
0758	New Haven	1933		Geometric-Skyscraper	Walnut w/Maple	175	102
0759	New Haven	1936		Hand Bag Watch	Black	75	102
0760	New Haven	1936	900	Boudoir Alarm	Walnut	75	102
0761	New Haven	1936	904	Keyless Alarm	Silver	125	102
0762	New Haven	1936	906		Grey	60	102
0763	New Haven	1936	927	Popeye	Ivory w/Black trim	300	102
0764	New Haven	1936	928	New Style	Black w/Nickel plated	75	102
0765	New Haven	1936	933	Midget Alarm	Chrome	90	103
0766	New Haven	1936	2781		Jade Catalin	225	103
					Amber Catalin	175	103
0767	New Haven	1936		Little Octagon	Ivory	80	103
					Ivory w/Luminous Dial	90	103
0768	New Haven	1936		Slumber Stopper	Chrome	110	103
0769	New Haven	1938	955	Spinning Wheel	Green	150	103
					Ivory	125	103
0770	New Haven	1938		Mars	Walnut	75	103
					Ivory	85	103
0771	New Haven	1938		Rhonda	Gold	200	103
0772	New Haven	1939	571	Ideal	Ivory	90	103
					Chrome	125	103
					Gold	110	103
0773	New Haven	1939	572	Seaman	Mahogany	100	104
0774	New Haven	1939			Walnut	75	104
0775	New Haven	1939			Walnut	75	104
0776	New Haven	1939			Walnut	90	104
0777	New Haven	1939			Blue Mirror	125	104
0778	New Haven	1939			Blue Mirror	150	104
0779	New Haven	1939			Ivory	125	104
					Brown	125	104
0780	New Haven	1939	378, 384	Ideal Junior	Ivory	90	104
					Chrome	125	104
					Gold	110	104

Plate #	Brand Name	Year	Model No.	Model Name	Variation(s)	Value	Page
0781	New Haven	1939		Silent Secretary	Walnut w/Gold	75	104
0782	New Haven	1939		Colonial Highboy	Mahogany	225	105
0783	New Haven	1939		Streamliner	Mahogany	500	105
0784	New Haven	1940	383	Bantry	Black w/Chrome	100	105
					Ivory w/Brass	90	105
0785	New Haven	1940	494	Lone Ranger	Black	275	105
0786	New Haven	1940	640		Walnut	110	105
0787	New Haven	1940	647		Walnut	150	105
0788	New Haven	1940	676	Tele-List and Clock	Walnut w/Brass trim	150	105
0789	New Haven	1940	1031	Tele-List and Clock	Walnut w/Brass trim	125	105
0790	New Haven	1940	1043	Gondolier	Chrome w/Blue Mirror	350	106
0791	New Haven	1940	1051	Four Hundred	Walnut w/Chrome	175	106
0792	New Haven	1940	1060	Nugget	Black	150	106
					Ivory	125	106
0793	New Haven	1940	1062	Nautical	Walnut	150	106
0794	New Haven	1940	1063	Ship's Wheel	Walnut	125	106
0795	New Haven	1940	1064	Arc	Walnut	250	106
0796	New Haven	1940	2069	Cigarette Server	Walnut	75	106
					Blue	80	106
0797	New Haven	1940	6861	Mem-O-Clock	Walnut	100	106
0798	New Haven	1940	6916	Swing Top Cig Case	Walnut	110	107
0799	New Haven	1940	6910		Walnut	125	107
0800	New Haven	1940	6906		Walnut	125	107
0801	New Haven	1940	8577		Mahogany	100	107
0802	New Haven	1940	6914		Ivory	75	107
0803	New Haven	1940	8583		Blue Mirror	150	107
0804	New Haven	1940	8584		Blue Mirror	175	107
0805	New Haven	1940	8585		Blue Mirror	200	107
0806	New Haven	1940	686, 687	Archon Mirror	Blue Mirror	250	108
					Peach Mirror	350	108
0807	New Haven	1940		Scottie	Walnut	200	108
0808	New Haven	1940	632		Gold w/Pink	110	108
0809	New Haven	1940	642, 643		Gold w/Pink Face	75	108
					Gold w/Blue Face	85	108
0810	New Haven	1940	1855, 1856		Pigskin	60	108
					Black	65	108
0811	New Haven	1940	6903, 6904	Tele-List and Clock	Walnut	110	108
0812	New Haven	1940		Cloister	Mahogany	200	108
0813	New Haven	1940		Durham	Mahogany	175	108
0814	New Haven	1942		Strato	Mahogany	150	109
0815	New Haven	1942		Culver	Walnut	75	109
0816	New Haven	1942		Irma	Walnut	125	109
0817	New Haven	1942	140		Maroon	125	109
					Ivory	110	109
0818	New Haven	1942	828	Mariner	Walnut	110	109
0819	New Haven	1942		Vista	Onyx	125	109
0820	New Haven	1942	345	Spica Jr Alarm	Ivory	70	109
0821	New Haven	1942		Regency Design	Mahogany	125	109
0822	New Haven	1942		Clock and Calender	Brass	90	110
0823	New Haven	1942		Echo	Walnut	60	110
0824	New Haven	1942		Library	Green Catalin	250	110
					Ivory (Butterscotch) Catalin	200	110
0825	New Haven	1942		Overnite	Black w/Chrome	90	110
					Ivory w/Brass trim	75	110
0826	New Haven	1942		Peerless	Walnut	70	110
0827	New Haven	1942		Seaman	Walnut	100	110
0828	New Haven	1948		Ideal	Chrome	80	110
					Gold	60	110
0829	New Haven	1957	424	Ideal	Black	80	110
					Chrome	75	110
0830	New Haven	1957	617	Whirl	Ivory	15	111
0831	New Haven	1957	633	Viking	Maroon	15	111
0832	New Haven	1957	671	Marlow	Mahogany	15	111
0833	New Haven	1957	685	Oxford	Green	50	111
0834	New Haven	1957		Halo	Ivory	20	111
0835	New Haven	1957		Pocket Travel Watch	Nickel	60	111

Plate#	Brand Name	Year	Model No.	Model Name	Variation(s)	Value	Page
0836	New Lux	1951	6833, 6860	Harvester	Ivory	20	111
					Ivory w/Luminous Dial	25	111
					Grey	20	111
					Grey w/Luminous Dial	25	111
0837	Old Reliable	1930	1119,20,21,22	Pedestal Base	Green w/Gold	75	111
					Green w/Gold w/Luminous Dial	80	111
					Blue w/Gold	75	111
					Blue w/Gold w/Luminous Dial	80	111
					Red w/Gold	75	111
					Red w/Gold w/Luminous Dial	80	111
					Nickel	70	111
					Nickel w/Luminous Dial	75	111
0838	Old Reliable	1930	1198, 1199		Nickel	75	111
					Nickel w/Luminous Dial	80	111
0839	Old Reliable	1931	1256		Walnut	75	112
0840	Old Reliable	1931	1151,52,57	DeLuxe Pedestal	Green	80	112
					Green w/Luminous Dial	85	112
					Blue	80	112
					Blue w/Luminous Dial	85	112
					Red	80	112
					Red w/Luminous Dial	85	112
					Nickel	75	112
					Nickel w/Luminous Dial	80	112
0841	Old Reliable	1931	1262,63	Regular	Nickel	50	112
					Nickel w/Luminous Dial	55	112
					Green	55	112
					Green w/Luminous Dial	60	112
					Black	55	112
					Black w/Luminous Dial	60	112
					White	45	112
					White w/Luminous Dial	50	112
					Blue	55	112
					Blue w/Luminous Dial	60	112
0842	Old Reliable	1932	1196		Walnut	75	112
0843	Old Reliable	1933	952		Black w/Chrome	115	112
0844	Old Reliable	1933	953		Black w/Chrome	150	112
0845	Old Reliable	1933	1174, 1175		Nickel	130	112
					Nickel w/Luminous Dial	140	112
0846	Old Reliable	1933	1262, 1263		Nickel	200	112
					Nickel w/Luminous Dial	215	112
0847	Old Reliable	1933	1264, 1265	Bell Top	Nickel	45	112
					Nickel w/Luminous Dial	50	112
0848	Old Reliable	1936	1365	Twin Face	Black w/Chrome	200	113
0849	Othello	1950	90A	Othello	Ivory	50	113
0850	Peerless	1933		Skyscraper	Black w/Chrome	110	113
0851	Pennwood	1934	528		Walnut	125	113
0852	Pennwood	1934	529		Black	125	113
0853	Pennwood	1936	1362	Numeral Dial	Walnut	150	113
0854	Pennwood	1936	1364	Numeral Dial	Walnut	350	113
0855	Pennwood	1938	100	Chieftain	Brown	100	114
					Black	125	114
					Ivory	140	114
0856	Pennwood	1937	1371, 1370	Century	Rosewood w/Ivory	275	114
0857	Pennwood	1937		Bronze	Bronze	150	114
0858	Pennwood	1940	AC-48	Frederal Moderne	Brown and Ivory	125	114
					Maroon and Silver	175	114
0859	Pennwood	1940	710	Moderne	Walnut or Ivory	75	114
0860	Pennwood	1940		Zephyr	Walnut	750	114
0861	Pennwood	1940	12A		Brown	75	115
					Ivory	100	115
					Marbled Ivory	150	115
0862	Pennwood	1960		Century Executive	Black w/Ivory	325	115
0863	Pennwood	1949	300	Topper	Walnut	125	115
					Ivory	125	115
0864	Pennwood	1963		Numechron Belvedere	Mahogany	65	115
					Blond	70	115
0865	Pennwood	1952	N	Timeter	Brown w/Ivory	75	115

Plate #	Brand Name	Year	Model No.	Model Name	Variation(s)	Value	Page
0866	Pennwood	1963		Numechron Satellite	Black	125	115
					Walnut	100	115
0867	Pennwood	1963		Numechron TV-Lamp	Walnut	65	116
0868	Pennwood	1948		Starlet	Walnut	60	116
					Ivory	60	116
0869	Pennwood	1963		Numechron Explorer	Walnut	50	116
0870	Phinney-Walker	1940		Desk Set	Walnut	125	116
0871	Phinney-Walker	1955	20	Clock/Cigarette	Walnut	75	116
0872	Phinney-Walker	1952	32		Gold	25	116
0873	Phinney-Walker	1952	39		Gold	40	116
0874	Phinney-Walker	1955	42		Gold	35	116
0875	Phinney-Walker	1957	30	Time For Royalty	Pink	40	117
					Clear	25	117
					White	30	117
					Amber	35	117
					Blue	40	117
0876	Phinney-Walker	1957	33	Calender Alarm	Gold	35	117
0877	Phinney-Walker	1957	34		Gold w/Blue	40	117
					Gold w/Crystal	35	117
					Gold w/Pink	40	117
0878	Phinney-Walker	1957	36	Desk Mates	Gold	50	117
0879	Phinney-Walker	1957	50		Walnut	35	117
					Blue	45	117
					Ivory	40	117
					Pink	45	117
0880	Phinney-Walker	1957		Tuck-Away	Gold w/Tan	35	117
					Gold w/Green	40	117
					Gold w/Walnut	35	117
					Gold w/Maroon	40	117
0881	Phinney-Walker	1963		Crown Jewel	Red	35	117
					Blue	35	117
					White	30	117
					Amber	35	117
0882	Phinney-Walker	1963		Premier	Brass	70	117
0883	Phinney-Walker	1963		Cirolet	White	40	118
					Black	45	118
0884	Phinney-Walker	1963		Heritage	Brass	40	118
0885	Plymouth	1940	654		Black	45	118
					Ivory	35	118
0886	Pyramid	1942	329	Pyramid	Ivory	125	118
					Black	150	118
0887	Ravenswood	1931			Walnut	75	118
0888	Relide	1962		Bell Companion	Gold	50	118
0889	Relide	1962		Beside Manner	Gold	45	118
0890	Relide	1962		Boudoir Quadrille	Gold	70	118
					Silver w/Gold	80	118
0891	Relide	1962		Calender	Brass	40	118
0892	Relide	1962		Celestial	Gold	50	119
0893	Relide	1962		Chairman	Gold	55	119
0894	Relide	1962		Chalet Suisse	Brass	65	119
0895	Relide	1962		Classique	Gold	50	119
0896	Relide	1962		Deluxe Mantle	Gold	45	119
0897	Relide	1962		Elite	Brass	40	119
0898	Relide	1962		Executive Director	Gold	45	119
					Silver	50	119
0899	Relide	1962		Globe Clock	Gold	75	119
0900	Relide	1962		Globemaster	Gold	60	119
0901	Relide	1962		Globemaster Deluxe	Gold	70	120
0902	Relide	1962		Globetrotter	Brass	50	120
0903	Relide	1962		Grandeur & Elegance	Gold	80	120
0904	Relide	1962		Horoscope	Gold	60	120
0905	Relide	1962		Host Time	Black	60	120
					Blue	65	120
					Maroon	65	120
0906	Relide	1962		Lantern	Brass	75	120
0907	Relide	1962		Miniature	Brass	50	120
0908	Relide	1962		Nocturne	Gold and Black	70	120

Plate #	Brand Name	Year	Model No.	Model Name	Variation(s)	Value	Page
0909	Relide	1962		Popular Quadrille	Gold	70	120
0910	Relide	1962		Rectangle Companion	Brass	40	121
0911	Relide	1962		Rippling Halo	Gold	40	121
0912	Relide	1962		Star-Time	Gold and Silver	125	121
0913	Relide	1962		Versatile	Gold	35	121
0914	Revere	1963		Carthage	Mahogany	25	121
0915	Rex	1933			Chrome w/Black	175	121
					Ivory	90	121
					Brown	80	121
0916	RFD	1932	930		Green	75	121
					Pink	75	121
0917	RFD	1935	925		Nickel	85	121
0918	RFD	1935	930		Nickel	85	121
0919	RFD	1935	930A		Walnut	75	122
0920	RFD	1935	931		Nickel	60	122
0921	RFD	1935	936		Green	70	122
					Blue	70	122
					Rose	75	122
					Lavender	80	122
0922	RIO	1942			Black	80	122
					Ivory	60	122
0923	Royal Kenmore	1929		Penn	Walnut	100	122
0924	Royal Kenmore	1929		Princess Pat/Kodel	Walnut	125	122
0925	Royal Kenmore	1930		Electric Utility	Walnut	125	122
0926	Royal Kenmore	1932	900	Anna-Belle	Blue	75	122
					Green	75	122
					Ivory	60	122
					Pink	80	122
0927	Royal Kenmore	1932	901	Irene	Walnut	125	122
0928	Royal Kenmore	1932	902	Vernamae	Brass	110	123
0929	Royal Kenmore	1932	903	Evelyn	Walnut	65	123
0930	Royal Kenmore	1932	905	Kenalarm Petite	Walnut	125	123
0931	Royal Kenmore	1932	906	Dowling	Walnut	350	123
0932	Royal Kenmore	1932	908	Montgomery	Walnut	60	123
0933	Royal Kenmore	1932	910	McDonald	Walnut	75	123
0934	Royal Kenmore	1933		Skyscraper	Brown	250	123
0935	Sears	1959	7128		Walnut	25	123
0936	Sears	1965	7100		White	10	123
0937	Sears	1965	7137, 7135		Walnut	60	124
					Walnut w/Luminous Dial	65	124
0938	Sears	1965	7194-97		Beige	20	124
					Walnut	20	124
					Blue	30	124
					Orange	40	124
0939	Sears	1965	7171		Cherry	15	124
0940	Sears	1965	7118-7121		Beige	10	124
					Blue	15	124
					White	10	124
					Walnut	10	124
0941	Semca	1950	1334		Satin-Gold	50	124
0942	Semca	1950	6820, 6821		Brass	50	124
0943	Semca	1952	113		Brass	45	124
0944	Semca	1952	718		Gold w/pink	35	124
					Gold w/blue	35	124
					Gold w/crystal	35	124
					Gold w/amethyst	35	124
					Gold w/peridot	35	124
					Gold w/topaz	35	124
0945	Semca	1952	741		Blue	40	124
					Maroon	40	124
					Walnut	35	124
					Green	40	124
					Ivory	35	124
0946	Semca	1952	773		Gold	25	125
0947	Semca	1952	7852		Gold	25	125
0948	Semca	1955	117		Gold	40	125
0949	Semca	1955	721		Gold w/Pink	35	125
					Gold w/Blue	35	125
					Gold w/Crystal	35	125

Plate #	Brand Name	Year	Model No.	Model Name	Variation(s)	Value	Page
0950	Semca	1955	737		Brass	50	125
0951	Semca	1955	744		Ivory	25	125
					Green	30	125
					Blue	30	125
0952	Semca	1955	780		Brass	20	125
0953	Semca	1955	790		Brass	30	125
0954	Semca	1955	795		Brass	30	125
0955	Semca	1955	796		Gold	25	126
0956	Semca	1955	7866		Brass	25	126
0957	Sentinel	1950		Sentinel Prince	Ivory	20	126
0958	Sentinel	1955		Capstan	Brass	40	126
0959	Sentinel	1955		Dapper	Ivory	35	126
0960	Sentinel	1955		Dawn	Ivory	40	126
0961	Sentinel	1955		Little Pal	Ivory	40	126
0962	Sentinel	1955		Pride	Brass	50	126
0963	Sentinel	1955			Brass	20	126
0964	Sentry	1957	6750	Miniature	Ivory	30	127
0965	Sentry	1958	6810, 6811		Ivory	30	127
0966	Sentry	1958	6813		Ivory	25	127
0967	Sentry	1957	6961		Ivory	15	127
0968	Sentry	1958	7061, 7062		Ivory	15	127
					Pink	20	127
0969	Sentry	1958	7052		White	20	127
0970	Sentry	1958	6812		Ivory	15	127
					Ivory w/Luminous Dial	15	127
0971	Sentry	1958	6952	Old Reliable	Ivory	45	127
					Ivory w/Luminous Dial	50	127
0972	Sentry	1958	7051, 7050	Spotlight	White	40	127
					White w/Luminous Dial	45	127
					Blue	60	127
					Blue w/Luminous Dial	65	127
0973	Sessions	1931		El Mode	Mahogany	150	128
					Walnut	140	128
0974	Sessions	1931		Elwyn	Mahogany	65	128
					Walnut	60	128
0975	Sessions	1931		Octagon	Nickel	125	128
					Cracked Green	150	128
0976	Sessions	1932	916M		Ivory	100	128
					Black	110	128
					Mahogany	100	128
0977	Sessions	1932	958M		Black	75	128
					Mahogany	65	128
0978	Sessions	1932	7037	A	Mahogany	75	128
0979	Sessions	1932	7064, 7065	Coronet	Mahogany	50	128
0980	Sessions	1932		Hamilton	Mahogany	90	128
0981	Sessions	1932		Jefferson	Mahogany	85	128
0982	Sessions	1932		Standish	Mahogany	70	129
0983	Sessions	1932	29	Westminster	Mahogany	85	129
0984	Sessions	1933	151	Cuckoo	Brass	200	129
0985	Sessions	1933	238	Airplane	Brass	250	129
0986	Sessions	1933	159, 160	Coach	Brass	125	129
0987	Sessions	1933	239A, 239B	Farm	Red w/Ivory	150	129
					Green w/Ivory	150	129
					Blue w/Ivory	150	129
0988	Sessions	1933	152, 153	New Coach	Brass	150	129
					Nickel	160	129
0989	Sessions	1933	154	Ship	Brass	175	130
0990	Sessions	1933	162	Windmill	Brass	150	130
0991	Sessions	1934		Gothic Design	Walnut	75	130
0992	Sessions	1935		Nordic	Mahogany	65	130
0993	Sessions	1935	W		Walnut	50	130
0994	Sessions	1935			Mahogany	60	130
0995	Sessions	1936		Manley, Stanley	Mahogany w/Chrome	90	130
					Maple w/Chrome	100	130
0996	Sessions	1936		Maxwell	Mahogany w/Chrome	80	130
					Maple w/Chrome	90	130
0997	Sessions	1936		Monroe	Curley Maple	65	130

Plate #	Brand Name	Year	Model No.	Model Name	Variation(s)	Value	Page
0998	Sessions	1936		Morgan	Maple w/Black	150	131
					Ivory w/Green	125	131
0999	Sessions	1936		Nevel	Mahogany w/Chrome	80	131
1000	Sessions	1936		Nixon	Ivory w/Green	75	131
1001	Sessions	1936		Norman	Mahogany w/Chrome	95	131
					Maple w/Chrome	105	131
1002	Sessions	1936		Onyx	Onyx	100	131
1003	Sessions	1936		Westminster	Mahogany	110	131
1004	Sessions	1936			Mahogany	90	131
1005	Sessions	1936			Mahogany	110	131
					Maple	125	131
1006	Sessions	1936			Mahogany	125	131
					Ivory	130	131
					Red	135	131
1007	Sessions	1936			Mahogany	110	132
					Ivory	115	132
					Red	120	132
1008	Sessions	1936	287, W		Walnut w/Black	225	132
1009	Sessions	1938	SK		Ivory	100	132
					Green	110	132
1010	Sessions	1938	279, A		Walnut	75	132
1011	Sessions	1938	439		Walnut	65	132
					Mahogany	70	132
1012	Sessions	1938	W		Walnut	30	132
1013	Sessions	1939		Stir-Up	Nickel	50	132
1014	Sessions	1939			Maple	125	132
1015	Sessions	1939			Mahogany	45	133
1016	Sessions	1939			Walnut	45	133
1017	Sessions	1939			Walnut	40	133
1018	Sessions	1942	134	DeLuxe Airliner	Walnut w/Chrome	250	133
1019	Sessions	1940		Yankee Clipper	Walnut w/Chrome	125	133
1020	Sessions	1939			Nickel w/Black	175	133
1021	Sessions	1940	297, 501	Capstan	Walnut	50	133
1022	Sessions	1940	290		Walnut	175	133
1023	Sessions	1940	294		Walnut	90	134
1024	Sessions	1940	298		Walnut	75	134
					Ivory	80	134
1025	Sessions	1940			Walnut w/Black	225	134
1026	Sessions	1940			Walnut	175	134
1027	Sessions	1940			Mahogany	50	134
1028	Sessions	1940			Walnut	60	134
1029	Sessions	1940			Walnut	125	134
1030	Sessions	1940		Scottie	Walnut	225	134
1031	Sessions	1941	200	Airliner	Walnut	250	135
1032	Sessions	1941		Modern Cabinet	Mahogany	50	135
1033	Sessions	1941		Capitol Dome	Chrome and Mahogany	150	135
1034	Sessions	1941		Moderne	Onyx	125	135
1035	Sessions	1942	135, 136	Golden Eagle	Walnut and Brass	175	135
1036	Sessions	1942	139, 140	Golden Girl	Walnut and Brass	250	135
1037	Sessions	1942	130, 131	Panther	Mahogany	300	135
1038	Sessions	1942	827	Waterman Set	Walnut	125	136
1039	Sessions	1942	132, 133	Winged Victory	Walnut	175	136
1040	Sessions	1942	385	Shelf Clipper	Walnut	75	136
1041	Sessions	1942	390		Walnut	75	136
1042	Sessions	1942	394		Walnut	125	136
1043	Sessions	1942	419		Walnut and Brass	60	136
1044	Sessions	1942	420		Walnut	60	136
1045	Sessions	1942	424		Ivory	50	137
					White	50	137
					Red	75	137
					Walnut	40	137
1046	Sessions	1942	434		Walnut	40	137
1047	Sessions	1942	435		Walnut	45	137
1048	Sessions	1947	4A	Pussyfooter	Ivory	75	137
					Ivory w/Luminous Dial	80	137
1049	Sessions	1948		Ballerina	Walnut w/Bronze	125	137
1050	Sessions	1948		Boy and Dog	Walnut w/Bronze	150	137

Plate #	Brand Name	Year	Model No.	Model Name	Variation(s)	Value	Page
1051	Sessions	1948		Horseshoe	Bronze	75	137
1052	Sessions	1949		Boat	Ivory	75	137
1053	Sessions	1949	136		Mahogany	110	137
1054	Sessions	1949			Mahogany	25	138
1055	Sessions	1949		Ship's Wheel	Mahogany	40	138
1056	Sessions	1950	134		Mahogany	25	138
1057	Sessions	1949			Walnut	45	138
1058	Sessions	1951		Occassional	Mahogany	60	138
1059	Sessions	1951		Mak-A-Clock	Walnut	25	138
1060	Sessions	1951		Western Horse	Walnut w/Brass	125	138
1061	Sessions	1951		Propellor	Walnut w/Brass	225	139
1062	Sessions	1957	73, 75	Enchantment, Escort	Honey	40	139
					Maple	40	139
1063	Sessions	1956		Aquarius	Brass	250	139
1064	Sessions	1956		Bravo	Mahogany	25	139
1065	Sessions	1956		Interlude	Mahogany	20	139
1066	Sessions	1957		Connoisseur	White w/Chrome	15	139
1067	Sessions	1957		Pixie	White	15	139
					White w/Luminous Dial	15	139
1068	Sessions	1957		Sweetheart	White	20	139
					White w/Luminous Dial	20	139
1069	Sessions	1957		Tee Vee	Mahogany	75	140
1070	Sessions	1960		Love Alarm	Pink	95	140
					Blue	95	140
1071	Sessions	1958		Bird	Walnut	225	140
					Onyx	250	140
1072	Sessions	1958		Flying Cloud	Walnut w/Chrome	125	140
1073	Sessions	1958		Swinging Playmates	Walnut	200	140
					Onyx	225	140
1074	Sessions	1962		Doze-On	White	15	140
					White w/Luminous Dial	15	140
					Pink	20	140
					Pink w/Luminous Dial	20	140
					Blue	20	140
					Blue w/Luminous Dial	20	140
1075	Sessions	1962		Shelton	Mahogany	10	140
					Cinnamon	10	140
1076	Sessions	1963		Limelite	White	45	140
					Yellow	60	140
					Blue	60	140
					Tan	50	140
1077	Sessions	1962		Lenox	Walnut	60	141
1078	Sessions	1962		Lorelei	White	60	141
					White w/Luminous Dial	90	141
					Pink	95	141
					Pink w/Luminous Dial	100	141
					Blue	105	141
					Blue w/Luminous Dial	100	141
1079	Sessions	1962		Sessionette	White	105	141
					White w/Luminous Dial	10	141
1080	Sessions	1963		Sessionglo	White	10	141
					Pink	15	141
					Blue	15	141
1081	Seth Thomas	1931		Durango	Green w/Black	150	141
					Pink w/Black	150	141
					Yellow w/Black	160	141
					Gold w/Black	160	141
					Walnut w/Black	140	141
1082	Seth Thomas	1931		Gibson	Mahogany	70	141
1083	Seth Thomas	1931		Hour-glass	Mahogany	100	141
1084	Seth Thomas	1931		Nanking	Walnut	80	141
1085	Seth Thomas	1931		Newton	Mahogany	75	142
1086	Seth Thomas	1931		Sonora	Onyx	110	142
1087	Seth Thomas	1931		Stetson	Mahogany	85	142
1088	Seth Thomas	1931		Upson	Mahogany	85	142
1089	Seth Thomas	1931		Westbury	Mahogany	90	142
1090	Seth Thomas	1933		Capstan	Mahogany	55	142

Plate #	Brand Name	Year	Model No.	Model Name	Variation(s)	Value	Page
1091	Seth Thomas	1933		Crest	Mahogany	70	142
1092	Seth Thomas	1933		Dalesbury	Mahogany	80	142
1093	Seth Thomas	1933		Floret	Mahogany	90	142
1094	Seth Thomas	1933		Lotus	White	150	143
1095	Seth Thomas	1933		Tabor	Mahogany	110	143
1096	Seth Thomas	1933		Woodmont	Mahogany	60	143
1097	Seth Thomas	1934		Budoir	Mahogany w/Maple	90	143
1098	Seth Thomas	1935		Plymouth	Mahogany	85	143
1099	Seth Thomas	1936			Mahogany	85	143
1100	Seth Thomas	1939		Console	Mahogany w/Brass	225	143
1101	Seth Thomas	1939	E-853	Echo-Luminous	Mahogany w/Brass	60	143
1102	Seth Thomas	1939	E-853	Echo	Mahogany w/Brass	50	143
1103	Seth Thomas	1940		Desk Set	Walnut	125	144
1104	Seth Thomas	1956		Baxter	Mahogany w/Brass	50	144
1105	Seth Thomas	1940	E-884	Lee	Ivory	65	144
1106	Seth Thomas	1942		Culver	Walnut	40	144
1107	Seth Thomas	1947		Carlisle	Black w/Brass	75	144
1108	Seth Thomas	1948		Yukon	Brass	60	144
1109	Seth Thomas	1951	7061	Severa	Mahogany w/Brass	30	144
1110	Seth Thomas	1952		Alcor	Brass	40	144
1111	Seth Thomas	1952		Northbury	Mahogany	30	145
1112	Seth Thomas	1952		Polaris	Brass	40	145
1113	Seth Thomas	1952		Vega	Brass	35	145
1114	Seth Thomas	1956		Cathay	Mahogany	20	145
					Mahogany w/Luminous Dial	25	145
					Blond	25	145
					Blond w/Luminous Dial	30	145
1115	Seth Thomas	1956	517	Compass	Mahogany w/Black	20	145
					Black w/Walnut	20	145
1116	Seth Thomas	1956		Penthouse	Cherry	60	145
					Blond	75	145
1117	Seth Thomas	1956		Poise	Mahogany	30	145
1118	Seth Thomas	1956		Rudder	Walnut	60	145
1119	Seth Thomas	1956		Sharon-Echo	Maple	25	145
					Mahogany	20	145
1120	Seth Thomas	1958		Leather Case	Leather	15	145
1121	Seth Thomas	1959		Wayne	Walnut	20	146
1122	Seth Thomas	1963		Beverly	Walnut	25	146
					Mahogany	30	146
1123	Seth Thomas	1963		Canewood	Walnut	15	146
					Mahogany	15	146
1124	Seth Thomas	1963		Facet	Crystal	25	146
1125	Silver	1937	200	Silver Swingtime	Ivory	225	146
					Walnut	225	146
1126	Silver	1937	50	Rotary	Ivory	300	146
					Brass	325	146
					Black	325	146
1127	Silver	1937	778		Ivory	75	146
					Green	85	146
1128	Silvertone	1932	2812	DeLuxe	Nickel w/Black	175	147
1129	Silvertone	1932	2813	DeLuxe	Nickel w/Black	80	147
1130	Spartus	1963		Time-O-Lite	Brass	125	147
					White	125	147
1131	Spartus	1962		Moon-Glo Planter	Copper	150	147
1132	Sunbeam	1958		Vari-Lite	White	45	147
					Tan	50	147
1133	Sunbeam	1958	7081		Ivory	10	147
1134	Sunbeam	1958	7084		Ivory	15	147
					Ivory w/Luminous Dial	20	147
1135	Sunbeam	1965		Preferred/Slumberwd	Walnut	10	147
					Gold	15	147
1136	Sunbeam	1965		Design	Tan	40	148
1137	Sunbeam	1965		Petite	Ivory	15	148
1138	Sundberg-Ferar	1965	7190		White	15	148
					Beige	20	148
					Pink	25	148
					Turquoise	25	148

Plate #	Brand Name	Year	Model No.	Model Name	Variation(s)	Value	Page
1139	Sun-Up	1936	6202	Gothic	Brown w/Copper	60	148
1140	Sun-Up	1936	6209		Ivory w/Nickel	85	148
					Black w/Nickel	115	148
1141	Sun-Up	1938	8959	Octagon	Rose	75	148
					Green	70	148
					Ivory	60	148
1142	Sun-Up	1938	8961	Ultra-Modern	Ivory	60	148
					Green	70	148
					Red	70	148
1143	Telechron	1928	370	Clinton	Mahogany	75	148
1144	Telechron	1929	431	Mantel	Bronze	125	148
1145	Telechron	1929	323	Petite	Ivory	60	149
					Red	75	149
					Green	75	149
1146	Telechron	1930	431	Modernique (Frankl)	Machined Silver and Gold	1250	149
					Chrome w/Purple & Black	1500	149
1147	Telechron	1929	522	Salem	Mahogany	60	149
1148	Telechron	1930	523	Patricia	Ivory	65	149
					Red	80	149
					Green	80	149
1149	Telechron	1930	524	Oxford	Mahogany	110	149
1150	Telechron	1930	700	Electro-Alarm	Walnut	250	149
					Ivory	375	149
					Green	600	149
1151	Telechron	1931	326	Bruce	Mahogany	60	149
1152	Telechron	1931	526	Bellevue	Mahogany w/Burl Maple	75	149
1153	Telechron	1931	530	Nottingham	Mahogany	150	149
1154	Telechron	1931	531	Lorraine	Mahogany w/Burl Maple	80	150
1155	Telechron	1931	602	Castleton	Mahogany	110	150
1156	Telechron	1931	603	Jefferson	Mahogany	70	150
1157	Telechron	1931	711	Telalarm	Dura Silver Alloy	100	150
1158	Telechron	1932	329	Colony	Mahogany	50	150
1159	Telechron	1932	532	Shelburne	Mahogany w/Lacewood	70	150
1160	Telechron	1932	605	Waverly	Mahogany	65	150
1161	Telechron	1932	606	Winchester	Mahogany w/Satinwood	75	150
1162	Telechron	1932	3A-51	Renault	Mahogany	65	150
1163	Telechron	1932	3F-51	Duke	Black	125	151
1164	Telechron	1932	R-930		Walnut	65	151
1165	Telechron	1933	4F-51B	Telart	Chrome w/Black	175	151
1166	Telechron	1933	8B-03	Minitman	Mahogany	200	151
1167	Telechron	1934	7F-53	Telebell	Nickel w/Black Base	150	151
					Black w/Ivory Base	110	151
1168	Telechron	1934	7B-01	Autolarm	Walnut	60	151
1169	Telechron	1934	3F-01	Commonwealth	Mahogany w/Chrome	225	151
1170	Telechron	1934	8B-01	Minitmaster	Black w/Brass	250	151
1171	Telechron	1934	8B-05	New Minitmaster	Black w/Chrome	250	152
					Ivory w/Chrome	325	152
1172	Telechron	1935	4F-59	Attache	Brass	100	152
					Chrome	125	152
1173	Telechron	1935	4F-61	Pharoah	Mahogany	90	152
1174	Telechron	1935	7F-63	Quacker	Black w/Orange	325	152
					Yellow w/Orange	375	152
					Blue w/Orange	375	152
1175	Telechron	1936	3F-53	Daphne	Butterscotch Catalin	250	152
					Black Catalin	275	152
					Red Catalin	300	152
					Green Catalin	275	152
					Rose Quartz Catalin	325	152
					Clear Catalin	325	152
1176	Telechron	1936	4F-63	Aztec	Brass	90	152
					Chrome	115	152
1177	Telechron	1936	4F-65	Luxor	Chrome & Brass, Blue Mirror	175	152
					Chrome & Brass, Silver Mirror	200	152
					Chrome & Brass, Lavender Mirror	250	152
1178	Telechron	1936	7F-01	Announcer	Black	80	152
1179	Telechron	1936	7F-03	Clarion	Black	90	152
1180	Telechron	1936	7F-149	Sparkler	Ivory	90	153
					Black	80	153

Plate #	Brand Name	Year	Model No.	Model Name	Variation(s)	Value	Page
1181	Telechron	1936	7F-57	Airlarm	Walnut	60	153
					Maple	70	153
1182	Telechron	1936	7F-65	Aladdin	Ivory	100	153
					Black	80	153
1183	Telechron	1936	7F-65	Deputy	Walnut	75	153
					Ivory	90	153
1184	Telechron	1936	7F-71	Gendarme	Walnut	70	153
					Ivory	80	153
1185	Telechron	1936	7F-73	Meadowlark	Black	40	153
					Cherry	50	153
1186	Telechron	1935	Special	Pelicans	Chrome, Catalin, Black Marble	1200	153
1187	Telechron	1936	8B-09	Tribute (Teague des.)	Walnut and Maple	400	153
1188	Telechron	1936	CF-363/769	Usher	Ivory	75	154
					Ivory w/Luminous Dial	80	154
					Black	75	154
					Black w/Luminous Dial	80	154
1189	Telechron	1937	4H-81	Statesman	White	90	154
1190	Telechron	1938	3F-67	Pageant	Ivory w/Brass	90	154
					Brown w/Brass	70	154
					Black w/Brass	80	154
1191	Telechron	1937	5F-51	Doric	Walnut and Maple	125	154
1192	Telechron	1938	3H-78	Basque	Ivory (Butterscotch) Catalin	225	154
					Black Catalin	250	154
1193	Telechron	1938	CH-783	Kleertone	Ivory (Butterscotch) Catalin	225	154
					Black Catalin	250	154
					Brown Catalin	250	154
1194	Telechron	1937	4B-79	Olympic	Walnut and Maple	110	154
1195	Telechron	1937	8B-07	Baron (Teague)	Black	225	154
					Ivory	275	154
					Walnut	200	154
1196	Telechron	1938	8B-11	Granada	Brown w/Maroon	150	155
					Black w/Maroon	175	155
1197	Telechron	1939	3F-71	Coronado	Walnut	100	155
1198	Telechron	1939	3H-73	Domino	Black	90	155
					Walnut	80	155
1199	Telechron	1939	3H-79	Croft	Walnut	90	155
1200	Telechron	1939	3H-81	Virginian	Walnut	75	155
1201	Telechron	1939	3H-83	Melbourne	Green Catalin	175	155
1202	Telechron	1939	4B-85	Cordova	Mahogany	60	155
1203	Telechron	1939	4F-55	Airlux	Onyx	70	155
1204	Telechron	1939	4F-67	Embassy	Chrome	125	156
1205	Telechron	1939	4F-73	Smartset	Walnut	90	156
1206	Telechron	1939	4H-77	Deauville	Black Mirror	150	156
					Blue Mirror	175	156
1207	Telechron	1939	4H-83	Naples	Walnut	75	156
1208	Telechron	1939	4H-91	Finesse	Faux Leather	50	156
1209	Telechron	1939	4H-93	Highland	Walnut	80	156
1210	Telechron	1939	4H-95	Kendall	Mahogany	50	156
1211	Telechron	1939	6B-01	Jubilee	Walnut	60	156
1212	Telechron	1939	6B-03	Seville	Walnut	75	156
1213	Telechron	1939	6B-05	Picardy	Mahogany	50	157
1214	Telechron	1939	7H-77	Mirolarm	Blue Mirror	110	157
					Pink Mirror	130	157
1215	Telechron	1939	7H-79	Butler	Black	90	157
					Black w/Luminous Dial	95	157
					Walnut	80	157
					Walnut w/Luminous Dial	85	157
1216	Telechron	1939	7H-85	Attendant	Walnut w/Nickel	100	157
					Walnut w/Luminous Dial	110	157
					Ivory w/Gold	125	157
					Ivory w/Luminous Dial	135	157
1217	Telechron	1939	8F-03	Explorer	Walnut	60	157
1218	Telechron	1940	3H-89	Bancroft	Walnut	80	157
1219	Telechron	1940	4B-07	Harwich	Ivory and Brown	175	157
1220	Telechron	1940	4B-153	Barclay	Ivory and Brown	175	157
1221	Telechron	1940	7F-75	Mayfair	Gold w/Black	110	158
1222	Telechron	1940	7H-109	Florilla	Brass w/Black	75	158

Plate#	Brand Name	Year	Model No.	Model Name	Variation(s)	Value	Page
1223	Telechron	1940	7H-91	Secretary	Ivory	60	158
					Ivory w/Luminous Dial	65	158
					Walnut	40	158
					Walnut w/Luminous Dial	45	158
1224	Telechron	1940	7H-93	New Telalarm	Brass	75	158
					Brass w/Luminous Dial	80	158
					Nickel	110	158
					Nickel w/Luminous Dial	120	158
1225	Telechron	1940	7H-99	Steward	Brass w/Walnut	100	158
1226	Telechron	1940	CH-387	Somerset	Walnut	80	158
1227	Telechron	1941	3H-97	Vassel	Walnut	50	158
1228	Telechron	1941	4B-151	Stoneham	Ivory and Brown	100	158
1229	Telechron	1941	4B-155	Hampshire	Ivory and Brown	125	158
1230	Telechron	1941	4H-89	Vagabond	Walnut w/Brass	90	159
1231	Telechron	1941	5H-57	Suave	Walnut w/Brass	110	159
1232	Telechron	1941	5H-59	Satellite	Brass	125	159
1233	Telechron	1941	6B-13	Magnolia	Mahogany	225	159
1234	Telechron	1941		Conductor	Ivory	70	159
					Walnut	55	159
1235	Telechron	1941	7H-101	Imp	Ivory (Butterscotch) Catalin	150	159
					Rose Catalin	200	159
					Brown Catalin	175	159
1236	Telechron	1941	7H-113	Custodian	Walnut	45	159
1237	Telechron	1941	7H-115	Fortress	Ivory	150	159
1238	Telechron	1941	7H-117	Reporter	Ivory	70	159
					Brown	60	159
1239	Telechron	1941	7H-119	Governor	Stained Pine	40	160
1240	Telechron	1941	7H-122	Serene	Ivory w/Clear	150	160
					Ivory w/Blue	175	160
1241	Telechron	1941	7H-89	Guest	Faux Leather	60	160
1242	Telechron	1941	8H-15	Instructor	Walnut	65	160
1243	Telechron	1941	8H-17	Registrar	Walnut	75	160
1244	Telechron	1942	4H-97	Forum	Walnut	75	160
1245	Telechron	1946	7H-125	Dispatcher	Brown	90	160
					Ivory	110	160
1246	Telechron	1949	7H-149	Sparkler	Ivory	60	160
1247	Telechron	1949	3H-157	Yachtsman	Brass	125	160
1248	Telechron	1948	7H133-S	Electric Executive	Walnut	150	161
1249	Telechron	1941	8B-13	Register	Walnut	90	161
1250	Telechron	1948	7H-137	Little Tel	Walnut	50	161
					Ivory	60	161
1251	Telechron	1951	3H-163	Swarthmore	Mahogany	30	161
1252	Telechron	1950	7H-09	Nocturne	Walnut	25	161
					Ivory	30	161
1253	Telechron	1950	7H-153	Serene	Ivory	75	161
1254	Telechron	1951	3H-159	Suave	Clear	110	161
1255	Telechron	1951	7H-07	Everset	Ivory	20	161
1256	Telechron	1951	7H-141	Airlux	Mahogany w/Brass	40	162
					Transparent w/Brass	75	162
1257	Telechron	1951	7H-157	Colonnade	Walnut	30	162
1258	Telechron	1951	7H-161	Tempo	Ivory	25	162
1259	Telechron	1951	7H-163	Kirkwood	Mahogany	25	162
1260	Telechron	1951	7H-165	Coronado	Walnut	50	162
1261	Telechron	1951	7H-169	Guest	Ivory	35	162
1262	Telechron	1951	7H-173	Tel-A-Glow	Ivory	35	162
1263	Telechron	1951	7H-179	Tribute	Gold	30	162
1264	Telechron	1951	7H-183	Imp	Ivory	20	162
					Brown	15	162
1265	Telechron	1951	7H-185	Tiara	Pink	30	163
					Green	30	163
					Blue	30	163
1266	Telechron	1951	7H-187	Personality	Clear	25	163
1267	Telechron	1951	7H-189	Alladin	Ivory	20	163
1268	Telechron	1952	7H-199	Minstrel	Ivory	15	163
1269	Telechron	1952	7HP-171	Bancroft	Ivory	15	163
1270	Telechron	1953	7H-195	Mirolarm	Ivory w/Brass	20	163
1271	Telechron	1953	7H-197	Illuminette	Ivory w/Brass	25	163

Plate #	Brand Name	Year	Model No.	Model Name	Variation(s)	Value	Page
1272	Telechron	1953	7H-201	Telegrain	Walnut	35	163
1273	Telechron	1953	7H-207	Lullaby	Ivory	10	163
1274	Telechron	1952	2H-33	Ivy	Red	50	164
					Green	40	164
					Grey	30	164
					Yellow	45	164
1275	Telechron	1953	7H-215	Decor	Beige	25	164
1276	Telechron	1953	7H-209	Gracewood	Mahogany	15	164
					Maple	20	164
					Blonde	20	164
1277	Telechron	1953	7H-211	Dorm	Ivory	15	164
					Ivory w/Luminous Dial	15	164
1278	Telechron	1954	8H-29	Telejour	Brass	40	164
1279	Telechron	1954	2H-47	Telechoice	Brown w/Brass	40	164
					White w/Chrome	50	164
					Red w/Chrome	60	164
					Yellow w/Chrome	55	164
1280	Telechron	1955	5H-69	Illumitime	Black and White	125	164
1281	Telechron	1955	5H-65	Outline	Maple	500	165
1282	Telechron	1955	5H-71	Panorama	Walnut w/Brass	325	165
1283	Telechron	1955	5H-67	Showpiece	Silver w/Brass	175	165
1284	Telechron	1955	7H-213	Perspective	Black w/Brass	275	165
1285	Time King	1933	160		Green	85	165
					Blue	85	165
					Pink	90	165
					Black	90	165
1286	Timemaster	1936	910	New Timemaster	Chrome	110	165
1287	Timeter	1934	4601		Black w/Chrome	250	165
1288	Timeter	1934	4602		Walnut	250	165
1289	Timeter	1934	4603		Chrome	300	165
1290	Timex	1954		Falcon	Ivory	15	166
					Ivory w/Luminous Dial	15	166
1291	Timex	1955		Radiolite	Ivory	20	166
1292	Timex	1957		Falcon	Green	15	166
					Ivory	15	166
					Gold	15	166
1293	Timex	1957		Falcon	Ivory	15	166
					Green	15	166
1294	Tuxedo	1933			Gold	80	166
					Bronze	85	166
					Green	80	166
1295	U.S. Time Corp	1950		Hoppalong Cassidy	Black	150	166
					Red	175	166
1296	United	1933		Futurist	Bronze	450	166
1297	Usalite	1932	700	Atlas	Nickel	300	166
1298	Usalite	1935	12	Pequot	Green and Amber	250	166
1299	Usalite	1935	704	Modernistic	Black w/Silver	250	167
1300	Victor	1931	1110	One Day Intermittent	Green w/gold	75	167
					Green w/gold w/Luminous Dial	80	167
					Blue w/gold	80	167
					Blue w/gold w/Luminous Dial	85	167
					Red w/gold	90	167
					Red w/gold w/Luminous Dial	95	167
					Nickel w/gold	100	167
					Nickel w/gold w/Luminous Dial	105	167
1301	Victor	1931	1135	One Day Intermittent	Nickel	65	167
					Nickel w/Luminous Dial	70	167
1302	Viking	1932	851	Electro-Glo	Black w/Chrome	750	167
1303	Viking	1932	1400	Electro-Glo	Black w/Chrome	500	167
1304	Viking	1932	1600	Electro-Glo	Black w/Chrome	400	167
1305	Viking	1933		Moon-Glo	Chrome	400	167
1306	Viking	1934			Chrome	150	167
1307	VIM	1930	1201-02,1219		Green	65	168
					Blue	65	168
					Nickel	70	168
1308	Waltham	1921	1207-8		Walnut	175	168
1309	Waltham	1921	1231-8	Nouveau	Walnut	225	168

Plate #	Brand Name	Year	Model No.	Model Name	Variation(s)	Value	Page
1310	Waltham	1932	3013		Gold	90	168
					Blue	100	168
1311	Waltham	1932	8300		Mahogany	200	168
1312	Waltham	1939	8574		Mahogany	100	168
1313	Waltham	1940	663	Parker Pen and Pencil	Walnut	125	168
1314	Waltham	1940	665	Parker Pen and Pencil	Walnut and Black	125	168
1315	Waltham	1940	666	Parker Pen and Pencil	Walnut	110	169
1316	Waltham	1940	3531		Green	160	169
					Cream	140	169
					Walnut	140	169
1317	Waltham	1940	1010	Cleopatra	Walnut	65	169
1318	Waltham	1940	1018		Green	175	169
1319	Waltham	1940	1857		Black	40	169
					Pigskin	40	169
					Blue	40	169
1320	Waltham	1940	8558		Mahogany	75	169
1321	Waltham	1940	644		Walnut	250	169
1322	Waltham	1940	646, 651		Pink Mirror	375	169
					Blue Mirror	325	169
1323	Waltham	1940	648, 649		Black w/Chrome	150	170
1324	Waltham	1940	8581, 8582		Blue & Black w/Chrome	225	170
1325	Ward	1934	951, 908, 909		Black w/Nickel	175	170
					Green w/Nickel	150	170
					Walnut w/Copper	150	170
1326	Ward	1935	903		Green	40	170
					Pink	50	170
1327	Ward	1936	924		Black	50	170
1328	Ward	1936	925		Black w/Nickel	45	170
					Black w/Nickel w/Luminous Dial	50	170
					Grey w/Nickel	35	170
					Grey w/Nickel w/Luminous Dial	40	170
					Ivory w/Gold	35	170
					Ivory w/Gold w/Luminous Dial	40	170
1329	Ward	1936	926		Green w/Brass	60	170
					Black w/Nickel	75	170
1330	Ward	1936	1051		Ivory w/Gold	60	170
					Black w/Gold	70	170
					Green w/Gold	70	170
1331	Ward	1936	1052		Ivory w/Gold	75	170
					Green w/Gold	85	170
1332	Ward	1936	972		Grey w/Nickel	50	171
					Ivory w/Gold	40	171
1333	Ward	1936	947, 948	Square	Black	35	171
					Green	35	171
1334	Ward	1937	974		Black	35	171
					Black w/Luminous Dial	40	171
					Ivory	30	171
					Ivory w/Luminous Dial	35	171
1335	Ward	1942	1000		Walnut w/Gold	45	171
					Ivory w/Gold	50	171
1336	Ward	1942	1002		Ivory w/Gold	60	171
1337	Ward	1950	6880	Square Case	Ivory	60	171
1338	Ward	1951	6839, 6881		Ivory	40	171
					Ivory w/Luminous Dial	45	171
1339	Ward	1950	6951, 6952		Ivory	40	171
					Ivory w/Luminous Dial	45	171
1340	Ward	1951	6953, 6954	Old Reliable	Ivory	60	171
					Ivory w/Luminous Dial	65	171
1341	Wards	1951	7075		Ivory	40	172
1342	Ward	1954	7055		Mahogany	20	172
1343	Ward	1954	7237		Mahogany	25	172
1344	Ward	1954	6951, 6952		Ivory	15	172
					Ivory w/Luminous Dial	20	172
1345	Ward	1954	7050, 7051		Ivory	20	172
					Ivory w/Luminous Dial	25	172
					Walnut	15	172
					Walnut w/Luminous Dial	20	172

Plate#	Brand Name	Year	Model No.	Model Name	Variation(s)	Value	Page
1346	Ward	1958	7145	Perky	Chrome	45	172
					Copper	40	172
1347	Ward	1951	6885		Ivory	60	172
1348	Wash. Elec.	1931	20, 25	Gothic	Walnut	80	172
1349	Wash. Elec.	1931	5	Ronell	Walnut	75	172
1350	Waterbury	1931	112	Current	Blue w/Gold	225	173
					Pink w/Gold	200	173
					Yellow w/Gold	200	173
					Black w/Chrome	225	173
1351	Waterbury	1931	113	Coil	Walnut	150	173
1352	Waterbury	1931	114	Modernistic	Black w/Chrome	300	173
1353	Waterbury	1931	115	Mayflower	Mahogany	100	173
1354	Waterbury	1931	119	Arcadia	Walnut	100	173
1355	Waterbury	1931	120	Bryn Mawr	Green	90	173
					Pink	90	173
					Ivory	80	173
					Blue	90	173
1356	Waterbury	1931			Nickel	60	173
					Nickel w/Luminous Dial	65	173
1357	Waterbury	1931		Correct Time Display	Mahogany	500	173
1358	Westclox	1910		Big Ben	Nickel	75	174
1359	Westclox	1930		Big Ben Deluxe	Cracked Green	110	174
					Cracked Green w/Luminous Dial	120	174
					Cracked Blue	110	174
					Cracked Blue w/Luminous Dial	120	174
					Cracked Rose	115	174
					Cracked Rose w/Luminous Dial	125	174
					Nickel	115	174
					Nickel w/Luminous Dial	125	174
1360	Westclox	1931	72	Bantam	Green	75	174
1361	Westclox	1931	200	Leg	Nickel	75	174
1362	Westclox	1931	261	Roman Arch Design	Walnut	125	174
1363	Westclox	1931	262	Modernistic Design	Walnut	125	174
1364	Westclox	1931	840	Big Ben	Mahogany	90	174
1365	Westclox	1931	141, 142, 143	Ben Hur	Blue	90	174
					Green	90	174
					Red	90	174
					Nickel	100	174
1366	Westclox	1931	20, 41, 42, 43	America	Blue	75	174
					Green	75	174
					Red	75	174
					Nickel	80	174
1368	Westclox	1931	401	La Salle Series	Duro Silver Alloy	150	175
1369	Westclox	1931	402	La Salle Series	Duro Silver Alloy	175	175
1370	Westclox	1931	403	La Salle Series	Duro Silver Alloy	175	175
1371	Westclox	1931	404	La Salle Series	Duro Silver Alloy	175	175
1372	Westclox	1931	405	La Salle Series	Duro Silver Alloy	180	175
1373	Westclox	1931	406	La Salle Series	Duro Silver Alloy	175	175
1374	Westclox	1931	320, 330	Big Ben	Nickel	100	175
					Nickel w/Luminous Dial	110	175
1375	Westclox	1931	521, 522, 523	Tom Thumb	Green	75	175
1376	Westclox	1931	820, 830	Big Ben	Mahogany	125	175
					Mahogany w/Luminous Dial	135	175
1377	Westclox	1932		Que-Tee	Mahogany	90	176
1378	Westclox	1931		Big Ben (Concave)	Black w/Nickel	125	176
					Black w/Nickel w/Luminous Dial	135	176
					Ivory w/Gold	100	176
					Ivory w/Gold w/Luminous Dial	110	176
1379	Westclox	1931		Baby Ben (Concave)	Black w/Nickel	100	176
					Black w/Nickel w/Luminous Dial	110	176
					Ivory w/Gold	80	176
					Ivory w/Gold w/Luminous Dial	85	176
1380	Westclox	1932		Big Ben (Convex)	Black w/Nickel	135	176
					Black w/Nickel w/Luminous Dial	145	176
					Ivory w/Gold	110	176
					Ivory w/Gold w/Luminous Dial	115	176

Plate #	Brand Name	Year	Model No.	Model Name	Variation(s)	Value	Page
1381	Westclox	1932		Baby Ben (Convex)	Black w/Nickel	110	176
					Black w/Nickel w/Luminous Dial	115	176
					Ivory w/Gold	90	176
					Ivory w/Gold w/Luminous Dial	95	176
1382	Westclox	1932	61B	Dura	Duro Silver Alloy	150	176
1383	Westclox	1934	827	Silent Night	Ivory w/Gold	100	176
1384	Westclox	1934	865	Andover	Chrome w/Blue	180	176
1385	Westclox	1934	868	Orb	Black w/Gold	150	177
1386	Westclox	1934	873	Bachelor	Brown w/Brass	80	177
					Black w/Brass	100	177
					Ivory w/Brass	90	177
1387	Westclox	1934		Siesta	Black w/Nickel	110	177
1388	Westclox	1936	949	Modern Square	Black w/Nickel	75	177
1389	Westclox	1934		Fortune	Black w/Nickel	75	177
					Black w/Nickel w/Luminous Dial	85	177
1390	Westclox	1934	814, 815	Country Club	Black with Nickel	80	177
					Black w/Nickel w/Luminous Dial	85	177
					Ivory w/Gold	60	177
					Ivory w/Gold w/Luminous Dial	65	177
1391	Westclox	1935	812	American	Black with Nickel	110	177
1392	Westclox	1935	828	Ben Bolt	Black with Nickel	90	177
					Black w/Nickel w/Luminous Dial	95	177
1393	Westclox	1935	846	Greenwich	Walnut	50	177
1394	Westclox	1935	850	Ben Franklin	Black w/Brass	60	178
1395	Westclox	1936	944	New Bantam	Green w/Black	40	178
1396	Westclox	1936	953	Tide	Black w/Nickel	75	178
					Ivory w/Gold	60	178
1397	Westclox	1936		Bingo	Ivory	40	178
					Walnut	40	178
1398	Westclox	1938	959, 960	Spur	Black w/Nickel trim	65	178
					Black w/Nickel w/Luminous Dial	70	178
1399	Westclox	1940	S5-F	Logan	Ivory w/Brass	60	178
1400	Westclox	1938		Leland	Smoke Glass w/Chrome Base	175	178
1401	Westclox	1939	S5-G, 871	Pittsfield	Brass w/Ivory	150	178
1402	Westclox	1939			Onyx w/Brass	110	178
1403	Westclox	1939			Walnut w/Burl Maple	65	179
1404	Westclox	1939			Walnut	50	179
1405	Westclox	1940	880	Big Ben	Black w/Nickel	130	179
					Ivory w/Gold	110	179
1406	Westclox	1940	880	Big Ben	Black w/Nickel	140	179
					Ivory w/Gold	120	179
1407	Westclox	1936		Baby Ben	Black w/Nickel	110	179
					Black w/Nickel w/Luminous Dial	115	179
					Ivory w/Gold	85	179
					Ivory w/Gold w/Luminous Dial	90	179
1408	Westclox	1939			Ivory	60	179
1409	Westclox	1941	987	Shelby	Ivory	50	179
					Walnut	40	179
1410	Westclox	1948	125, 135	General	Ivory w/gold	40	179
					Ivory w/Gold w/Luminous Dial	45	179
1411	Westclox	1948	74-3	Clock of Tomorrow	Brass	125	179
1412	Westclox	1948	904, 907	Moonbeam	Ivory	125	180
					Ivory w/Gold w/Luminous Dial	130	180
1413	Westclox	1948	S7-H	Sphinx	Walnut	50	180
1414	Westclox	1949		Big Ben	Black w/Nickel	90	180
					Black w/Nickel w/Luminous Dial	100	180
					Ivory w/Gold	75	180
					Ivory w/Gold w/Luminous Dial	80	180
1415	Westclox	1949		Baby Ben	Black w/Nickel	80	180
					Black w/Nickel w/Luminous Dial	85	180
					Ivory w/Gold	60	180
					Ivory w/Gold w/Luminous Dial	65	180
1416	Westclox	1950	943	Ardmore	Walnut	40	180
1417	Westclox	1950	980	Switch Clock	Ivory w/Gold	45	180
1418	Westclox	1950		Big Ben	Walnut w/Gold	40	180
					Walnut w/Gold w/Luminous Dial	45	180

Plate#	Brand Name	Year	Model No.	Model Name	Variation(s)	Value	Page
1419	Westclox	1950	960, 962	Barry	Black	40	180
					Ivory	30	180
1420	Westclox	1951		Bantam	Ivory	25	180
1421	Westclox	1957		Tide (Flamingo)	Pink	100	181
					Yellow	80	181
1422	Westclox	1956	656, 692	Sheraton	Mahogany	20	181
					Mahogany w/Luminous Dial	20	181
					Maple	20	181
					Maple w/Luminous Dial	20	181
1423	Westclox	1955		Big Ben	Black w/Nickel	40	181
					Black w/Nickel w/Luminous Dial	45	181
					Ivory w/Gold	30	181
					Ivory w/Gold w/Luminous Dial	35	181
1424	Westclox	1955		Baby Ben	Black w/Nickel	40	181
					Black w/Nickel w/Luminous Dial	45	181
					Ivory w/Gold	30	181
					Ivory w/Gold w/Luminous Dial	35	181
1425	Westclox	1958		Glendale	White	20	181
1426	Westclox	1957		Ellsworth	Grey	25	181
					Red	45	181
1427	Westclox	1957		Piper	Ivory	35	181
					Ivory w/Luminous Dial	40	181
					Black	40	181
					Black w/Luminous Dial	45	181
1428	Westclox	1958		Lace	White	20	182
					White w/Luminous Dial	25	182
					Pink	30	182
					Pink w/Luminous Dial	35	182
					Blue	30	182
					Blue w/Luminous Dial	35	182
1429	Westclox	1962		Legend	Walnut w/Gold	50	182
1430	Westclox	1962		New Dune	Brass	25	182
1431	Westclox	1962		Dynamic	White	75	182
					Pink	100	182
1432	Westclox	1962		Drowse	Tan	15	182
					Green	20	182
					Pink	20	182
1433	Westclox	1962		Award	Walnut w/Brass	60	182
1434	Westclox	1965		Double Bell	Brass	20	182
1435	Westclox	1962		Isotron	Brass w/Silver	25	182
1436	Westclox	1962		Big Ben	Black w/Nickel	35	183
					Black w/Nickel w/Luminous Dial	40	183
					Ivory w/Gold	30	183
					Ivory w/Gold w/Luminous Dial	35	183
1437	Westclox	1962		Baby Ben	Black w/Nickel	30	183
					Black w/Nickel w/Luminous Dial	35	183
					Ivory w/Gold	25	183
					Ivory w/Gold w/Luminous Dial	30	183
1438	Westclox	1965			Beige	20	183
1439	Westclox	1965		Quiet tick	Tan	15	183
					Tan w/Luminous Dial	20	183
1440	Westclox	1965			Grey	15	183
					Grey w/Luminous Dial	20	183
1441	Westinghouse	1932	WM611-68A	Nelson	Black w/Chrome	125	183
1442	Westinghouse	1932	WM611-51AB	Magnus	Blue	125	183
					Green	125	183
					Rose	125	183
1443	Westinghouse	1932	WM611-56A	Cunard	Black w/Nickel	110	183
1444	Westinghouse	1932	WM611-63T	Futurist	Black w/Gold	225	183

APPENDIX NO. 2

MARKET VALUES: WEATHER METERS AND GUIDES, APPLIANCE SWITCHES AND TIMERS

Plate#	Brand Name	Year	Model No./Name	Variation(s)	Value	Page
1457	Airguide	1934		Black w/Chrome	60	187
1458	Airguide	1939	Air Condition Indicator	Black w/Chrome	65	187
1459	Airguide	1940	Forecast Barometer	Black	110	187
1460	Airguide	1940	York	Black w/Chrome	60	187
1461	Airguide	1942	Tempid Teller	Black, Chrome	65	187
1462	Airguide	1954	Argyle	Black	60	187
1463	Airguide	1942	3-in-1 Airguide	Black w/Chrome	125	187
1464	Airguide	1956	Corsair	Brass	75	187
1465	Airguide	1951	Princeton Air Pilot	Grey	70	188
1466	Airguide	1954	Princeton Air Pilot	Grey	70	188
1467	Airguide	1956	Princeton Air Pilot	Grey	65	188
1468	Airguide	1957	Corsair	Grey	50	188
1469	Airguide	1963	Director	Aluminum	60	188
1470	Airguide	1963	Princeton	Grey, Brass Base	75	188
1471	Airguide	1963	Sherwood	Fruitwood w/Brass	35	189
1472	Airguide	1963	Zonar Comfort Coordinator		40	189
1473	Air-O-Meter	1938			65	189
1474	Bugle Boy	1936		Ivory w/Green	150	189
				Ivory w/Red	175	189
1475	Bugle Boy	1937	Thermometer Alarm	Green	110	189
				Ivory	100	189
1476	Bugle Boy	1940	Smart Dome	Ivory	400	189
				Bronze	425	189
1477	Bugle Boy	1940	4-In-1 Calendar	Ivory	450	189
				Bronze	500	189
1478	Bugle Boy	1940	Cloisonne Modern	Ivory	110	189
				Mahogany	80	189
1479	Bugle Boy	1940	Globe	Ivory w/Brass	90	190
				Black w/Chrome	125	190
1480	Bugle Boy	1940	Thermometer Alarm	Brown	110	190
				Green	125	190
1481	Bugle Boy	1951	Sunrise	Ivory	35	190
1482	Clock-Trola	1933	Radio Switch	Walnut	150	190
1483	DeLuxe	1938	Minute Call (Footed)	White	125	190
				Ivory	125	190
				Green	150	190
				Red	150	190
1484	DeLuxe	1939	Thermo-Alarm	Ivory w/Brass	125	190
1485	DeLuxe	1940	Thermo-Alarm	Ivory	110	190
1486	DeLuxe	1942	Thermometer		20	190
1488	Everhot	1950	Appliance Timer	Baked Enamel	75	191
1489	Flex-Seal	1942	Flex-Seal Timer	Black	20	191
1490	General Electric	1930	TM8-30	Chrome/Black	250	191
1491	General Electric	1939	7F-64, Utility Timer	Black	75	191
				Ivory	90	191

Plate#	Brand Name	Year	Model No./Name	Variation(s)	Value	Page
1492	General Electric	1939	8B-52, Voyager	Walnut	80	191
1493	General Electric	1949	Chef	White	35	191
1494	General Electric	1949	Select-O-Switch	Mahogany	40	191
1495	General Electric	1950	8H-66, Little Chef	White	35	191
1496	Gilbert	1933	Highlander	Brown w/Chrome	200	191
				Ivory w/Chrome	225	191
				Green w/Chrome	250	191
				Black w/Chrome	325	191
1497	Havlin	1930	Time Switch Clock	Walnut	100	192
1498	Hull	1940	Desk Thermometer	Black w/Chrome	60	192
1499	Intermatic	1958	A401, Clock-Timer	Green	25	192
1500	Intermatic	1958	A211, Time-All	Grey	20	192
1501	Intermatic	1963	Time-All	Ivory	15	192
1502	Jason	1962	Executive	Walnut w/Brass	60	192
1503	Jason	1962	Consultant	Mahogany w/Brass	125	192
				Maple w/Brass	150	192
1504	Jason	1962	Diplomat	Fruitwood	45	192
1505	Jason	1962	VIP	Walnut w/Brass	95	193
1506	Klok-Tenna	1930	Klok-Tenna	Walnut	125	193
1507	Lux	1933	Thermo-Squire	Black w/Nickel	85	193
1508	Lux	1949	Minute-Minder	White	15	193
1509	Lux	1949	Minute-Minder	White	15	193
1510	Lux	1963	Minute Minder	White	15	193
1511	National Call	1938	Kitchenette	Ivory w/Red	150	193
				Ivory w/Green	175	193
				Ivory w/Black	175	193
1512	New Haven	1931	Switchman	Walnut	150	193
1513	New Haven	1935	Switchman	Walnut	125	193
1514	New Haven	1957	Minitimer	White	20	194
1515	Nutone	1942	Weather Man	Ivory/Brass	125	194
1516	Pilot	1942	Desk Thermometer	Mahogany	45	194
1517	Pilot	1942	Mate	Brass	50	194
1518	Pilot	1942	Ship's Wheel	Brass	50	194
1519	Pilot	1942	Weather Man	Brass	40	194
1520	Presto	1963	Long-Ring Minute Minder	Ivory w/Black	20	194
1521	Racine	1929	Automatic Time Switch	Black	35	194
1522	Relide	1962	L'Heure Book Clock	Walnut	40	194
				Black	45	194
				Red	50	194
1523	Relide	1962	Satellite	Gold	275	195
1524	Rochester	1934	Humiditherm	Black w/Chrome	90	195
1525	Royal Kenmore	1932	Radiolarm Petite	Walnut	135	195
1526	Selsi	1940	Admiral	Mahogany	110	195
1527	Selsi	1940	Forecaster	Walnut	115	195
				Mahogany	125	195
1528	Sessions	1940	Combination Set	Walnut w/Brass	275	195
1529	Seth Thomas	1940	Anchor Bookend Set	Brass	250	195
1530	Sessions	1940	Kloxit	White w/Chrome		196
				Ivory w/Chrome		196
				Red w/Chrome		196
				Black w/Chrome		196
1531	Stellar	1962	General	Brass	100	196
1532	Stellar	1962	Weather Station	Walnut w/Brass	75	196
1533	Sun-Up	1936	Automatic	Ivory	150	196
				Green	160	196
				Black	175	196
1534	Sun-Up	1936		Green w/Nickel	90	196
				Black w/Nickel	110	196
1535	Sun-Up	1936		Green	110	196
				Black	125	196

Plate #	Brand Name	Year	Model No./Name	Variation(s)	Value	Page
1536	Swift & Anderson	1940	Ship's Wheel	Brass	75	196
1537	Swift & Anderson	1940	Ship Wheel (2 Unit Set)	Bronze	110	197
				Chrome	125	197
1538	Swift & Anderson	1942	Desk Penometer	Mahogany w/Brass	125	197
1539	Swift & Anderson	1940	Ship Wheel (3 Unit Set)	Bronze	125	197
1540	Swift & Anderson	1940	American Combination	Black w/Chrome	150	197
1541	Swift & Anderson	1940	Biometer	Black w/Chrome	75	197
1542	Swift & Anderson	1940	Forecaster Barometer	Walnut	60	197
1543	Swift & Anderson	1940	Marine Design Barometer	Brass	90	197
1545	Swift & Anderson	1942	Desk Weather Station	Brass	125	198
1546	Swift & Anderson	1940	New Capstan	Mahogany w/Brass	75	198
1547	Swift & Anderson	1942	Biometer	Mahogany w/Brass	75	198
1548	Swift & Anderson	1957	Fisherman	Walnut w/Brass	40	198
1549	Swift & Anderson	1957	Chelmsford	Walnut w/Brass	40	198
1550	Swift & Anderson	1957	Comet	Grey	75	198
				Ivory	75	198
1551	Swift & Anderson	1956	Sherwood	Fruitwood w/Brass	100	198
1552	Swift & Anderson	1956	Lowell	Mahogany w/Brass	65	199
				Maple w/Brass	90	199
1553	Swift & Anderson	1963	Sierra	Cherry w/Brass	65	199
1554	Swift & Anderson	1957	Huntsman	Walnut w/Brass	40	199
1555	Swift & Anderson	1957	German Barometer	Walnut w/Brass	45	199
1556	Swift & Anderson	1957	Windlass	Brass	70	199
1557	Swift & Anderson	1963	Chatham	Mahogany w/Brass	60	199
1558	Taylor	1931		Walnut	65	199
1559	Taylor	1938	Baroguide	Black w/Chrome	175	199
1560	Taylor	1938	Humiguide	Black w/Chrome	150	200
1561	Taylor	1939	Combination Weather Stand	Walnut	175	200
				Mahogany	195	200
1562	Taylor	1939	Marlboro Stormguide	Walnut w/Brass	75	200
1563	Taylor	1940	Fleetwood Baroguide	Green w/White	90	200
				Blue w/White	125	200
1564	Taylor	1939	Taylor Clyde Stormoguide	Mahogany w/Brass	100	200
1565	Taylor	1940	Ashton	Ivory	50	200
1566	Taylor	1940	Argyle	Black w/Chrome	125	200
1567	Taylor	1940	Belmont Humiguide	Lacquer	110	200
1568	Taylor	1940	Darien	Ivory	125	201
1569	Taylor	1940	Fairfax Stormguide	Black w/Chrome	75	201
1570	Taylor	1940	Hampton Humiguide	Black	100	200
1571	Taylor	1940	Fairmont Stormguide	Black w/Chrome	125	201
1572	Taylor	1940	Winton Combination	Black w/Chrome	225	201
1573	Taylor	1940	Fisherman's Barometer	Black w/Chrome	100	201
1574	Taylor	1940	Kenmore Baroguide	Bronze	110	201
1575	Taylor	1940	Renwick Baroguide	Ivory w/Bronze	110	202
1576	Taylor	1940	Stratford Stormguide	Black Lacquer w/Chrome	70	202
1577	Taylor	1940	Ultra Humiguide	Walnut	85	202
1578	Taylor	1940	Tremont Combination	Walnut w/Gold	325	202
1579	Taylor	1940	Warwick Stormguide	Mahogany w/Brass	70	202
1580	Taylor	1940	Voyager Baroguide	Walnut w/Brass	50	202
1581	Taylor	1940	Yacht Stormguide	Brass	75	202
1582	Taylor	1940	Yacht Stormguide	Walnut w/Brass	60	202
1583	Taylor	1942	Combination	Black w/Chrome	70	203
1584	Taylor	1950	Baroguide	Clear Top, Gold Base	60	203
1585	Taylor	1950	Baroguide	Ivory w/Gold	40	203
1586	Taylor	1947	Humidiguide	Ivory w/Chrome	110	203
1587	Taylor	1951	Combo Stormguide	Black w/Chrome	120	203
1588	Taylor	1959	Combo Stormguide	Dark	110	203
				Blonde	120	203
1589	Taylor	1963	Ambassador	Mahogany w/Brass	110	203
1590	Taylor	1963	Aquila	Mahogany w/Brass	35	204

Plate#	Brand Name	Year	Model No./Name	Variation(s)	Value	Page
1591	Taylor	1963	Consul	Gold Lacquer	75	204
1592	Taylor	1963	Fremont	Walnut w/Brass	95	204
1593	Taylor	1965	Combination	Grey	40	204
1594	Telaire	1935	Telaire	Walnut	125	204
				Black	150	204
1595	Telechron	1939	8B-51, Controlla	Walnut	75	204
1596	Telechron	1939	8B-53, Organizer	Walnut	75	204
1597	Telechron	1947	8HA-55, Selector	Walnut	60	205
1598	Telechron	1947	8HA-61, Switch Alarm	Walnut	40	205
1599	Telechron	1948		White	45	205
1600	Temp Alert	1942	Air Pilot	Ivory	70	205
1601	Temp Alert	1942	Bath Thermometer	Pink	60	205
				Blue	60	205
1602	Tel-Tru	1940	Desk Thermometer	Ivory w/Chrome	95	205
1603	Thermodex	1942	Fountain Pen	Walnut	100	205
				Black	125	205
1604	Time Lite	1929	Electric Time Switch	Bronze	125	205
1605	Tork-Time	1929	Time Clock		175	205
1606	Tower	1954		Ivory	15	206
				Black	20	206
1607	Tower	1954		Ivory	15	206
				Black	20	206
1608	Tower	1954		Ivory	15	206
				Black	20	206
1609	Waltham	1939	Combination	Walnut w/Silver	125	206
1610	Waltham	1940	Barometer Set	Mahogany	125	206
1611	Ward	1941		Grey	80	206
1612	Westclox	1952	Switch Alarm	Ivory	40	206
1613	Westinghouse	1950	Appliance Timer	Baked White Enamel	50	206

APPENDIX NO. 3

MANUFACTURERS AND BRAND NAMES

As used within this reference, a "brand name" is a marketing name for a specific product line. This may not be the same name as that of the product manufacturer. The brand name may also be a "house" name: a product line manufactured for a specific large wholesaler or retailer using their name or brand. Such brands might often use more than one supplier. As a result, the actual manufacturer may be difficult to discern. Additionally, smaller mail order and specialty houses, often called "jobbers", operated by purchasing excess inventories of cases and/or movements from various manufacturers. They then modified, mixed and matched parts, and applied their private brand. Several clock companies such as Ingraham and Lux catered to the jobber and house markets while also selling clocks under their own brands.

The distinction between clock brand names and their manufacturers has become further complicated over time. The American clock industry initially developed in the mid-nineteenth century and was dominated by seven clockmaking companies, all located in Connecticut. The industrial revolution, introduction of electricity as an alternate power source, several economic downturns and two world wars assured a continually unstable market from the turn of the 20th century forward. Resultant business failures, acquisitions, mergers, partnerships, and name changes make the clock industry of the 20th century quite difficult to follow. The introduction of inexpensive quartz movements in the 1970's virtually ended the industry. There remain only two American clock companies: Timex (US Time Corp.) and General Time Corp. (Westclox/Seth Thomas). Most of their manufacturing is conducted outside the US. Other American brands remain as ghosts, their trademarks having been purchased after their closure.

The following section provides basic information about American clock brand names which appear in this book. Ownership and affiliation histories are furnished where known.

Aldine	Sears Roebuck house brand early 1930's
Apollo	Lux brand name 1930's-40's
Aristocrat	Montgomery-Ward house brand early 1950's. Known Supplier(s): Ingraham
Artcraft	Unknown Jobber brand 1930's. Known Supplier(s): Lux
Autodex	Seth Thomas brand name
Barr	Unknown Jobber brand 1930's. Known Supplier(s): Pennwood
Belmont	Unknown Jobber brand 1930's
Bugle Boy	Spiegel house brand 1930's-50's. Known Supplier(s): Ingraham; Lux; Mastercrafters
Bulova	European brand manufacturer. 1930's US clocks made by Ingraham
Chieftain	Pennwood brand name
Chelsea	Montgomery-Wards house brand 1940's. Known Supplier(s): Ingraham, Seth Thomas
Clinton	Unknown Jobber brand 1950's
Comet	Montgomery-Wards house brand 1930's
DeLuxe	Lux brand line 1930's-40's
Dinson	Montgomery-Ward house brand 1950's Known Supplier(s): Gilbert
Duokron	Hammond brand name
Fashion	Unknown jobber brand name c.1930's. Known Supplier(s): Lux
Forestville	Early Connecticut clockmaker acquired by E.N.Welch late 1800's Acquired by Sessions in 1903 through purchase of E.N. Welch. Retained as Sessions brand.
Gable	Ingraham brand name 1930's

General Electric	General Electric Co. formed 1902 by merger of Edison Electric and Thomson Houston Electric. 1917 acquired half interest in Telechron. Telechron produced GE brand clocks beginning 1930. 1943 GE purchased controlling interest in Telechron. Both brands continued in production by GE until 1960's. 1979 Clock manufacturing unit sold to Timex (formerly U.S. Time).
Gilbert	Wm. Gilbert Clock Corp., Winsted CT. Est'd. 1828 as Marsh, Gilbert & Co., Bristol, CT. 1866 renamed Wm. L Gilbert Clock Co. 1964 clock division was sold to Spartus Corp. which was acquired by General Time Corp. in 1996.
Haddon	Haddon Products, Inc., Chicago, IL. Produced primarily 'Mystery' and animated motion type clocks early 1950's through early 1960's.
Hamilton	Hamilton Sangamo Corp., Springfield, IL. Founded c.1890 as Sangamo Electric. 1927 sold to Hamilton Watch Co. and renamed Hamilton-Sangamo Corp. Produced electric clocks exclusively 1928-1930. 1931 Acquired by General Time Corp. and eventually merged into their Seth Thomas Division.
Hammond	Hammond Clock Co., Chicago, IL. Produced electric clocks 1928 until 1941. Did not resume production after WWII.
Harmony House	Sears Roebuck house brand Post WWII through 1950's. Known Supplier(s): Seth Thomas; New Haven; Ingraham
Havlin	Brand name associated with Royal Kenmore and Lincoln.
Herman Miller	Exclusive brand name manufactured by Howard Miller Clock Co., Zeeland, MI, for Herman Miller Furniture. Established late 1920's with emphasis on traditional design. 1930 Gilbert Rohde began modern design cabinets, utilized Hammond movements. In the 1950's the Eames designed many clocks. Still in operation this date.
Herschede	Herschede-Hall Clock Co. Inc., Cinn., OH. Est'd. 1877, Incorporated 1902. Specialized in ornamental chime and strike clocks. 1929/30 established Revere brand for electric clock line utilizing Telechron movements. 1932/33 introduced Herschede brand electric clocks. 1934/35 ceased clock sales. Operated as cabinet supplier to GE/Telechron. In 1987 operations ceased.
Imperial	Imperial Sales Co. National jobber company 1930's-40's. Known Supplier(s): Pennwood

Ingersol Ingersol Clock Co., Waterbury, CT. Est'd c.1880's. Operated as sole agent for Waterbury 1908-1922. Acquired by Waterbury 1922. Refer to Waterbury listing for further history.

Ingraham E. Ingraham & Co., Bristol, CT. Est'd. 1857. Specialized in cabinet making. 1920's developed steam press molding technology allowing elaborate contouring of plywood cases. 1931 began producing small radio cabinets for Emerson Radio & Television, NYC. 1936 established as key cabinetmaker in radio while continuing clock production. 1967 ceased operations. Brand name sold and remains in use.

Jefferson Jefferson Electric Co., Bellwood, Il. Known for production of novelty 'mystery' type clocks c.1955-1965.

Lawson Lawson Clock Co., Los Angeles, CA. Established c.1930 and produced cyclometer digital clocks until early 1940's. Known for relationship with Kem Weber, German industrial designer, who championed new streamline styling.

Lincoln Brand name associated with Royal Kenmore and Havlin.

Lux Lux Clock Co., Inc, Waterbury CT. Est'd 1917 Specialized in 'novelty' clocks. 1931 marketed exclusively by A.C. Keebler. Brand names included Lux, DeLuxe and Keebler. Also marketed to catalog houses and jobbers, selling under their brands.

Manning-Bowman Manning-Bowman & Co., Meriden, CT. Manufacturer of high style kitchen and decorative items (similar to Chase). Produced electric clocks from late 1920's until early 1930's.

Marlboro Unknown jobber brand name c.1930's.
Known Supplier(s): Lux

Mastercrafters Mastercrafters Clock Co., Chicago, IL. Est'd. 1946/47 and remained in business through 1970's. Specialized in novelty lighted, motion and mystery clocks.

National Call Sears Roebuck house brand 1920's - 1960's.
Known Supplier(s): Ingraham, Lux, Hammond, Haddon, Mastercrafters, Seth Thomas, Havlin

New Haven New Haven Clock Co., New Haven, CT. Est'd 1853. Continued in operation until 1959.

New Lux Lux Brand Name c.1950's

Old Reliable	Montgomery-Ward house brand 1930's. Known Supplier(s): Ingraham, Lux
Peerless	Sessions brand name c.1930's
Phinney-Walker	Est'd. c.1907 specializing in keyless wind clocks. No production evident 1920 forward. Name resurfaced 1940's - 1960's with clocks distributed primarily by jewelers.
Pyramid	Lux Brand Name c.1930's
Pennwood	Pennwood Co., Pittsburgh, PA. Specialized in cyclometer clocks early 1930's - 1960's. Brand names included Pennwood, Federal and Numechron.
R.F.D.	R.F.D. ('Ready For Duty') unknown jobber brand c.1930's Known Supplier(s): Ingraham and Lux
Relide	**Wholesale house brand.** Distributed primarily to jewelers c.1950's - 1960's.
Rio	Ingraham brand name c.1940's
Royal Kenmore	Royal Kenmore Electric. Marketed electric clocks late 1920's until the early 1930's. Associated with Lincoln and Havlin Brands.
Sears	Sears Roebuck house brand begun use on clocks late 1950's
Semca	**Wholesale house brand.** Distributed primarily to jewelers c.1950's - 1960's.
Sentinel	unknown jobber brand c.1930's - 1940's Known Supplier(s): Westclox and Ingraham
Sessions	Sessions Clock Co., Forestville, CT. Established 1903 when Sessions family acquired E.N. Welsh (est'd. 1864) and changed name to Sessions. Ceased operations c.1960.
Seth Thomas	Seth Thomas Clock Co., Plymouth Hollow, CT. Est'd. 1853. 1932 acquired by General Time Corp., retaining Seth Thomas as subsidiary.
Silver	National catalog jobber house brand. Known Supplier(s): Lux
Silvertone	Deluxe/Lux brand line c. early 1930's

Sunbeam	Montgomery-Ward house brand late 1950's - 1960's
Sun-Up	Spiegel house brand name c. 1935 - 1939 Known Supplier(s): Lux and Ingraham
Telechron	Warren Telechron Co., Ashland, MA., Est'd 1916. 1917 GE acquired half interest (non-controlling). 1930/31 began production GE brand clocks. 1943 GE acquired controlling interest, continued production of both Telechron and GE clocks. 1979 Timex (US Time Corp.) acquired remaining clock operations.
USALite	Novelty clock jobber 1930's Known Supplier(s): New Haven (movements)
United	**United Clock Corp., Brooklyn, NY. Incorporated 1931. Operations in New York and California. Acquired by United Metal Goods Manufacturing Co.**
Victor	Montgomery-Ward house brand early 1930's
Waltham	Waltham Clock Co., Waltham, MA. Est'd.1859 as American Watch Co. in Waltham, CT. 1925 renamed Waltham Clock Co. 1957 ceased operations. Waltham trade name purchased and continues in use.
Waterbury	Waterbury Clock Co., Waterbury, CT. Est'd. 1857. 1892 became primary supplier to Ingersol. 1922 purchased Ingersol. 1932 reorganized. 1942 purchased by Norwegian investment group. 1944 named changed to US Time Corp. c.1970's name changed to Timex.
Westclox	Founded as United Clock Co., Peru, IL, 1885. Reorganized in 1887 as Western Clock Co. Westclox brand introduced 1909 and formally organized as a division of Western Clock Co. in 1923. 1931 acquired by General Time Corp. Merged to become Division beside Seth Thomas. In 1936 Division name changed from Western Clock to Westclox. 1996 General Time acquired Spartus Corp. (which included the operations of Gilbert Clock Co., acquired by Spartus in 1964).

BIBLIOGRAPHY

Bailey, Chris. *Two Hundred Years of American Clocks and Watches*. Englewood Cliffs, New Jersey: Prentice-Hall, 1975.

Coggins, Frank. *Clocks-Construction, Maintenance and Repair*. Blue Ridge Summit, PA: TAB Books, 1984.

Fiell, Charlotte and Peter. *Design of the 20th Century*. Koln, Germany: Benedict Taschen Verlag GmbH, 1999.

Kingsey, Sian. *The Collector's Corner: Clocks*. London, England: Quantum Books, Ltd., 1999.

Linz, Jim. *Electrifying Time: Telechron and G.E. Clocks, 1925-1955*. Atglen, Pennsylvania: Schiffer Publishing Co., 2001.

Marshall, Percival (Editor). *Electric Clocks and Chimes, A practical Handbook*. Kings Langley, Herts, England: Argus Books Ltd., 1976.

Miller, Martin. *Antiques Source Book*. London, England: Carlton Books, Ltd., 2000.

Noblet, Jocelyn de (Editor). *Industrial Design: Reflection of a Century*. Paris, France: Flammarion/APCI, 1993.

Roberts, Derek. *Collecting Clocks*. London, England: Quantum Books, Ltd., 1992.

Schorsch, Anita. *The Warner Collector's Guide to American Clocks*. New York, New York: Warner Books, Inc., 1981.

Schwartz, Marvin. *Collectors' Guide to Antique American Clocks*. Garden City, New York: Doubleday & Co., Inc., 1975.

Shenton, Alan and Rita. *Collectable Clocks, 1840 - 1940, Reference and Price Guide*. Woodbridge, Suffolk, England: Antique Collectors' Club Ltd., 1994.

Swedberg, Robert and Harriett. *American Clocks and Clockmakers*. Radnor, Pennsylvania: Wallace-Homestead Book Co., 1989.

Tyler, E. J. *American Clocks for the Collector*. New York, New York: E. P. Dutton, Inc., 1981.

Wilson, Guy, Dianne Pilgrim and Dickran Tashjian. *The Machine Age in America, 1918-1941*. New York, New York: Harry N. Abrams, Inc., 1986.

WEBSITES

Timex Corporation. *The Timex Website*. www.timex.com. ©2000

Historical Clock and Watch Research. *Historical Clock and Watch Research Website*. www.clockswatches.com. ©2001

FTL Design. *History of Electric Clocks*. www.electric-clock.com. ©2000